CHOPIN'S POLISH BALLADE

CHOPIN'S POLISH BALLADE

Op. 38 as Narrative of National Martyrdom

Jonathan D. Bellman

OXFORD
UNIVERSITY PRESS
2010

OXFORD
UNIVERSITY PRESS

Oxford University Press, Inc., publishes works that further
Oxford University's objective of excellence
in research, scholarship, and education.

Oxford   New York
Auckland   Cape Town   Dar es Salaam   Hong Kong   Karachi
Kuala Lumpur   Madrid   Melbourne   Mexico City   Nairobi
New Delhi   Shanghai   Taipei   Toronto

With offices in
Argentina   Austria   Brazil   Chile   Czech Republic   France   Greece
Guatemala   Hungary   Italy   Japan   Poland   Portugal   Singapore
South Korea   Switzerland   Thailand   Turkey   Ukraine   Vietnam

Copyright © 2010 by Oxford University Press, Inc.

Published by Oxford University Press, Inc.
198 Madison Avenue, New York, New York 10016

www.oup.com

Oxford is a registered trademark of Oxford University Press.

All rights reserved. No part of this publication may be reproduced,
stored in a retrieval system, or transmitted, in any form or by any means,
electronic, mechanical, photocopying, recording, or otherwise,
without the prior permission of Oxford University Press.

Library of Congress Cataloging-in-Publication Data
Bellman, Jonathan, 1957–
Chopin's Polish ballade: op. 38 as narrative of national martyrdom / Jonathan D. Bellman.
   p. cm.
Includes bibliographical references and index.
ISBN 978-0-19-533886-7
1. Chopin, Frédéric, 1810–1849. Ballades, piano.   2. Ballades (Instrumental
music)—History and criticism.   3. Piano music—History and criticism.   I. Title.
ML410.C54B22 2009
786.2'1896—dc22   2008046842

Publication of this book was supported by the Otto Kinkeldey Publication
Endowment Fund of the American Musicological Society

In memory of my father
Dr. Samuel Irving Bellman (z"l; 1926–2009)
Professor Emeritus of English,
California State Polytechnic University, Pomona

For Deborah Ann Kauffman
and Benjamin Howard Bellman
Mihi vita cariores sunt

PREFACE

We have always valued instrumental music as it has *spoken to us*, and can never listen to the delightful works of Beethoven, Mozart, Haydn, Ries, Onslow, and some others, without having their sentiment—nay, when we are in a fanciful humor—their *story*, as clearly impressed upon our minds as if it had been told in words.

Henry F. Chorley, The Athaneum, 15 March 1834

This is the meaning of this poem, and all Chopin's works are poems. Only seek and you will find, and you will be a thousandfold rewarded for your researches.

Jean Kleczyński, The Works of Frederic Chopin:
Their Proper Interpretation, 1880

The age of description is over.

Hans Keller, "The Chamber Music," in The Mozart
Companion, ed. H. C. Robbins Landon and
Donald Mitchell, 1956

The Second Ballade, op. 38, of Frédéric Chopin (composed in 1836–39 and first published in 1841) occupies a secure position on piano recital programs, yet seems to be one of the most incompletely understood pieces in the entire nineteenth-century repertoire. It is known to have existed—to have been performed by the composer, in fact—in at least two radically different versions, though he published only one, and such basics as the key and the proper ending are still matters of debate. The form of op. 38 as published is notoriously problematic, so much so that completely contradictory views of it go back more than a century. There is probably no other work of similar stature about which there is so little consensus on the most fundamental issues.

No artwork appears in a vacuum. Some reflected light is shed on op. 38 by a group of almost offhand remarks made about the work by certain of Chopin's contemporaries—remarks that both open windows into the ballade's cultural and musical worlds and (predictably) raise further questions. More may be gleaned from the work's musical style and style referents, from its relationship to the contemporary Parisian operatic and amateur repertories, and from the cultural milieu and nationalistic aspirations of the diasporic Polish community in 1830s Paris, a community with which Chopin associated. The Second Ballade is a piece in which aesthetic, popular, cultural, and personal realms intersect in striking ways, yet the work's very familiarity has tended to obscure its radical and unique aspects. To pianists and music scholars it is completely familiar, one passage proceeding predictably after the next; anything radical and interesting has virtually to be reimagined because of the music's secure and familiar place in our piano culture.

The critical literature on Chopin in general and the ballades in particular has grown in recent decades, but it seems that many core issues are still being wrestled with, and that the ballade as a musical genre shares its secrets far less willingly than the sonata or the symphony. In the course of this study, the work most helpful to me has been that of Jeffrey Kallberg (on Chopin in a variety of musical and cultural contexts in Paris), Halina Goldberg (on Chopin in the context of broader Polish culture and literature), Jim Samson (on the ballades as a genre and Chopin's biography), James Parakilas (on Chopin's ballades in relation to poetic models and the genre of the instrumental ballade that evolved after Chopin's op. 23), David Kasunic (on Chopin's ballades and their formal and aesthetic relationships to opera), and John Rink (on the reception history of Chopin's ballades). Not only has the work of these scholars provided a wealth of raw material and discerning thought for me to mine and reflect upon, but they have all been unfailingly generous with their time and resources as, in the long gestation of this project, I returned repeatedly with questions and requests for advice.

The decision to concentrate on Chopin's Second Ballade without assuming the responsibility of formulating a coherent view of the four ballades as a group was made because of my unwillingness to forgo—as must be the case in all genre studies—the full examination of a single work's unique qualities in order to identify broader generic patterns: not what makes a work special, in other words, but what defines the family resemblances of a group of works. I do devote a chapter to Chopin's First Ballade, op. 23, but that is necessary background in that it is the first—unavoidably, Chopin's first essay in a new genre will provide crucial context for his second. The two works are related in general aesthetic and narrative ways yet very different with respect to form and musical procedure, and in any case a study of the Second Ballade that ignored the first would be impossible. As the subject of my story is the Second in its time, though, there was no need to expand the picture to encompass the Third and Fourth, except in certain tangential ways.

If nothing else, Chopin's Second Ballade serves to illustrate the complexity of the ways in which in a single, relatively brief musical work—a justly celebrated work, though (less sentimentally) but one of myriad piano pieces from the 1830s that takes at most eight minutes to perform—engaged with its time, and with listeners ever after. It is a unique masterpiece. I hope this study will demonstrate how studies of other masterpieces that foreground the individual works rather than the other members of their generic families might contribute to a better understanding of each, rather than less helpfully reinforcing the more common view of The Repertoire as a great jumble of works that are examples of this or that template, approach, or pattern.

My love affair with op. 38 dates back decades, to my years as an undergraduate piano major at the University of California, Santa Barbara; a certain young pianist named Deborah Kauffman performed it on her senior recital. Perhaps the original impetus for this study, though, was an almost offhand remark by Jeffrey Kallberg in his 1982 doctoral dissertation. He mentioned a couple of intriguing contemporary remarks made about the Second Ballade by people close to the composer but then needed to return to other matters in his already titanic study of the Chopin sources and manuscripts. Before shutting the door on the subject of op. 38, though, he made the observation (on p. 100) that "a thorough study is warranted." To him, then, goes the credit for the original nudge in this direction.

ACKNOWLEDGMENTS

It is with the deepest pleasure that I acknowledge Professor Alejandro E. Planchart, formerly of the University of California at Santa Barbara, and Leonard Ratner, formerly of Stanford University, as mentors and friends who encouraged both thick-context approaches to music and nonstandard ways of thinking about it, and whose work continues to be a model and an inspiration to me after several decades. Jean Pang Goyal and Steve Swayne very generously shared with me their early work on the two versions of op. 38. Maja Trochimczik, Jolanta Pekacz, and (again) Halina Goldberg were extremely helpful to me with regard to Polish sources and translation. Helpful suggestions and reactions to earlier versions of this work were offered by John Michael Cooper, Will Crutchfield, Russell Guyver, Marie Sumner Lott, and William Marvin. Stephen Luttmann has been the very Platonic ideal of a music librarian, providing advice and demonstrating wonderful generosity and resourcefulness in procuring sources. My difficulties in rendering the nuances of connotation of early nineteenth-century German into modern English were eased considerably by his attention, and by the substantial help of Gabriele Menz.

Two friends never saw the end of this project. The pianist Walter Schenkman (z"l), with whom I had animated discussions on these and related subjects, made his final departure (at the piano, in fact) one evening at the time I was readying the manuscript for first submission; his lively reactions will be missed. And let this book also be to the memory of my friend Jonathan Pevsner (z"l); the focused writing phase occurred simultaneously with the final stages of Jonathan's heroic battle against lung cancer, and our almost daily correspondence throughout this time will remain a lasting memory for me.

Finally, with deepest love, my gratitude to my wife, Dr. Deborah Kauffman, who not only puts up with me, both when I'm writing books and when I'm not, but who also produced all my musical examples on Finale. She and our son, Benjamin Howard Bellman, make my life ever joyful and invigorating.

CONTENTS

	List of Musical Examples	xv
1	Two Versions, Two Keys, and "Certain Poems of Mickiewicz"	3
	Two Versions	6
	Two Keys	14
	"Certain Poems of Mickiewicz"	19
2	Genesis of a Narrative Process	35
	Stories in Tones	35
	Amateur Program Music	40
	Ballad Poetry and Musical Form	50
3	Hearing *Konrad Wallenrod*: The First Ballade, Op. 23	55
	Overview and Stylistic Summary of the First Ballade	55
	Konrad Wallenrod: Plot and Structure	67
	Konrad Wallenrod as Ballade Scenario	72
	The Lay of Aldona's Fate	78
4	Op. 38 and the Genre Issue	86
	A Formal Overview of Chopin's Second Ballade	86
	The Second Ballade and the Sonata Problem	90
	Ballade as Genre	94
	The Operatic Ballade to 1831	97

5   The Polish Pilgrims and the Operatic Imperative   111
        A Pilgrims' Ballade; a Polish Ballade   111
        The Great Migration and Polish Culture in Exile 114
        Personal Anguish and Literary Apotheosis   123
        Sapienti Pauca   132

6   Martyrdom and Exile: The Narrative of Chopin's
    F Major Ballade   145
        Internal Evidence I—the A Material: Siciliano   145
        Internal Evidence II—the B Material: Storm   152
        Internal Evidence III—the C Theme   156
        Chopin's Second Ballade as Narrative of
        National Martyrdom   160
        Versions, Tonic Keys, and Mickiewicz Revisited 170
        The Forest and the Trees   173

    *Appendix: "A M. F. Chopin, sur sa Ballade
    polonaise," by Félicien Mallefille*   176

    Bibliography   185

    Index   193

LIST OF MUSICAL EXAMPLES

Ex. 1.1.	Felix Mendelssohn, *St. Paul*, "How Lovely Are the Messengers," mm. 1–8.	8
Ex. 1.2.	Fryderyk Chopin, Ballade no. 2, op. 38, mm. 1–11.	9
Ex. 1.3.	Chopin, "Baladine," close.	10
Ex. 1.4.	Maria Szymanowska, "Świtezianka," mm. 1–12.	29
Ex. 3.1.	Chopin, Ballade no. 1, op. 23, mm. 1–7.	59
Ex. 3.2.	Chopin, Ballade no. 1, op. 23, mm. 8–16.	60
Ex. 3.3.	Chopin, Ballade no. 1, op. 23, mm. 66–76.	62
Ex. 3.4.	Chopin, Ballade no. 1, op. 23, mm. 106–114.	63
Ex. 3.5.	Chopin, Ballade no. 1, op. 23, mm. 138–141.	64
Ex. 3.6.	Chopin, Ballade no. 1, op. 23, mm. 208–212.	65
Ex. 3.7.	Chopin, Ballade no. 1, op. 23, mm. 242–250.	65
Ex. 3.8.	Vincenzo Bellini, "L'Abbandono," piano introduction.	79
Ex. 3.9.	Chopin, Ballade no. 1, op. 23, mm. 243–248.	83
Ex. 4.1.	Chopin, Ballade no. 2, op. 38, mm. 47–58.	87

Ex. 4.2.	Chopin, Ballade no. 2, op. 38, mm. 98–102.	88
Ex. 4.3.	Chopin, Ballade no. 2, op. 38, mm. 195–end.	89
Ex. 4.4.	François-Adrien Boïeldieu, *La dame blanche*, act 1, "Ballad of the White Lady," mm. 10–29.	100
Ex. 4.5a.	Louis Hérold, *Zampa*, act 1, Camilla's ballade, first couplet.	102
Ex. 4.5b.	Hérold, *Zampa*, act 1, Camilla's ballade, third couplet.	103
Ex. 4.6.	Giacomo Meyerbeer, *Robert le diable*, act 1, Raimbaut's ballade, mm. 1–20.	104
Ex. 4.7.	Meyerbeer, *Robert le diable*, act 1, Raimbaut's ballade, mm. 32–42.	105
Ex. 4.8.	Meyerbeer, *Robert le diable*, act 1, Raimbaut's ballade, second stanza, mm. 51–60.	106
Ex. 4.9.	Meyerbeer, *Robert le diable*, act 1, Raimbaut's ballade, third stanza, mm. 91–98.	107
Ex. 6.1.	Chopin, Ballade no. 2, op. 38, mm. 1–46.	146
Ex. 6.2.	Chopin, Mazurka in C Major, op. 24 no. 2, mm. 1–4.	147
Ex. 6.3.	Meyerbeer, *Robert le diable*, act 1, Raimbaut's ballade, opening of vocal line.	148
Ex. 6.4.	Meyerbeer, *Robert le diable*, act 1, first reminiscence of Raimbaut's ballade.	149
Ex. 6.5.	Meyerbeer, *Robert le diable*, act 1, second reminiscence of Raimbaut's ballade.	150
Ex. 6.6.	Chopin, Ballade no. 2, op. 38, mm. 47–52.	152
Ex. 6.7.	Gioachino Rossini, *Guillaume Tell*, overture, mm. 92–116.	155
Ex. 6.8.	Chopin, Ballade no. 2, op. 38, mm. 169–183.	156
Ex. 6.9.	Rossini, *Guillaume Tell*, instrumental postscript to the finale of act 1.	157
Ex. 6.10.	Chopin, Ballade no. 2, op. 38, mm. 95–102.	158
Ex. 6.11.	Rossini, *Guillaume Tell*, act 2, "Oui, vous l'arrachez à mon âme," mm. 28–34.	160
Ex. 6.12.	Chopin, Ballade no. 2, op. 38, mm. 108–115.	163

CHOPIN'S POLISH BALLADE

1

TWO VERSIONS, TWO KEYS, AND "CERTAIN POEMS OF MICKIEWICZ"

Three persistent issues have bedeviled the reception of Fryderyk Chopin's Second Ballade, op. 38, and all three were first raised in Robert Schumann's review of the newly published work. In the 2 November 1841 issue of the *Neue Zeitschrift für Musik*, Schumann recalled his first encounter with the piece in 1836, when Chopin had visited Leipzig and played it for him (among other works); at that time, it had ended in a different key and been structurally very different from the version later published. Schumann also remembered that Chopin had made an apparently offhand remark about drawing inspiration for the First and Second Ballades from the poetry of Adam Mickiewicz. In what would become one of the most frequently quoted passages from the entire Chopin literature, Schumann wrote:

> We must direct attention to the ballade as a most remarkable work. Chopin has already written one composition of the same name—one of his wildest and most original compositions; the new one is different—as a work of art inferior to the first, but equally fantastic and inventive. Its impassioned episodes seem to have been inserted afterwards. I recollect very well that when Chopin played the Ballade here, it ended in F major; now it closes in A minor. At that time he also mentioned that certain poems of Mickiewicz had suggested his *Ballades* to him.[1]

---

1. "Wir haben noch der Ballade als eines merkwürdigen Stückes zu erwähnen. Chopin hat unter demselben Namen schon eine geschrieben, eine seiner wildesten eigentümlichsten Kompositionen; die neue ist anders, als Kunstwerk unter jener ersten stehend, doch nicht weniger phantastisch und geistreich. Die leidenschaftlichen Zwischensätze scheinen erst

Schumann had recorded his immediate impressions of the meeting with Chopin in two places: his diary and a letter to his old teacher, Heinrich Dorn. The diary entry for 12 September 1836, the day Chopin visited, is disappointingly fragmentary and vague. The piece that most caught Schumann's fancy was the Ballade no. 1 in G Minor, op. 23, which had been published just two months previous: "In the morning, Chopin.... 'His *Ballade* I like best of all.' I am very glad of that; I am very glad of that. Doesn't like his works being discussed. [Noting pieces played:]...two new ones—a *Ballade*—*Notturno* in D flat....[I] bring him Sonata and Etudes by me; he gives me *Ballade*."[2]

Chopin would have given him a copy of the new publication, the Ballade no. 1 in G Minor, op. 23, as a gesture of professional courtesy, particularly because he was being given copies of Schumann's works. What might not immediately be clear from Schumann's cryptic notes is which Ballade Schumann liked "best of all," since—as we know from the 1841 review— he knew both: he was *given* the one but heard the other (albeit in different form). His inclusion of a ballade among the "two new ones" does not clarify which it was; he had mentioned a ballade already, but because the "D-flat Notturno" (the Nocturne, op. 27 no. 2) had also recently seen print, both publications might have been considered equally "new." So we know from the 1841 review that he preferred the First Ballade and that he heard the Second on this visit, but his jotted notes yield nothing more definite.

The matter of what Schumann was given versus what he had heard is clarified somewhat by his description of the meeting in a letter to Dorn of 14 September, two days after the visit:

---

später hinzugekommen zu sein; ich erinnere mich sehr gut, als Chopin die Ballade hier spielte und in F-dur schloss; jetzt schliesst sie in A-moll. Er sprach damals auch davon, dass er zu seinen Balladen durch einige Gedichte von Mickiewicz angeregt worden sei. Umgekehrt würde ein Dichter zu seiner Musik wieder sehr leicht Worte finden können; sie rührt das Innerste auf." *Neue Zeitschrift für Musik* 15 (1841), 141–42. The English translation is from Robert Schumann, *On Music and Musicians*, ed. Konrad Wolff, trans. Paul Rosenfeld ([New York]: Pantheon, [1946]), 143, although I emend Rosenfeld's translation to include Schumann's plural, *Balladen*; he inexplicably gives the singular ("daß er zu seinen Balladen durch einige Gedichte von Mickiewitz angeregt worden sei"). If we take it literally, Chopin told Schumann in 1836 that "some poems of Mickiewicz" inspired both ballades, the recently published op. 23 in G Minor and the version Schumann heard of what would become op. 38, which apparently already had the title "Ballade." For whatever reason, Schumann does not comment much on the novelty and generic significance of an instrumental work titled "Ballade," as many other commentators have done.

2. Quoted in Jean-Jacques Eigeldinger, *Chopin: Pianist and Teacher*, 3rd ed., ed. Roy Howat, trans. Naomi Shohet, with Krysia Osostowicz and Roy Howat (Cambridge: Cambridge University Press, 1986), 268–69.

From Chopin I have a new ballade. It seems to me to be the work which shows most extraordinary genius (if not greatest inspiration); and I told him that I like it the best of all his works. After a long pause to reflect, he said emphatically: "I am glad of that, for it is my favorite also." He also played me a host of newer etudes, nocturnes, and mazurkas—all incomparable.[3]

So the favored ballade was the one Schumann *had*, as opposed to the one he had simply heard, which would have been the G Minor, and it was probably one of the "new ones" mentioned in the diary entry; F. Gustav Jansen, who published this letter in his 1904 anthology of Schumann's correspondence, even inserts "G moll" in brackets after the "new ballade" reference.[4] Still, we know that after Chopin's visit Schumann knew two ballades: the one he preferred above all and received a copy of, and the one ("inferior to the first") he later described having heard Chopin play in a form different from what it would later become. The only explicit reference to a "ballade" other than the G Minor lies in Schumann's plural from 1841; Chopin said that "some poems of Mickiewicz" suggested *seine Balladen* to him. This—though it is at five years' distance from the actual conversation—is the clearest indication that the early version of op. 38 had already acquired the title "Ballade."

Painstaking examination of these fossil shards of memory is necessary because so much has been extrapolated from them, and not always judiciously. All we can say for sure from Schumann's accounts is that he preferred the G Minor Ballade but did hear a different version of op. 38 in 1836. Although the Second Ballade did not speak to Schumann as the First did, he still thought highly of it, at least in its published version. Although it might appear that Chopin's dedication (in 1841) of op. 38 to

---

3. "Von Chopin habe ich eine neue Ballade. Sie scheint mir sein genialischstes (nicht genialstes) Werk; auch sagte ich es ihm, daß es mir das liebste unter allen. Nach einer langen Pause Nachdenken sagte er mit großem Nachdruck—'das ist mir lieb, auch mir ist es mein Liebstes.' Außerdem spielte er mir eine Menge neuer Etüden, Notturnos, Masureks—alles unvergleichlich" (my translation). *Robert Schumanns Briefe: Neue Folge*, ed. F. Gustav Jansen (Leipzig: Breitkopf und Härtel, 1904), 1:78. This passage is also quoted in series 8, vol. 1, of the supplemental volumes of Robert Schumann, *Neue Ausgabe sämtlicher Werke*: Ernst Burger, *Robert Schumann: Eine Lebenschronik in Bilden und Dokumenten* (Mainz: Schott, 1998), 151. Translation is a bit of a problem here; the German words *genialisch* and *genial* mean "possessing genius," but with *genialisch* there is also the implication of unconventional, high-flown, boundless, and extravagant genius. Schumann seems to be suggesting not an either/or relationship between the terms, but rather that the first is somewhat more accurate than the second. I am grateful to Stephen Luttmann for his help with this knotty little phrase.

4. Schumann, *Robert Schumanns Briefe*, 1:78.

Schumann was in some way connected to the latter's affection for it, the dedication was probably just Chopin's professional reciprocity for to Schumann's 1838 dedication ("To his friend F. Chopin") of his *Kreisleriana*. Ultimately it does not matter that much. For our purposes, that Schumann heard Chopin's op. 38 in an earlier form from the composer's own fingers is a good starting point, and the absence of further information is very instructive, in a kind of negative way, when we consider the speculations and theories that have grown up around it.

Two Versions

Chopin's early performance for Schumann in Leipzig was not the only time the Ballade was heard in a form notably different from the published one, though; he played it this way at other times as well, as did those close to him. This well-documented point is relevant to all the problematic issues concerning the piece and is by no means a mere odd historical footnote. In this case, "versions" implies something quite different from the localized variants in ornamentation, phrasing, or chord voicing that emerge, say, from a comparison of different manuscripts and publications of Chopin's nocturnes, originating with the composer and those around him. It seems instead that the two versions of op. 38 reflected radically different conceptions of what the form, dramatic trajectory, affect, and even genre of the piece ought to be. Moreover, because the composer continued to perform the alternate version well after the piece was published in its now-familiar form, he was clearly not troubled by the coexistence of two such fundamentally different concepts of the work, any more than he was by the many variants that survive for his other works (many of which he provided himself).

There has been a good deal of speculation about the two versions, so a thorough reexamination of the available evidence will indicate what if anything concrete there is to be ascertained. The published version of this ballade is well-known and widely played; the phantom alternate version tantalizes because of the persistence of discussion coupled with the almost total lack of hard information about it, though such performance history as can be assembled seems to suggest that the composer preferred playing it. I would argue that the early history of the Second Ballade means that both versions have to be considered "works" in some sense, complete enough for performance. (It is not impossible that more than one additional version existed, though there is no particular reason to suppose so.) Although many of the items that follow have been published before, it seems appropriate to assemble them once and for all and compare them, to see if a plausible solution to the mystery might emerge.

In its published form, op. 38 begins in F major (with a B-flat in the key signature, which remains until the closing section) and ends in A minor.[5] Schumann's statement that the fiery A minor episodes originally were entirely missing means that, when he heard it, this other, non-G Minor Ballade was a much shorter and more monochromatic piece than the First Ballade. Such a piece is also at least generally consistent with the later descriptions of an alternate version of op. 38, which in turn may mean that what Schumann heard in 1836 may have remained a viable alternative rather than an early, incomplete, or superseded version. Reviews of Chopin's 1848 performances in England and Scotland suggest that this is the version he was playing at the end of his life (perhaps having been too weakened from the wasting effects of the illness that would ultimately kill him to play the larger version). For example, on 8 July 1848 an anonymous reviewer from the London *Examiner* wrote:

> Perhaps there is no one who at all who knows the works of Chopin, but knows and loves the Ballade in F Major, Op. 38. It opens with a tone repeated and swelled like a sound of nature—a breeze or a stream—out of which a song develops itself, as the witch of the Alps is shaped from the rainbow of the waterfall; but it still retains the character of a thing that grows up and is not made. It is short, simple, single; always fresh. In the last piece [meaning the last program group] this was set between the graceful whim of the Mazurka, first of Op. 5th, and the marvelous intertexture of an undulating Valse [probably op. 7 no. 1 is meant].[6]

Three months later Chopin was in Edinburgh. In the *Edinburgh Evening Courant* of 7 October 1848, a reviewer mentioned two other works, an "Andante et Largo," that

> were also very beautiful, introducing two Polish melodies, somewhat peculiar in style, yet very pleasing. That they went home to the hearts of such of the performer's compatriots as were present was evident from the delight with which they hailed each forgotten melody with all its early associations, as it rang in their ears. The

---

5. The ending itself was not unproblematic, though; between the manuscripts and early publications there are several different voicings of the subdued and fatalistic i–V7–i, A minor closing cadence, a gesture that clearly gave the composer a good deal of trouble.

6. Quoted in William Atwood, *Fryderyk Chopin: Pianist from Warsaw* (New York: Columbia University Press, 1987), 248.

concluding piece was also national, the ballad, reminding us somewhat of one of the choruses in Mendelssohn's *St. Paul* ("How Lovely are the Messengers," we think) and consequently having less originality than the other.[7]

"Short, simple, single," according to the *Examiner*, while the notably "national" ballade was, according to the *Edinburgh Evening Courant*, less original than the specifically Polish works. Example 1.1 gives the opening of Mendelssohn's "How Lovely," and example 1.2 gives the opening of op. 38.

Another contemporaneous review (published anonymously in the *Glasgow Herald* on 29 August 1848) seems to describe the same work, though it is not specifically identified: "Again in another subject, one single note of the key was heard with its monotonous pulsations moving through [a] peculiar series of musical embellishments. One thing...must have been apparent to every one of the audience, namely the melancholy

Ex. 1.1. Felix Mendelssohn, *St. Paul*, "How Lovely Are the Messengers," mm. 1–8.

---

7. Quoted in Atwood, *Fryderyk Chopin: Pianist from Warsaw*, 256. For what it's worth, just before the op. 38 Ballade took shape Chopin had heard Mendelssohn's *St. Paul* (and therefore the chorus in question); the composer had played it for him in the fall of 1835. In Mendelssohn's words, "It really was a sight to be seen on Sunday evening when I had to play [Chopin] my oratorio while inquisitive Leipzigers crowded on tiptoe into the room so as to be able to say they had seen Chopin. Between the first and second parts of the oratorio he dashed off his new studies and latest concerto to the astonishment of the Leipzigers, and then I went on with my *St. Paul* just as if an Iroquois and a Kaffir had met and conversed." Arthur Hedley, ed. and trans., *Selected Correspondence of Fryderyk Chopin* (London: Heinemann, 1962), 130.

Ex. 1.2. Fryderyk Chopin, Ballade no. 2, op. 38, mm. 1–11.

and plaintive sentiment which pervaded his music."[8] These descriptions might well describe something like one of the op. 28 preludes: a short, single-affect piece programmed as part of a group. It seems highly unlikely that anything like the published version of op. 38 would have resulted in these descriptions, all of which omit any discussion of the blistering A minor sections and off-tonic close.

Leaving the question of an alternate version aside for the moment, we can identify at least a limited tradition of performing only the first section of the piece, the F major siciliano of mm. 1–46. Chopin's childhood friend Józef Brzowski described the composer's performance, in late spring or early summer 1837, of—among other works—"the beginning of the Ballade no. 2 in F Major."[9] This is definite: not an earlier or alternate version, but instead just the first part of the version we know. Camille Saint-Saëns mentions the same approach: in his essay "A Chopin M.S.: The F Major Ballade in the Making," Saint-Saëns (who had never actually heard Chopin play) explained that his friend, the opera singer Pauline Viardot-Garcia, who had been both a close friend and a student of Chopin, "told me that [Chopin] had often played for her the Andantino of the beginning, but he had never continued and finished the piece."[10]

---

8. Ibid., 254.

9. Tad Szulc, *Chopin in Paris: The Life and Times of the Romantic Composer* (New York: Scribner, 1998), 182. Chopin and Brzowski were paying a visit to Chopin's friend the Marquis de Custine. This must have been written after 1841, when the ballade's final form was revealed to the world through its publication, and when it acquired its opus number.

10. Camille Saint-Saëns, "A Chopin M.S.: The F Major Ballade in the Making," in *Outspoken Essays on Music* [1922], trans. Fred Rothwell (Westport, CT: Greenwood Press [1970]), 102.

Ex. 1.3. Chopin, "Baladine," close.

Two musical documents testify further to the tradition of playing only the first forty-six measures of op. 38 as a complete work. The first is a marking the composer made in Jane Wilhelmina Stirling's score of op. 38. Stirling was a Scottish admirer and student of Chopin in the mid-1840s who remained his friend and supporter during and after his 1848 voyage to England and Scotland. In the words of Jean-Jacques Eigeldinger, she "remains famous for her devotion to the person, the works, and the memory of Chopin."[11] At the end of the first section in her score, Chopin simply marked an "X," as if to indicate "No further; you should only play to here."[12] What is more, there is an English publication (Chappell & Co., [1876]) of Chopin's "Baladine, Op. 38" that consists of *only* the first section; the final cadence is expanded over two measures, maintaining the melodic cadence on the prime but omitting Chopin's decorative arpeggio that ends on the third scale degree (see ex. 1.3).[13] Though this publication may signify no more than a publisher's attempt to bring the piece to a wider market of novice students and amateurs, it still hints—particularly in the context of the Stirling score and Chopin's English and Scottish performances—at a performance tradition in which the opening forty-six measures of the piece were treated as a completed whole. It seems that those in England and Scotland were most aware of this tradition, though

11. Eigeldinger, *Chopin: Pianist and Teacher*, 179.

12. Jean-Jacques Eigeldinger and Jean-Michel Nectoux, *Frédéric Chopin: Œuvres pour piano; Facsimile de l'exemplaire de Jane W. Stirling avec annotations et corrections de l'auteur* (Paris: Bibliothèque nationale, 1982), 247. Eigeldinger explains this particular meaning of Chopin's notated "X" in *Chopin: Pianist and Teacher*, 207 n. 21. He also uncritically repeats the similar story about the Princess Czartoryska and A. J. Hipkins as reported by Arthur Hedley (see n. 20 below), noting simply that the Viardot/Saint-Saëns version "finds some confirmation" with the Czartoryska/Hipkins/Hedley one.

13. There were actually two versions of this Chappell publication: the first consisted of only the first section, as described, and the second—a "Complete Version" [*sic*]—closing the first section with the same rewritten cadence, and appending the rest of the piece in a separate "movement" (thus, two "movements": one clearly in F major, the other beginning and ending in A minor). I am grateful to John Rink for directing my attention to these publications.

certain others (at least two near to the composer, Brzowski and Viardot) were aware of it also.

To my knowledge, that is the sum total of contemporary information about an alternate performance tradition. Later, though, more fanciful views of the single-key version began to be advanced. Gerald Abraham, in his 1939 book *Chopin's Musical Style*, tried to imagine what a version that ended in F major might have been like. His starting point for examining the form of the Second Ballade was the assumption that it was originally similar to that of the First, op. 23 in G Minor, which he had mapped out in this way:

Introduction: *Largo*.
First subject (*moderato*): G minor.
Second subject (*meno mosso*): E-flat major.
Development (*a tempo*): beginning in A minor and passing through various keys.
Second subject: E-flat major.
First subject (drastically shortened): G minor.
Coda (*presto con fuoco*): G minor.[14]

He then quotes the 1841 Schumann review, suggesting that while it is not clear what Schumann meant by "impassioned episodes," he might have meant

perhaps the powerful sequential passage that crowns the *presto con fuoco* second subject, perhaps the more strenuous incidents in the working out of the first subject, which follows this, or perhaps the stormy coda. But the return of the first subject is foreshadowed in the bass octave passage just before the coda and does actually occur, with dramatic effect, as a fleeting wistful reminiscence when this coda has reached its climax. Imagine, then, that, instead of the coda, heralded and rounded off by fragments of the first subject, Chopin had here simply written out the first subject in full and in F Major; we should have a form almost exactly like that of the G-Minor Ballade. And it seems to me highly probable that this or something like it *was* the original form of the piece that Schumann heard.[15]

Problems with Abraham's view include the facts that his definitions of "impassioned episodes" are neither straightforward nor stylistically

---

14. Gerald Abraham, *Chopin's Musical Style* [1939] (London: Oxford University Press, 1968), 55.
15. Ibid., 56–57.

consistent, and that the formal strategy of dispersing all the accrued energy at the end of op. 38 in a full statement of the opening F major siciliano would strike many (including me) as, to borrow a concept from Donald Francis Tovey, suicidal. Moreover, since Abraham has just described the final statement of the first subject of the First Ballade as "drastically shortened," it is hard to see why the first subject of the Second Ballade would have been "written out in full" if (as he states) he was taking op. 23 as a basic model. (Jim Samson's view is that Schumann's impassioned episodes "meant of course the figuration of Theme II,"[16] which makes more logical and intuitive sense.) Nonetheless, Abraham evidently considered this plan, which would have resulted in a much more extended version of the work that somehow still remained in F major, to reflect Chopin's original intent.

Still with a speculative element, yet even more vaguely, Arthur Hedley wrote in his 1947 Chopin biography that "he (and Princess Marcelline Czartoryska after him) used to play an extended version [N.B.] of the first section only, in F major. (A. J. Hipkins heard the princess play this in the fifties.)"[17] I know of no other source for this information, and Hedley provides none, so there is neither any actual documentation for this "extended version" of the opening section nor corroboration from a known source closer to Chopin's lifetime. One possible point of origin for this information is given by Hedley in an extraordinary statement:

> The book *How Chopin Played*, based on the recollections [of] A. J. Hipkins, has given a new lease of life to some of the most deplorable of the Chopin legends. Just how much of Chopin's playing Mr. Hipkins was acquainted with has lately been revealed to the writer by the acquisition of his annotated copies of Chopin. Mr. Hipkins was in no position to make *ex cathedra* pronouncements on the subject.[18]

Hipkins's account of the Second Ballade and Czartoryska's playing of it is nowhere to be found, neither in *How Chopin Played: From Contemporary Impressions Collected from the Diaries and Note-Books of the Late A. J. Hipkins* (London: J. M. Dent and Sons 1937), nor in an unpublished paper by Hipkins on Chopin in England from which Joseph Bennett quotes liberally in his serialized Chopin biography, which stretched across several numbers of the *Musical Times* in 1882.[19] The

---

16. Jim Samson, *Chopin: The Four Ballades* (Cambridge: Cambridge University Press, 1992), 53.
17. Arthur Hedley, *Chopin* [1947] (New York: Collier Books, 1962), 188.
18. Ibid., 119 n. 1.
19. Edith J. Hipkins and A. J. Hipkins, *How Chopin Played: From Contemporary Impressions Collected from the Diaries and Note-Books of the Late A. J. Hipkins*

scores seem to be untraceable, and it is more than a little interesting that they are cited nowhere else in the literature.[20] One might imagine some skepticism that the opening section alone—two and a half minutes maximum, at quite a slow tempo—really would be the entirety of the alternate version, but shorter Chopin pieces do exist, and the other sources state explicitly that this was the case. Because the mention of such a tradition stemming from Hipkins and the Princess Czartoryska shows up nowhere else, then, the influential Hedley is the sole source of the view of the alternate form of the ballade that consists of an "extended version" of the opening section.

The existence of a version of op. 38 that consisted of an extended treatment of the opening section, with or without some of the A minor material but still convincingly ending in F major, has, despite the absence of credible evidence for it, become part of the lore surrounding the piece. Attempts to trace or compose such a version are not uncommon, mostly owing (one suspects) to a general musicological I-love-a-mystery feeling about ghost versions, incomplete works, and

---

(London: J. M. Dent and Sons, 1937); Joseph Bennett, "The Great Composers: Chopin," *Musical Times*, 1 January 1882, 12–15; 1 February 1882, 70–74; 1 March 1882, 132–35; 1 April 1882, 191–94; 1 May 1882, 256–59; 1 June 1882, 314–17; and 1 July 1882, 372–75.

20. The similarity of the anecdote to the established one—Hipkins supposedly hearing the princess play precisely what Saint-Saëns heard from Pauline Viardot—renders it, to me, less plausible rather than more, and there are some odd loose ends associated with it. Fabricated plausibility based on extant, verifiable sources is a familiar strategy of those who would falsify; Richard D. Altick devotes an entire chapter of *The Scholar Adventurers* (New York: Macmillan, 1950) to a couple of famous cases of literary forgery where source plausibility was increased via the forger's knowledge of the subjects' biographies. The circumstance that Hedley had "recently acquired" the supposed Hipkins scores, which evinced enough musical ignorance to offend him, stretches credulity rather far, particularly because said scores seem to have disappeared without a trace and the Hipkins/Czartoryska anecdote is otherwise absent from the literature. Hipkins was an accomplished piano technician and musical scholar who had tuned for Chopin and heard him play; Hedley's waspish attack on his expertise seems oddly unmotivated. Sadly, the area of Chopin studies certainly has not been free of opportunistic pseudo-scholarship, and as much as one would not want to believe it of Hedley, this might be another case of it. (Jean-Jacques Eigeldinger has noted another troubling inconsistency in relation to Hedley's work: the letters of Joseph Filtsch, brother of the prodigiously talented Chopin student Carl Filtsch, are nowhere to be found outside Hedley's own edition of Chopin's correspondence, and they offer virtually nothing unavailable elsewhere; Eigeldinger, *Chopin: Pianist and Teacher*, 142 n. 157). The least attractive possibility, of course, is that some of this might be the product of Hedley's creativity. A more benign explanation for the scores' subsequent disappearance without a trace might be that at some later point Hedley realized he had probably been deceived at the time of purchase and, perhaps ashamed of his own credulity, disposed of the scores without further discussion.

so on.[21] Taken together, though, the published reactions to Chopin's 1848 performances in England and Scotland, the accounts of Viardot and Brzowski, the Stirling score, and perhaps even the Chappell publication strongly suggest that a short, uninterrupted F major version of the op. 38 Ballade—the opening andantino, in other words, and no phantom at all—not only existed but remained a viable option for the composer and at least two of his students (Stirling and Viardot), despite the fact that the 1840 publication of op. 38 is much more elaborate. In addition to being consistent with the surviving contemporary testimony (including that of Schumann), of course, a collateral benefit to this view is that the alternate version does survive intact, save perhaps for the final bar or two. My feeling, then, is that we can put this mystery in the "solved" column.

Two Keys

That there was an incontrovertibly F major version of the ballade is highly relevant to the debate about whether the tonic of the published version is really F major or A minor. The Second Ballade has long been called "the F Major" by pianists (cf. the title of the Saint-Saëns essay mentioned earlier), in reference to the single-flat key signature that is maintained for about five-sixths of the length of the work, the long opening section in F major that ends with a thoroughly prepared and coherent formal articulation (with several extensions to the cadence itself), and the clear return to that key (and initial thematic material) in

---

21. My thanks go to Jean Pang Goyal for sharing with me an early seminar paper she wrote on the subject. I have heard of a version by the Polish scholar Mieczyslaw Tomaszewski that received a performance by Murray Perahia (interestingly, in view of Perahia's stated belief that the true tonic of the piece is A minor), and Professor Steven Swayne of Dartmouth generously shared his own early efforts in this area with me. David Witten, taking a different approach, dismisses Gerald Abraham's conjecture with a "preposterous, hypothetical version of mm. 164–171, if indeed Schumann heard the *entire* Ballade with an ending in F major" (though he seems to be willfully misreading Schumann's account). David Witten, "The Coda Wagging the Dog: Tails and Wedges in the Chopin Ballades," in *Nineteenth-Century Piano Music: Essays in Performance and Analysis*, ed. Witten (New York: Garland, 1997), 149–50. The precise nature of this phantom version is often seen as an inviting compositional problem rather like, in a small way, that of completing Bach's *Kunst der Fuge*; the challenge of combining compositional creativity and historical awareness for a solution is seen as an inviting one. As was observed to me by William Marvin, the strength and structural positioning of the descending bass line that cadences into the ballade's closing section (mm. 167–169) precludes, once and for all, any coherent return to F major.

m. 83. What remains unexplained by this designation, of course, is the fact that the piece actually ends in A minor, a key briefly visited in the opening section and the key of the contrasting material that shatters the gentle pastoral mood in m. 47. Johannes Brahms seems to be the first on record to have had a different view of the tonality of op. 38; in a letter of 1 November 1877 to Ernst Rudorff, one of the editors for Breitkopf und Härtel with whom he was working on a complete edition of Chopin's works, he referred to a puzzling passage (the closing cadence of the opening section) of the "A Minor Ballade."[22]

In recent years, other commentators—including the pianist Murray Perahia and the scholars Joel Sheveloff and David Witten—have adopted the Brahmsian view. In the notes to his 1994 recording of the ballades, Perahia wrote: "I have requested that the Second Ballade, listed traditionally in the key of F major, be listed on the present release in the key of A minor. It is a fantasy, wherein the sub-mediant key of F major is prolonged, reverting to the tonic A minor only in the Coda."[23] Perahia does not explain why Chopin called the work a ballade and not a fantasy, despite the fact that he chose to call other works fantasies (opp. 49 and 61). Joel Sheveloff describes op. 38 as a work that

> prolongs F major stubbornly for forty-five measures, before suddenly shifting to A minor. It circles back to F in measure 82, but that merely teases. By the time the Ballade's 203 measures have passed by, we know the piece's real key to be A minor, and that the opening F functioned as submediant of an incomplete progression; the "key" of the beginning turns out to be illusory, but we do not know that until the very end.[24]

And David Witten, before offering the aforementioned newly composed retransition to F major as a counterargument to Schumann and Abraham, opines, "Clearly, Brahms the composer understood the A-minor destiny of the piece."[25] The inescapable corollary to that statement, of course,

---

22. The letter to Rudorff is translated in Styra Avins, ed., *Johannes Brahms: Life and Letters* (Oxford and New York: Oxford University Press, 1997), 533.

23. Murray Perahia, notes to his *Chopin: 4 Ballades* (1994), CD, Sony Classical SK 64399, 6.

24. Joel Sheveloff, "A Masterpiece from an Inhibition: Quashing the 'Inquisitive Savage,'" in Witten, *Nineteenth-Century Piano Music*, 286. Whether the opening section of op. 38 is 45 or 46 measures long, or the piece is 203 or 204 measures long, or the return to F major occurs on m. 82 or 83 depends on whether or not the incomplete opening measure is counted, and there is widespread editorial disagreement on this point. I count it, and Sheveloff does not.

25. Witten, "Coda," 140.

would have to be that Saint-Saëns the composer did not. This is not a comparison that we have any business making.

The view that posits A minor as the tonic key of the piece requires proponents (such as Perahia) to dismiss the opening forty-six measures, a complete F major AABA + coda song form that concludes with a fully prepared cadential passage (complete with phrase extensions) and fermata, as merely "the submediant of an incomplete progression," which is a demotion I consider to be counterintuitive and unpersuasive. It is also hard to see these forty-six measures as "stubborn" prolongation when we have so far had no other tonic, no other key to which we feel we should be returning. Rather, it is the finished and reposeful nature of that section—something akin to a self-standing character piece, longer than several of the op. 28 Preludes—and its context in the work as published that make Brahms's idea of the A minor tonic and the theoretical arguments subsequently constructed to support it insufficient. To boil the issue down: an A minor tonic for op. 38, as defended by Perahia, Witten, and others, would require the following statement to be true:

> A piece that begins in F major, maintaining a structure consistent with that tonic key for five-sixths of its length but closing in A minor, is somehow really in A minor.

Additionally, since this piece was performed in two versions, then one statement from the following pair would also have to be true:

> A forty-six-measure piece that begins and ends in F major and does not modulate is somehow really also in A minor.
> Or:
> The two versions of Chopin's op. 38 Ballade somehow are really in different keys and have different tonics.

The first statement is untenable, the second silly, and the third perverse.

Another, more recently propounded way of addressing the issue is to allow that there is simply a two-key plan, and to adduce preexistent piano works that begin and end in different keys (Jim Samson has offered Hummel's op. 18 Fantaisie and N. B. Challoner's *Battle of Waterloo* as examples) as possible models or influences.[26] Certain generic

---

26. On Hummel's op. 18, see Samson, *Chopin: The Four Ballades*, 16–18. Hummel's Fantaisie alternates, in its later stages, between E-flat major and G minor/major tonics. Surely, though, the generic disparity between fantasy (=evocation of pianistic extemporization) and ballade (=evocation of storytelling within certain poetic conventions) raise more issues than can be explained by the commonality of fluctuating tonics. Samson's brief reference to Challoner's *Battle of Waterloo* is found in Samson, "Chopin's Alternatives to Monotonality," in *The Second Practice of Nineteenth-Century*

assumptions make these somewhat uneasy comparisons, though. By virtue of its title, the ballade genre, even at this nascent point, implied a kind of narrative coherence and completion, as would be characteristic of a poetic ballad. The fantasy, by contrast, was a more diffuse genre that evoked a variety of free approaches: the introductory prelude or intonation, the creative treatment of a variety of themes from a certain work (such as an opera), or the aesthetic inspirations of the upper ether as realized in an in-the-moment improvisation. Even in this last case, the underlying coherent structure of such a piece was to be masked by apparent wildness and caprice.[27] Beethoven's Fantasy op. 77 for piano, for example, begins in G minor but ends, after many contrasts of material and tonality and after a series of variations on a theme, in B major; I at least would not make the argument that all the prior material, improvisatory and harmonically unfixed as it is, still somehow inevitably leads to B major. Earlier piano works with a migratory tonal center will not necessarily, it seems, be of much help unless there is a generic relationship.

Vocal literature provides some more apposite examples. Schubert's early song *Der Liedler* (1815) begins with two strophes in A minor about a minstrel's departure from home and hearth because of unrequited love, then moves to A-flat major and other keys to narrate his worldly travels, and (after a return to A minor, as he returns to his homeland), ultimately ends in A-flat major after an act of selfless heroism that ends in his own death. The repeated strophe in A minor, the centrality of those verses to the story, and that key's return mean that it is rather more than just an introduction, while the close in A-flat major, a very important key established early in the song but one entirely unrelated to A minor, means at the very least that there were more harmonic possibilities available to early nineteenth-century composers than we seem to be willing to acknowledge today. The same composer's "Ganymed" (1817) moves from an exultant awakening in A-flat major through E major to end in a pastoral F major as the boy wafts up through blue skies to Zeus. And "Thränenregen" (1823), the tenth song of Schubert's *Schöne Müllerin* cycle, begins in A major but, despite its three-sharp key signature, ends in A minor as the poet's hopes are dashed. Each of these three songs has a compelling dramatic reason for a progressive tonality; no two are the same, and I know of no obsessive anxiety in the

---

Tonality, ed. William Kinderman and Harald Krebs (Lincoln: University of Nebraska Press, 1996), 42. Programmatic piano pieces of the time likewise could end in different keys from those in which they began (*The Battle of Waterloo* begins in G major and ends in D major). More on this genre will follow in chapter 2.

27. See Annette Richards, *The Free Fantasy and the Musical Picturesque* (Cambridge: Cambridge University Press, 2001), a brilliant disquisition on the free fantasy genre.

literature (to match that for Chopin's Second Ballade) that seeks to account for these harmonic approaches.[28] Too often, perhaps because of the relatively small number of such pieces, we accord the tonic key the irrevocability of the basic laws of physics. James R. Gaines, writing specifically about the Baroque concerto but with much more in mind, put it this way: "The knowledge that in the end we would always return to the place, or key, where we began offered a kind of reassurance that the tension ... would be resolved, that all would be well in the end. (When music could no longer be relied upon to end up where it started, two world wars and the atomic bomb had taken away the assurance of such happy endings.)"[29] But the aforementioned vocal works and other examples of *Hausmusik* could end in keys other than those in which they began, without scandal or cultural upheaval. That op. 38 did not end in its initial key does not seem to have bothered its contemporary listeners, which should give us pause; if listeners of the time somehow had the vocabularies to understand such a piece and were not unduly troubled by a migrating tonic, then perhaps we, from the twentieth century on, are making entirely too much of the issue.

For what it's worth, I propose that most pianists, including Saint-Saëns, have always had this one right. Chopin's op. 38 is a ballade *in F major* that existed in at least two versions. One version was harmonically unproblematic: this is the phantom alternate version just discussed, played for Schumann in 1836 and other documented times since. The other version is, of course, the published version, which is in F major and functions like a work in F major right up to the preparations for the explosive final section; by that point it becomes clear that something has gone terribly wrong and there will be no solution, no escape from the second key area, A minor, which is clearly the wrong key. Rather than forcing the work to fit a model inappropriate to it, a more commonsensical view might be that the harmonic journey from a bucolic F major siciliano to a catastrophic A minor might have an analog in tragedy, the dramatic genre where all things do *not* come out all right in the end, and it might have to do with the story Chopin's ballade sought to tell. This would make the migrating tonic analogous to the Schubert examples cited above and suggests that when the subject of a narrative has traveled some psychological or even physical distance and there is no real or figurative return, there is no reason to suppose that the initial key must

---

28. Maurice J. E. Brown and Eric Sams, in the *New Grove* Schubert worklist, assign without further comment the opening keys of these songs as their tonics: "Der Liedler" is in A minor, "Ganymed" in A-flat major, and "Thränenregen" in A major. In the absence of all other argument, of course, this reasoning would put Chopin's op. 38 in F major.

29. James R. Gaines, *Evening in the Palace of Reason: Bach Meets Frederick the Great in the Age of Enlightenment* (New York: HarperCollins, 2005), 131.

again be reached before the piece can end. The point is not whether or not Chopin knew Schubert's music to any great extent, but rather that such strategies were being used at the time as part of the general compositional toolbox, especially for narrative music more associated with home use and enjoyment than professional venues.

What is needed is an explanation for the singular form of op. 38, not a tortuous argument that seeks to deny that a problem with the tonic even exists. Part of the answer might lie with the inspiration for the ballade, which Chopin alluded to in his early conversation with Schumann. Samson has perceptively suggested that the harmonic plan is tied to the narrative itself: "I am suggesting that, given the music's referential code, we do not need a Mickiewicz poem to read the Second Ballade's narrative of innocence under threat, a narrative that in turn presents confrontation, mediation, and transformation. The two-key scheme is part of that narrative."[30] At risk of overstating the case: it would take a special kind of stubbornness and anachronistic approach to a work from the mid-nineteenth century titled "Ballade" to presume that it is *not* telling a story of some kind. My own view of that narrative will be advanced in later chapters; for now, let us proceed with the assumption that a specific Mickiewicz poem is not necessary to provide a key or solution to the meaning of this ballade. Chopin, after all, never implied such a thing. Still, there is no reason not to take him at his word regarding his general inspiration, to doubt Schumann's account of their earlier conversation, or to regard the comment as insignificant. The presence of Mickiewicz in discussions of the ballades and, more generally, in Chopin's biography needs another look, because to this point much of the discussion in the Chopin literature on this matter has been as inconclusive as that regarding versions and keys, and even more wrongheaded. For this reason, we will briefly broaden the discussion to all four ballades, because it will enable us to see how the widespread but questionable practice of identifying specific poems with specific pieces evolved, and how some really unsupported speculations gradually came to be regarded as components of an authoritative tradition.

"Certain Poems of Mickiewicz"

Adam Mickiewicz (1798–1855), though himself of Lithuanian birth, was both the major figure in Polish literary Romanticism and the most

---

30. Samson, "Chopin's Alternatives to Monotonality," 42.

prominent literary tribune of embattled Poland, which was in a state of near subjugation to the Russian czar after the disastrous insurrection of December 1830 and Russia's 1831 reprisal. (Lithuania and Poland had been a single political entity from the late fourteenth century until 1795, when a partition put much of this territory under Russian domination.) By the early 1830s Mickiewicz—still several years shy of forty—already held an honored position among Polish writers and was seen by the sympathetic Europeans as something of a standard-bearer for Polish national aspirations. Mickiewicz and Chopin knew each other from Polish émigré circles in Paris, though their personalities and responses to the Polish crisis were very different: Mickiewicz yearned for an organized Polish response, inspired by the finest Polish artists, while Chopin had a strong personal reaction to his nation's circumstances but was not inclined to involve himself with broader nationalistic activities. Still, the Parisian connection between Poland's Psalmist (as Mickiewicz has been called) and Poland's Bard (a traditional image of Chopin) was highly suggestive. Schumann's 1841 recollection of Chopin's 1836 remark that "certain poems of Mickiewicz had suggested his *Ballades* to him" somehow eventually became a received tradition found, with variations, throughout the Chopin literature: that because Mickiewicz wrote certain poems that he called *ballady* (ballads), each of Chopin's four ballades for piano must therefore have been based on a particular Mickiewicz poem. Further weakening the sloppy logic that underlies this tradition is the odd point that the poems usually offered as models were not necessarily those Mickiewicz designated as ballads, and that even though Chopin made his remark when only two of his ballades had been written, yet it has always been considered to apply to the second two as well. A collective sense of *se non è vero, è ben trovato* is perhaps the only reason for a broad-brush interpretation of Chopin's comment, vestiges of which are found even to the present day. Because of this tradition's persistence and influence, it will be necessary to trace its development, which makes for a cautionary tale about the need for sober scrutiny and evaluation of historical sources.

Until 1900 sources suggesting a connection between Mickiewicz and Chopin's ballades were fragmentary and inconclusive. Marceli Antoni Szulc, later one of Chopin's first biographers, mentioned the idea in his review of the Third Ballade, op. 47, in 1842. He seems to have read Schumann's review, though he did not recall the precise source, and the relevant comment seems to have been embellished. Note that even though both the First and Second Ballades had already been published by that time, Szulc does not seem aware of any specific poetic associations, which—we have to assume—would otherwise have appeared in the discussion:

We read somewhere that now and then Mickiewicz's poems, specifically his *Ballady* and *Piosnki*, gave origin to some of the most charming works by Mr. Chopin. If it can be believed, this detail would provide an extraordinary testimony to a spiritual affinity between our two greatest bards and would throw much light on Mr. Chopin's artistic development. The ballade under consideration [is] so fresh, fragrant, charming, airy, [and] full of grace that one cannot resist the thought that Mr. Chopin captured in harmonious sounds the impression taken from reading of one of these beautiful works by Mickiewicz. Particularly that stanza [the first return of the F minor theme, mm. 81 ff.] returning several times reminds us of these unimaginable stories, full of marvels, with which a nanny inspires the dreaming imagination of a child. Its mysterious circles surround us closer and closer with their charming power, lead us into unknown realms, into the realm of dreams and illusion; suddenly a more sorrowful note reveals itself, growing slowly, in a turmoil of fantastic and frantic passages, to extraordinary violence. That stanza, however, knows how to cast a spell on it, to console it, calm it down; only the bass wanders in chromatic passages looking for peace. At last it calms down too, and the initial theme appears in all the splendor of harmony and victorious chords and ends that marvelous poem, full of life and truth.[31]

Schumann's comment from the previous year, whether Szulc saw it or became acquainted with it second- or thirdhand, thus became a basis for speculation. Poland's two most celebrated artists are compared, and because one has gone silent, the other (inspired by the first) steps to the fore. Szulc, still living in Poland, seems to have been unaware that Mickiewicz

---

31. "Czytaliśmy gdzieś, że nierzadko poezye, mianowicie *Ballady* i *Piosnki* Mickiewicza, niejednemu z najpowabniejszych utworów p. Chopina dają początek. Jeśli zawierzać można, niepospolite dałby szczegół taki świadectwo o duchowym pokrewieństwie dwóch naszych największych wieszczów, i znacznie-by rozświetlił drogę rozwoju p. Chopina. *Ballada* niniejsza, tak świeża, wonna, powabna, napowietrzna, pełna wdzięku, iż nie można się oprzeć myśli, jakoby p. Chopin wrażenie powzięte z czytania jednego z owych cudnych utworów Mickiewicza w harmonijne złowił dźwięki. Osobliwie owa zwrotka [strona 7, system 1 i 2], powracająca kilka razy, przypomina nam owe powiastki niepojęte, pełne dziwów, któremi niańka rozmarzoną wyobraźnię dziecięcia kołysze. Jej czarodziejskie koła coraz bliżej swą uroczą potęgą nas osnuwają, wiodą w nieznane krainy, w dziedzinę marzeń i ułudy; z nienacka boleśniejsza przebija się nuta, wzbierając zwolna w wirze fantastycznych i szalonych pochodów, do niezwyczajnej gwałtowności." Marceli Antoni Szulc, "Przegląd ostatnich dzieł Chopina," *Tygodnik Literacki* (Poznań), 7 and 14 March 1842, quoted in Ferdynand Hoesick, *Chopin: Życie i twórczość* (Warsaw: F. Hoesick; Cracow: G. Gebethner & Spółka, 1910–1911), vol. 2, 483–84. I am indebted to Jolanta Pekacz for this excerpt and its translation.

and Chopin did not occupy similar places in the Parisian Polish community and that their relations were not really warm.[32] What was most important was that Poland itself had an artistic voice heard by the rest of Europe. Still, he makes no specific identification of the poetic source of the Third Ballade, nor does he allude to a Polish tradition that posited one.

The year 1849 saw both Chopin's death and an article written in response to it by Józef Sikorski, a critic who was a bit younger than Chopin but had studied with the same composition teacher, Józef Elsner. The article was titled "Recollections of Chopin" and begins with the closing lines of Mickiewicz's narrative poem *Konrad Wallenrod*: "Such is my lay of Aldona's fate / Let a soft-hearted reader, an angel on high / Compose an end that may heavenward fly."[33] The article briefly mentions Chopin's Second Ballade, which is felt to correspond more closely to German legends than those of Poland, but makes no direct connection between Mickiewicz's poems and any particular Chopin piece. We will have occasion to revisit both Sikorski's article and that particular Mickiewicz poem and passage, which enter our story very early.

Neither of the early Chopin biographers Hippolyte Barbedette (1861; 2nd ed. 1869) and Moritz Karasowski (3rd ed. 1879) says anything about any specific Mickiewicz works. As nearly as may be ascertained, the first identification of a specific Mickiewicz poem as the inspiration for one of Chopin's ballades was made by Jean Kleczyński (1837–95). Kleczyński was a Chopin "grandstudent" (he studied with three different important Chopin students and two of the composer's other associates when he lived in Paris during the years 1859–66) who wrote two books about Chopin's music and edited a ten-volume edition of it.[34] "There is no doubt that the impulse to create the ballads was given to Chopin by the ballads of Mickiewicz," he tells us, slightly distorting Schumann's original comment without acknowledging it, "and the third ballade is evidently inspired by Undine."[35] He does not attribute this "evident" connection to any of his teachers or other Chopin acquaintances. "Undine" is the French title of one of Mickiewicz's two poems about the haunted lake Świteź, *Świtezianka* and *Świteź*. The first is about a water nymph ("Undine," translated in English as "The Nixie") who punishes an unfaithful knightly lover

---

32. See Jolanta T. Pekacz, "Deconstructing a 'National Composer': Chopin and Polish Exiles in Paris, 1831–49," *Nineteenth-Century Music* 24/2 (Fall 2000), 161–72.

33. Józef Sikorski, "Wspomnienie Chopina" [Recollections of Chopin], *Biblioteka Warszawska* 4 (1849), 544. The translation is from Adam Mickiewicz, *Konrad Wallenrod* [1828] *and Grazyna* [1823], trans. Irene Suboczewski (Lanham, MD: University Press of America, 1989), 63.

34. Eigeldinger, *Chopin: Pianist and Teacher*, 102–3 n. 34.

35. Jean Kleczyński, *Chopin's Greater Works: How They Should Be Understood*, trans. and with additions by Natalie Janotha (London: William Reeves, 1896), 68.

by drawing him beneath the surface of her lake in a terrible whirlpool, and the second (called in French "Le lac de willis") is about a group of maidens who flee the lusts of conquering Russian soldiers and cast themselves into the lake, preferring suicide to defloration, becoming the lilies that surround it. Kleczyński's identification is odd, given that he quotes no more authoritative source (indeed, his wording implies that this is his own idea) and that Chopin's Third Ballade is the only one to end in a major key, following the triumphant statement of the opening theme—an odd realization of a poem that ends with the tragic consequences of a woman (or, in this case, a nixie) scorned.

That Kleczyński identified *Świtezianka* with the Third Ballade—the earliest specific identification I know—is relevant because the "traditional" association of the Second Ballade, op. 38, also involves one or the other of these two Świteź poems. This suggestion is first made in the next discussion of the Chopin-Mickiewicz "tradition" to appear in print, by the imaginative American Chopin arts critic, biographer, and sometime pianist James Gibbons Huneker (1857–1921), who in 1900 somehow had more information to offer. Of the First Ballade, op. 23, he writes: "That Chopin had a program, a definite one, there can be no doubt; but he has, wise artist, left us no clue beyond [the Lithuanian poems of Mickiewicz], the Polish bard." So far so good, but he immediately continues: "The G minor Ballade[,] after *Konrad Wallenrod*, is a logical, well-knit and largely planned composition. The closest parallelism may be detected in its composition of themes."[36] Huneker does not acknowledge the obvious inconsistency between these two comments. If Chopin, the "wise artist," left no clue beyond Mickiewicz's name, what is the source of the "after *Konrad Wallenrod*" comment, which is offered as fact, not speculation? Perhaps these are vestiges of different stages of the writing process or an editing oversight. Of the Second and Third Ballades, Huneker has this to say:

[The Second Ballade, op. 38] is really in the keys of F major–A minor. Chopin's psychology was seldom at fault. A major ending would have crushed this extraordinary tone poem, written, Chopin admits, under the direct inspiration of Adam Mickiewicz's "Le Lac de Willis."

[The Third Ballade, op. 47], the "Undine" of Mickiewicz, published November, 1841, and dedicated to Mlle. P. de Noailles, is too well-known to analyze. It is the schoolgirls' delight, who familiarly

---

36. James Huneker, *Chopin: The Man and His Music* [1900], with new introduction, footnotes, and index by Herbert Weinstock (New York: Dover, 1966), 156.

toy with its demon, seeing only favor and prettiness in its elegant measures.[37]

Huneker's florid prose style and too-ardent love of clever wordplay have left him vulnerable to accusations of dilettantism, but he did have a substantial piano background, even if his ambitions in this area were ultimately to be disappointed. While in Paris in 1878–79 he had been an auditor of the piano classes of Georges Mathias, piano professor for more than thirty years at the Paris Conservatory;[38] Mathias had been a long-time Chopin pupil and one of only two (the other was Karol Mikuli) to have had a distinguished teaching career after Chopin's death.[39] Huneker did understand French, so it is certainly possible that he was privy to Mathias's thoughts about the ballades and Mickiewicz, including perhaps information that originated with Chopin himself. Still, no surviving source justifies Huneker's statement that Chopin himself admitted a connection between the Second Ballade and Mickiewicz's *Świteź*, and his statement about the Third simply echoes Kleczyński. About all we can tell for sure from Huneker's comments is that people were interested in the poetic inspiration for the ballades.

Huneker provides no poetic identification for the Fourth Ballade. It is certainly possible that his book, translated into Polish and published in 1901, was the primary source (or print source, at least) of this reputedly but not demonstrably "Polish" tradition of associating specific Mickiewicz poems with the ballades. The monumental two-volume Chopin biography by Frederick Niecks (1888; 2nd ed. 1890, and 3rd ed. 1902) mentions no such connections, despite Niecks's extensive interviews with surviving Chopin students and friends in Paris. It is no great leap to suggest that if there were more to the Chopin-Mickiewicz tradition, one of the early biographers would have ferreted it out; yet in the surviving sources from the first half century after Chopin's death neither explicit connections between Chopin ballades and Mickiewicz poems nor a particular desire for them are to be found. The nineteenth century, it seems, was content to read Schumann literally: some poems of Mickiewicz inspired Chopin. And, for a number of decades, there the matter lay.

---

37. James Huneker, *Chopin: The Man and His Music* [1900], with new introduction, footnotes, and index by Herbert Weinstock (New York: Dover, 1966), 158–59.

38. Arnold T. Schwab, *James Gibbons Huneker: Critic of the Seven Arts* (Stanford, CA: Stanford University Press, 1963), 21, 121.

39. For more on Mathias, see Eigeldinger, *Chopin: Pianist and Teacher*, 170–71. Although Huneker never realized his pianistic ambitions (a subject about which he was somewhat sensitive), he was pianist enough to have taught for ten years (1888–98) at the National Conservatory in New York, having been hired by Rafael Joseffy as part of his six-person piano staff. Schwab, *James Gibbons Huneker*, 51–52.

Before we move beyond the nineteenth century, and in the interests of completeness, here is a program for op. 38 that Huneker attributes to the superpianist Anton Rubinstein: "Is it possible the interpreter does not feel the necessity of representing it to his audience—a field flower caught by a gust of wind, a caressing of the flower by the wind; the resistance of the flower, the stormy struggle of the wind; the entreaty of the flower, which at last lies there broken; and paraphrased—the field flower a rustic maiden, the wind a knight."[40] This program draws in some ways on gendered views of instrumental music that occasionally moved from relatively bland vocabulary of "masculine themes" and "feminine cadences" to really disturbing images, such as this summary of sonata form by Vincent D'Indy: "It is as if, after the active battle of the development, the being [*l'être*] of gentleness and weakness has to submit, whether by violence or by persuasion, to the conquest of the being of force and power."[41] Perhaps programs that are unsupported by such clearly identifiable musical phenomena as musical topics or references to other pieces are like Rorschach inkblot tests: indicators more of aspects of the commentator's personal psychology than of anything inherent in the objects themselves, and as such best left to mental health professionals. Contemporary musicologists will note that Adrienne Rich's poem *The Ninth Symphony of Beethoven Understood at Last as a Sexual Message* (1971–72) or interpretations built upon it were not the first suggestions of rape as subtext to a canonical instrumental work; the rape metaphor clearly has a longer history. Fortunately, it is a subject that disappears from our study right here.

In 1902, shortly after Huneker's book appeared, the pianist Edward Baxter Perry published his *Descriptive Analyses of Piano Works*, a book that includes lengthy treatments of the first three ballades. Some of the author's introductory words on method are worth quoting:

> Few among English-speaking musicians are able to read Mickiewicz in the original Polish; translations of his works are meager, imperfect, and very difficult to obtain. It is therefore not without a certain glow of satisfaction that the present writer is able, after diligent, unwearying inquiry and voluminous reading, covering a period of some fifteen years, confidently to affirm that he has at last traced back to their inspirational sources three at least of the four ballades; and he submits to the reader the results of his research, in the hope

---

40. Huneker, *Chopin: The Man and His Music*, 281–82.
41. Quoted as part of Marcia Citron's discussion of music as gendered discourse in her *Gender and the Musical Canon* (Cambridge: Cambridge University Press, 1993), 132–45.

that some degree of the interest and pleasure he has himself derived from this line of investigation may be shared by others.

Should any question arise with regard to the accuracy of the statements and conclusions here advanced, I would say that the authority on which they are based is derived partly from definite historical data, existing, though widely diffused, in print; partly from direct traditions gathered from those who enjoyed the personal acquaintance of the composer; and partly from the carefully considered internal evidence of the works themselves, when critically compared with the poems to which they presumably had reference.[42]

Surely the author protests too much, particularly when no actual sources are identified; for all its length this explanation is still quite vague. (Perry is at least honest enough to offer a plea to his readers to send him anything they can find out about the Fourth Ballade.) Besides being a pianist and author, Perry was a poet (of a kind), and he begins his book with not one but two poems, "My Keys" and "Only an Interpreter," which do little to inspire confidence in his approach. What little is available about him suggests that he was Boston based and, interestingly, blind (e.g., "the famous blind musician"),[43] so one wonders just what kind of reading he could have been doing, and what kinds of sources he could encounter as he indefatigably toured the United States.

There is a useful element in his method, though, whether it helps with identification or not: in an opening discussion of his approach, Perry says, "Long practice in perceiving and grasping what may be termed the 'internal evidence' of the music itself will develop, in the musician, a susceptibility to such impressions, which will often lead him to a knowledge elsewhere sought in vain."[44] If we take "internal evidence" to mean musical topics and styles and "susceptibility to such impressions" to imply linguistic competence in understanding a composer's stylistic idiom—these are not far-fetched glosses—we are probably close to what Perry meant, and it is an approach too rarely taken with the ballades. The actual linking of musical features with plot happens only rarely in Perry's discussion, however, and he only identifies the same poems as does Huneker. His writing is far too purple—these are less analyses than pseudo-literary effusions—and what he seems to enjoy most is the lengthy retellings of the poems.

---

42. Edward Baxter Perry, *Descriptive Analyses of Piano Works* (Philadelphia: Theodore Presser, 1902), 122–23.
43. *Nashville Globe*, 25 January 1907.
44. Ibid., 31.

The next development in this tradition originated in 1924 but was not published until later; it is described in the preface to Alfred Cortot's edition of Chopin's ballades (Editions Maurice Senart, 1929). I quote from David Ponsonby's English translation (Editions Salabert, 1931):

> The interpreter would be depriving himself of one of his most precious resources if he did not attempt to probe beneath the expressive magnificence of the musical language, and, in spite of its being sufficient unto itself, there discover the secret of the impression which first gave birth to it.
> In this we feel that we shall help him by reproducing here, after the version provided by Laurent Ceillier [sic; Cellier][45] in his commentaries on our series of concerts given in 1924, the brief account of the four poems which, according to tradition[,] suggested to Chopin the conception of his immortal works. May they bring to light the true reflection of the emotion by which these pages were dictated to the sublime musician of the soul of Poland.[46]

Thus adducing "tradition," Cortot quotes or paraphrases Cellier to the effect that the First Ballade is based on *Konrad Wallenrod*, but specifically the one episode that Mickiewicz subtitled *Ballad* ("The Ballad of Alpuhara"), a lay of Moorish Spain sung at a feast by the thoroughly inebriated title character, wherein a defeated Moorish king surrenders to his Christian enemies but exacts a terrible vengeance by infecting them with the plague. There seems to be no motivation beyond the word "Ballad" for this identification, because there is nothing in the music of op. 23 that identifies it with medieval Spain or the Muslim-Christian power struggle. Cellier and Cortot assign the Second and Third Ballades the same poems as did Huneker and Perry: op. 38 is associated with *Świteź*, the story of the Lithuanian virgin suicides, and op. 47 with *Undine* (*Świtezianka*), the jilted water sprite. Now, however, Chopin's Fourth Ballade is assigned a poem: *Trzech Budrysów* (Three Budrys), a lighthearted tale of a Lithuanian father who sends his three sons forth for adventure, acquisition, and manly quests, after which each returns with a bride, so the poem ends with three weddings. (Those who know the Fourth Ballade, with its aching melancholy and virtuosic minor-mode tempest of a closing section, will have their own thoughts about this identification.) The capsule summaries are vague and inexact. The Cellier/Cortot identifications were further

---

45. Laurent Cellier was the author of a book on Roger-Ducasse and editor of a collection of Breton folk songs.
46. Alfred Cortot, *Chopin Ballads (Students' Edition)*, trans. David Ponsonby (Paris: Editions Salabert, 1931), iii.

disseminated in the English-speaking world by way of the 1931 edition of Chopin's letters, collected by Henryk Opieński, which has a prefatory note by the translator, E. L. Voynich, that cites Cortot (without mentioning Cellier) and expands the summaries.

Meanwhile, on the Polish side, in 1926 Zdzisław Jan Jachimecki (1882–1953) published a Chopin biography (French translation by the author, 1930) in which he provided "descriptive analyses" of the ballades, including the close linking of, now, *Świtezianka* with the Second Ballade. It included his view of the work's wan closing melodic fragment as a setting of the closing words of the poem: "And who is the maiden? I know not." (To the Third Ballade Jachimecki assigns Heinrich Heine's *Lorelei*, so for him the Second and Third Ballades form a kind of pair, sharing the theme of malevolent fairies of the deep.)[47] Jachimecki's conception is considered to have been highly influential on the interpretations of pianists who came after him.[48] So, by 1931, specific Mickiewicz-Chopin connections had been disseminated, in a tone of specialist knowledge and certainty, in Polish, French, and English. Further, because of the disagreements between Jachimecki and Cellier/Cortot and the similarity in title and content, the matter of which precise poems were to be associated with the Second and Third Ballades was now becoming hazy. Still, a sense of mysterious yet authentic arcana came to be attached to the entire issue.

It is possible that Jachimecki was swayed to associate the Second Ballade with *Świtezianka* rather than *Świteź* by an earlier work, the vocal setting (1828) of the *Świtezianka* poem by Maria Szymanowska, a Polish pianist and composer (and, as it happened, Mickiewicz's mother-in-law; see ex. 1.4). The key is F major, the meter is 6/8, and the texture bears more than a passing resemblance to that found in the opening section of Chopin's Second Ballade. There the relationship ends, however; Szymanowska's setting seems to be a late derivative of Blondel's romance "Un fièvre brûlante" from André-Ernest-Modeste Grétry's *Richard Coeur-de-Lion* (1784), a studiedly simple and naive (and highly influential) number that evoked a kind of antique innocence, to the utter delight of Parisian audiences. Still, the superficial resemblance between the Second Ballade and an obscure Polish vocal setting of one of the two Mickiewicz poems tradition declared it to be based upon is suggestive, particularly when there is so little else of a concrete nature and the tradition itself gives the impression of grasping at straws.

---

47. Zdzisław Jachimecki, *Frédéric Chopin et son œuvre* (Paris: Librairie Delagrave, 1930), 131–32.

48. The Web site of the Narodowy Chopin Institute in Poland, http://www.nifc.pl/chopin/persons/text/id/679/lang/en, accessed 19 February 2007.

Ex. 1.4. Maria Szymanowska, "Świtezianka," mm. 1–12.

[musical score with lyrics:]
Ja-kiz to chło-piec pie-kny i mło-dy? Ja-ka to o-bok dzie-wi-ca?
Brze-ga-mi si-nej Świ-te-zi wo-dy i-da przy świe-tle ksie-ży-ca.
O-na mu z ko-sza da-je ma-li-ny, a on jej kwia-tki do wia-nka;

    The year 1934 saw an obscure publication, by one J. Stan, which enraged Lubov Keefer to the point that she published a contemptuous rebuttal to it in the *American Slavic and East European Review* in 1946 (incidentally, Keefer is the one who provides Stan with the first name of "Jean," otherwise unattested).[49] This ambitious little work reads like the product of an enthusiast, from its opening philosophy about describing music, its one-line apologia ("our sole excuse is to have wanted to be useful"), its impressionistic quotation of poetry, and its illustrations. Each ballade is given its own chapter; Stan begins by describing the circumstances of its genesis, then summarizes the assigned poem, and finally

---

49. Lubov Keefer, "The Influence of Adam Mickiewicz on the *Ballades* of Chopin," *American Slavic and East European Review* 5/1–2 (May 1946), 35–80.

matches musical elements to points in the poem. He does admit, wisely, that "it would surely be in vain to look, in the Chopin Ballade, for a line-by-line translation of a poem by his friend Mickiewicz," and he does note the oddity of imagining that the First Ballade was based on a Spanish episode from *Konrad Wallenrod* when there is nothing in the music to suggest Spain.[50] That observation is stylistically well founded, unlike some of his narrative readings, such as that the stark opening octaves of the First Ballade indicate the protagonist's drunkenness.[51] Stan's poem identifications follow Cellier/Cortot rather than Jachimecki: *Konrad Wallenrod* for no. 1, *Świteź* (about the mass suicide) for no. 2, "Ondine" (*Świtezianka*) for no. 3, and *Trzech Budrysów* for no. 4. This pamphlet lends additional apparent weight to the tradition of associating a specific poem with each ballade by devoting an entire publication to it, but it offers nothing new by way of historical justification for doing so.

By 1939, the year Gerald Abraham's short and mostly perceptive book *Chopin's Musical Style* was published, the author knew Huneker's book but was only generally aware of anything that had happened since (he noted "a sort of legend" linking the Fourth Ballade and the *Trzech Budrysów* but does not mention Cellier, Cortot, Jachimecki, Voynich, or Stan), and he fixed a gimlet eye on the authenticity of Huneker's reportage. Following a mention of Chopin's original comment to Schumann, Abraham offered the following evaluation of Huneker's method:

> As far as I can discover, Chopin himself never admitted anything more definite than this. But Huneker, in *Chopin: the Man and his Music*, first commends him as a "wise artist" for giving no more definite clue, and then goes on, without quoting any authority, to speak of "the G minor Ballade, after *Konrad Wallenrod*," to assert that the Second Ballade was "written, Chopin admits, under the direct inspiration of Adam Mickiewicz's *Le Lac de Willis*," and to speak of the A flat Ballade as "the *Undine* of Mickiewicz." (On the F minor he says nothing, though there is a sort of legend connecting it with the poem *Trzech Budrysów*.) Now Huneker was cursed not only with an unduly florid prose style but with a tendency to intellectual pretentiousness that only too often arouses suspicion that he was something of a charlatan. If he had ever read *Konrad Wallenrod*, he would have known that there is about as much connection between the G-Minor Ballade and Mickiewicz's grim narrative poem, with its exceedingly tough and unpleasant hero, as

---

50. J[ean?] Stan, *Les ballades de Chopin* (Paris: Parisis Éditions, [1934]), 27, 28.
51. Ibid., 30.

between *Macbeth* and Chopin's Barcarolle. As for *Le Lac de Willis* and *Undine*, I strongly suspect that they are one and the same poem: namely Mickiewicz's ballad, *Świtezianka*, of which a translation is given, as *The Nixie*, in *Konrad Wallenrod, and other writings of Adam Mickiewicz*, translated by various authors and published in 1925 by the University of California Press. (On the other hand, by *Le Lac de Willis* Huneker may have meant *Świteź*, which is also a poem about a haunted lake.) *Świtezianka*, which Rimsky-Korsakov long afterwards set as a cantata, might conceivably have inspired the Second Ballade, but it is absolutely preposterous to suggest that it has any connection with the Third.[52]

So in 1939, Abraham is calling all the identifications into question, including the one that—though he seems unaware of this fact—dates back to before Huneker (*Undine/Świteź*, first advanced by Kleczyński). In the meantime, the disparate views of Cortot/Cellier and Jachimecki had confused the *Świteź* and *Świtezianka* poems and (correspondingly) the Second and Third Ballades, probably beyond correction, so Abraham chose the poem he found more likely and decided that it was the intended candidate. Abraham's mention of a "sort of legend" linking Mickiewicz's "Three Budrys" with the Fourth Ballade suggests that the Cortot/Cellier approach had gained some traction, probably among pianists, though he was unaware of its precise source.

What is baffling is that even while registering skepticism about the specific identifications, reputable writers continued to repeat them, presumably out of reluctance to ignore extant literature and seem uninformed thereby. Arthur Hedley's Chopin biography managed to confuse the situation further in 1947 in his impatient recension of Jachimecki:

> Not content with insisting that this work illustrates the story of how the inhabitants of Switez were engulfed in the enchanted lake, Jachimecki goes so far as to make the last bars a setting of the actual text of Mickiewicz's poem: "And who is the maiden? I—know—not"—*finis*. The listener who has never heard of Mickiewicz or his poem need not worry. The Ballade exists for the whole world as beautiful and convincing music in its own right.[53]

For his confusion of the two poems (*Świteź* features the engulfed maidens; *Świtezianka* the given closing lines), Hedley was painstakingly

---

52. Abraham, *Chopin's Musical Style*, 57–58.
53. Hedley, *Chopin*, 174–75.

taken to task in 1967 by Adam Harasowski. Harasowski did not otherwise address or evaluate the tradition itself, and he noted with regret that the revised edition (1966) of Hedley's book had not corrected the point.[54] The extent to which individual Mickiewicz poems became unavoidable in ballade-related discussions may be seen in Camille Bourniquel's 1957 French Chopin biography (translated into English in 1960), which dutifully repeats the associations—without source citations—but immediately negates them with remarks such as "The subject [of the First Ballade] is supposed to be the story of a Lithuanian hero, Konrad Wallenrod, but with all due reservations this seems to be a quite unacceptable contention" and "it is difficult to see on what basis attempts have been made to connect [the Fourth Ballade] with the Lithuanian legend of *The Three Brothers Budrys.*" The Second Ballade is linked to Świteź, with no doubts, while the Third is linked to *both* Heine's *Lorelei* and Mickiewicz's *Undine* (= Świtezianka).[55] So, as was the case with Gerald Abraham, the author's distrust of the entire tradition was not sufficient to prevent the recounting of it. As ought to be clear by now, the tradition is essentially folkloric, with no real sources, yet people cannot quite bring themselves to let go of it completely.

Today one or another vague version of this "tradition" still appears regularly in program and CD notes and on Web sites worldwide, source uncited. For example, Murray Perahia wrote in 1994, "Personally, I have found the Schumann attestation regarding Mickiewicz's poems convincing, and I feel that an acquaintance with the musical facts surrounding these Ballades renders the poems even more relevant and evocative."[56] That Schumann's handful of words says almost nothing definite, that Perahia doesn't specify which "musical facts" he means or which poems are supposedly now more relevant and evocative—none of this matters; the hoary myth, now legitimized, is as familiar as George Washington's cherry tree. Yet if the linkage between specific Mickiewicz poems and Chopin's ballades really were of Polish provenance, or at any rate if it originated in the composer's lifetime, it would have received more attention in print before Kleczyński's isolated, offhand sentence about the Third Ballade, the Polish translation of Huneker's too-imaginative work, and a Polish biography published two years after Laurent Cellier's highly dubious commentaries on Alfred Cortot's 1924 concert season. It may be that because there is so much disagreement about how to analyze

---

54. Adam Harasowski, *The Skein of Legends around Chopin* (Glasgow: MacLellan, 1967), 175–77.
55. Camille Bourniquel, *Chopin*, trans. Sinclair Road (New York: Grove Press, 1960), 148–55.
56. Perahia, notes to *Chopin: 4 Ballades*, 6.

the form and structure of the ballades, writers are drawn to the possibility that specific poems can provide convenient answers instead. It is clear, though, that the Mickiewicz tradition as it has been handed down began a half century and more after Schumann's sole remark—unless Huneker really was relaying information he got from Georges Mathias—and besides being suspiciously late and distant from the composer is both anecdotal and contradictory. If anything at all is to be found in a link between Chopin's ballades and Adam Mickiewicz, an approach that goes beyond the reflexive quoting of earlier sources will be necessary.

The issues that so confuse the early history of Chopin's op. 38 thus touch upon the most fundamental aspects of the piece: how many versions of it there were, the identification of the true tonic, and whether this ballade is, once and for all, based on a poem by Adam Mickiewicz (and if so, which one). The most plausible and defensible answers to these questions would seem to be (1) that the phantom alternate version of op. 38 is no more than the opening section, mm. 1–46, played perhaps with a slightly different final cadence and without continuing on; (2) the progress of the piece shows it to be more "in" F major than any other key, regardless of the way it ends (for which there will have to be another explanation); and (3) just because Schumann said that Chopin told him that the First and Second Ballades were inspired by some poems of Adam Mickiewicz, we cannot extrapolate the same conclusion about the second two ballades, and there is no reason to assume that each Ballade is based on a *specific* poem[57]—Chopin's sole surviving remark cannot be stretched this far. Absent further information or analytical insights, little more can be said at this point.

In 1994 John Rink published an article in *Music Analysis* that provided a much-needed overview of the different historical approaches to analyzing the Chopin ballades.[58] These have ranged from nineteenth-century descriptive "analyses" and their descendants (such as those of Perry), to motivic and form-based approaches (such as the groundbreaking but much-criticized analyses of Hugo Leichtentritt [1922]), to a variety of later approaches. Oddly, it seems that no one had pursued the idea of rigorous style analysis—that is, identifying topics and styles in the Ratnerian sense of those terms and drawing conclusions based upon those identifications—beyond, say, describing the opening section of op. 38 as "bucolic."

---

57. This is the view of Jean-Jacques Eigeldinger, who archly asks if we require a specific individual as model for each and every character in Proust's *Remembrances of Things Past*. Eigeldinger, *Frédéric Chopin* (Paris: Fayard, 2003), 60–61.

58. John S. Rink, "Chopin's Ballades and the Dialectic: Analysis in Historical Perspective," *Music Analysis* 13/1 (1994), 99–115.

Nonetheless, recognizable musical styles were, in the eighteenth and early nineteenth centuries, the primary tools in musical narrativity, and Chopin's music has a strong basis in those stylistic vocabularies: examples include several funeral marches (both pieces so titled and otherwise), the F major pastorale and F minor storm scene that make up the Nocturne op. 15 no. 1, and the chorales at the end of the G Minor Nocturne op. 15 no. 3, and in the middle of the G Minor Nocturne op. 37 no. 1. Given Chopin's musical inheritance, it would be difficult to say that a siciliano such as the one that opens op. 38 does *not* have bucolic associations, or that F major was *not* a pastoral key, so a more potentially productive approach to the analysis of the F Major Ballade, for example, would be to ask what a bucolic F major siciliano is doing there, and how it relates to the rest of the piece and other works of its time and musical culture. What would Chopin have wanted to communicate, in other words, with a narrative work such as this one, which opens with a pastoral, innocent, yet slightly melancholy section that is suddenly almost obliterated by music of great violence? An approach that proceeds from such solid stylistic identifications, given the currency of those styles in Chopin's lifetime, might yield more promising results than have previous approaches, which do not offer any truly satisfactory, widely accepted conclusions.

The ways in which music might recount a narrative were evolving in the first half of the nineteenth century. Before we can look at Chopin's music in greater detail, we will need to know the musical strategies for storytelling—the rules of the game, in other words—as they were practiced, understood, and enjoyed in his time and immediately before. We are gradually becoming aware, here in our own time, that the familiar view of virtually all instrumental music as blandly "absolute" is anachronistic, inconsistent with both eighteenth- and nineteenth-century repertoire and contemporary analytical discussions of it,[59] so a better sense of the traditions Chopin could draw upon is fundamental to the question of how he would approach the composition of a piece titled "Ballade." As preparation for addressing a ballade narrative, then, let us proceed to an overview of contemporary musical narratives per se.

---

59. One important recent contribution in this is Sanna Pederson, "The Missing History of Absolute Music," paper given at the Seventy-Third Annual Meeting of the American Musicological Society, Québec City, Canada, 1–4 November 2007.

2

GENESIS OF A NARRATIVE PROCESS

Stories in Tones

By the time Chopin was composing his Ballade no. 1 in G Minor, op. 23 (according to Samson, "certainly no sooner than 1833, and probably 1834–5"),[1] the idea of instrumental music that told or evoked a story was well established. The few famous examples of such music that tend to be remembered today, however, are not necessarily the most relevant for Chopin, who worked in a variety of musical spheres. He was undoubtedly closer to amateur and consumer music than to the German symphonic tradition that still dominates the Western historical view, and the protocols of the one were far different from those of the other. Moreover, we are hampered by the fact that a great deal of the relevant middlebrow commercial music from his time (particularly from his youth in Poland) has all but disappeared. Because the cultivated concert tradition is very much alive in our own concert halls and music history curricula, we tend to rely upon it in understanding all strata of historical music, including that of Chopin. This is a mistake.

Programmatic music played a central role in the consumer realm, and the composers of the early Romantic era built upon the somewhat tentative developments of the previous centuries. Descriptive and narrative strategies in instrumental music date back at least to the later Renaissance, when depictions of battles and other phenomena (e.g., "The Fall of the Leafe," by Martin Peerson [c. 1572–1651]) enjoyed a certain popularity. One fairly well-known (and for our purposes apposite) example is William Byrd's

---

1. Jim Samson, *Chopin* (New York: Schirmer, 1997), 94.

series of short pieces titled *The Battell*, which is included in the 1591 collection *My Lady Nevells Book*. Byrd's work mostly concerns itself with the musical aspects of war: marches, fanfares, "Bagpipe and drone," "Flute and droome," and so on, though there are also a "March to the fighte" and a "Retreat." Each little scene, from "The souldiers summons" to "The buriing of the dead" and "The galliarde for the victorie," is evoked with depictive or characteristic gestures, and so the story of the battle is told in what amounts to a series of little musical postcards.

This anthology-of-miniatures approach to musical narrative was for a long time definitive: stories were recounted via several separate episodes, and scenes might be indicated by short titles or descriptions and then evoked by various musical means. Familiar examples from the Baroque era include the *Biblical Sonatas* of Johann Kuhnau (1660–1732), the young J. S. Bach's Capriccio in B-flat Major, BWV 992 ("On the Departure of His Beloved Brother"),[2] and the four violin concertos of Vivaldi's *Four Seasons*. These are not purely depictive, but rather are a mix of depictive gestures and typical dances that are then assigned programmatic significance, as when a Vivaldi pastorale becomes "Nymphs and shepherds dance to the bagpipe in their favorite spot" or a galliard in Kuhnau's sonata based on the David and Goliath story is designated the "Victory Dance and Festival." (A galliard had also served as a victory dance in Byrd's *Battell*.) At this early stage, composers used relatively neutral musical markers as specific signifiers in musical narratives, while the little subtitles and descriptors enabled them to function, topically, as plot signposts in the unfolding action.

One of the most familiar pieces of this type is the third movement of Vivaldi's "Autumn" from the *Four Seasons*. The story, as noted in the score, runs roughly as follows: The hunters emerge at dawn, departing with guns and dogs to the sound of the horn.—The beast flees and they follow its trail.—Wearied and dismayed by the din of guns and dogs, the wounded beast feebly attempts to flee . . .—but, worn out, dies.

Admittedly, this is hardly a mature, completed narrative, but as a kind of plot outline it was well suited to musical description, because while a codified musical vocabulary for depiction (horns, chase) already existed

---

2. Kuhnau's second sonata, "Saul Cured through Music by David," has movements or subsections that are titled "Saul's melancholy and madness," David's refreshing harp-playing," and "The king's restored peace of mind." Bach's work is divided into six short movements: "This describes the affectionate attempt of his friend to deter him from embarking on his journey," "This is a description of the misfortunes which could befall his friend in a sojourn in distant climes," "This is a mutual lamentation of both friends," "At this point the friends bid each other farewell, since they see that the departure cannot be avoided," "Aria of the postilion," and "Fugue in imitation of the postilion's horn call."

in basic form, musical strategies to suggest the passage of time or transitions between places or episodes (analogous to a cinematic dissolve or fade) really did not. The artistic retelling of a story via separate episodes already had, by that point, a long history in the realms of both musical and visual art—for example, series of paintings of episodes from the life of Jesus or the images from the medieval *Hunt of the Unicorn* tapestry—but a static approach is more successful in a static medium. Musical works organized this way seem straitened, and until compositional strategies enabled a move beyond episodic, set-piece formats, musical storytelling would remain in this fairly two-dimensional state.

By the early Romantic era, narrative strategies in instrumental music had not changed a great deal. A well-known case in point is Carl Maria von Weber's *Conzertstück* (1821; published 1823), a work for piano and orchestra in the post-Classical brilliant style (the Mendelssohn piano concertos, for example, share the same aesthetic). Weber's own program—with its elapsed time and operatic emotional content—amounts to more of a story than does the aforementioned Vivaldian series of outdoor scenes. Still, a comparison of this program with the music reveals less narrative than four discrete tableaux, and little in the way of transition between them:

A lady, a chatelaine [mistress of the castle], sits alone in her tower, gazing away into the distance. Her knight has gone on a crusade to the Holy Land. Years have passed and battles been fought. She wonders whether he is still alive and whether she will ever see him again. In her excited imagination she sees a vision of her knight lying wounded and forsaken on the battlefield. If only she could fly to his side and die with him! She falls back unconscious. Then, from the distance there is a sound of a trumpet, there is a flashing and fluttering in the forest coming nearer and nearer (Tempo di Marcia). It is the crusaders, knights, and squires, with banners waving and people shouting. And he is among them. She sinks into his arms. Love is triumphant. The woods and waves sing of their love, and a thousand voices proclaim his victory.[3]

As with certain passages in earlier programmatic works, one sometimes wonders if Weber later decided to retrofit a fairly typical plot to

---

3. Quoted in Donald Francis Tovey, *Essays in Musical Analysis*, vol. 4, *Illustrative Music* [1937] (London: Oxford University Press, 1956), 61–62. Significantly, this piece was a favorite of Chopin's, and two of his most prominent students (Karol Mikuli and Georges Mathias) remembered studying it with him. Eigeldinger, *Chopin: Pianist and Teacher*, 50, 276.

some stylistically conventional music in order to make it more accessible—this program was relayed by Weber's student Julius Benedict, and there is no record of its having been communicated to audiences. The second movement is a sort of mad scene, and a march follows, but the relationship between program and music remains fairly tenuous, particularly given a conspicuous absence of topical content (archaism, for example, is nowhere to be found in this tale of the Crusades) and Weber's too frequently indulged taste for busy surface textures, a kind of pianistic *horror vacui*. (Donald Francis Tovey said that "in moments of jubilation, [Weber's] characters sometimes seem to borrow their rhythms from the poultry-yard,"[4] and the busy pecking and clucking that results when the "woods and waves sing of their love" would be a prime example.) What the composer's program for a piece like the *Conzertstück* illustrates more than anything else is a known audience taste for narrative, a story to hang on to, whether the compositional strategy for realizing it is persuasive or not.

To take a more famous work, though, the 1830 *Symphonie fantastique* of Hector Berlioz was premiered with a printed program outlining an obsessive love affair that implodes in the paranoia of opium visions. Still, with the exception of such depictive elements as a head being lopped off by a guillotine at the end of the fourth movement, the piece remains close to the scenes-from-a-novel strategy (indeed, the work's subtitle is "Episodes in the Life of an Artist"). For all the *bizarrerie* of the program and creativity of orchestration, in fact, the formal outlines of this symphony are not far from something like Beethoven's Sixth, a suite of characteristic movements that roughly follow the typical four-movement symphonic cycle with an additional movement—in Beethoven's case, a storm scene before the final movement. Berlioz has a big opening Allegro, a dance movement, and a pastoral slow movement before the March to the Scaffold (the added movement) and Dream of a Witches' Sabbath. Still, the *Symphonie fantastique* does begin to evoke the passage of time in certain of the episodes. One strategy is to have at least two events depicted, one later than the other and in some way dependent on the first, and to place a certain amount of more neutral music in between. For example, in the third movement, one shepherd's shawm call is initially answered by another, but toward the end of the movement the first shepherd's call fades off into silence alone, reflecting the artist's growing sense of isolation. Large-scale passage of time or change of scene is effected, though, only by the pause between movements. In this respect,

---

4. Tovey, *Essays*, 63.

the narrative strategies of the piece are more refined than those of, say, Weber, but they are still somewhat primitive.[5]

After summarizing Berlioz's symphony and its tale, Robert Schumann wrote, in a long and serialized review of 1835:

> Such is the program. All Germany sniffed: to our minds such indications have something undignified and charlatanic about them! In any case the five principal titles would have sufficed; the more exact circumstances, although interesting on account of the personality of the composer who experienced the events of his own symphony, would have spread by word of mouth. In brief the sensitive German, averse to the subjective as he is, does not wish to be led so rudely in his thoughts; he was already sufficiently offended that Beethoven in the Pastoral Symphony did not trust him enough to divine its character without assistance....
>
> But Berlioz wrote for his own Frenchmen, who are not overly impressed by modesty. I can imagine them reading the program as they listen and applauding their countryman who so accurately pictured the whole. By itself, music does not mean anything to them.[6]

Schumann's appreciative but careful piece, though not terribly sympathetic to the work's programmatic aspects, was a response to the rough critical treatment of Berlioz by François-Joseph Fétis, the Belgian music critic and encyclopedist. Interestingly enough, though, Schumann had some years before allowed himself—writing in character, and followed by the gentle and sober reproof of another character—to be far more specific about a proposed program for Chopin's op. 2 Variations on Mozart's "La ci darem la mano."[7] Don Giovanni flirting and fleeing, Leporello behind the hedge, the "first kiss of love" taking place in B-flat major: the identification of all of these episodes in the music testifies to an intuitive and probably common way of hearing music at the time, whether such a program was specifically intended or not, or for that matter whether Schumann was endorsing it or merely characterizing the way a certain kind of personality heard music. It thus seems that while

---

5. For more on the "characteristic" symphony as a genre, see Richard Will, *The Characteristic Symphony in the Age of Haydn and Beethoven* (Cambridge: Cambridge University Press, 2002). Of course, this genre didn't disappear with the flowering of Romanticism; William Henry Fry's *Santa Claus Symphony* (1853) and Karl Goldmark's *Rustic Wedding Symphony* (1876) are later examples.

6. Robert Schumann, *On Music and Musicians*, ed. Konrad Wolff, trans. Paul Rosenfeld (New York: Pantheon Books, 1946), 180.

7. Ibid., 126–29.

Schumann's critical discomfort with raw programmaticism may accord with more modern aesthetic sensibilities, there are indications that narrative *hearing* was not exceptional in the 1830s, and thus that music that was in some measure narrative was not out of the ordinary.

The Vivaldi, Weber, and Berlioz programs (and Schumann's critical anxiety) are staples of any discussion of the growth of narrative music. Relying on this relatively small number of examples gives a skewed picture of the musical aesthetic of the time, however; we come away with the feeling that programmatic music was exceptional, an atypical way of hearing and writing by comparison with the more purely absolute symphonies, string quartets, and piano sonatas. This is hardly the case; another genre of program music flourished at the time but is now almost never discussed, despite its being far more proximate to Chopin's ballades than were orchestral works of Beethoven, Weber, and Berlioz. Examples were to be found on numerous late eighteenth- and early nineteenth-century music stands and in piano benches, and they testify to a widespread consumer taste for musical storytelling.

Amateur Program Music

It is one of the odd biases of the received tradition of Western music history that art or concert music is often considered a cultural artifact unto itself: the only influence on art music that receives serious attention, by and large, is other art music. By now it is a historiographic commonplace to view—"discipline"—music history as a very limited parade of masterworks, each relating to each other in limited, predictable, cause-and-effect kinds of ways. It is nonetheless undeniable that virtually all composers experienced musical life in a much broader way, including not only the art music of the concert hall, but also perhaps theater music (opera and ballet as well as more vernacular forms), the light entertainment music played in cafés, actual folk music (to whatever extent composers might have been exposed to it; several famous figures published arrangements), and music intended for home entertainment and performance. Such consumer music might be piano and piano-vocal arrangements of opera music, individual songs, collections of charming dances, or other specific works composed for middlebrow amateur musicians. What is more, the distinctions between various musical strata are by no means clear, especially because levels of amateur musicianship have evolved in various ways over the centuries, and clear-cut distinctions between highbrow art music and lowbrow popular music have probably been of far-reaching hermeneutic value only to the narrow-minded.

Musical works of the past do not separate themselves neatly into discrete categories, and it is a mistake to ignore the role played by consumer music in influencing both what is perceived to be authentic folk and popular music on the one hand and the music of the concert hall on the other.

Ralph P. Locke has argued eloquently for the study and awareness of *all* musical strata of a given historical time and place in order to understand concert music in its full context.[8] One specific example of such a study relating to Chopin is that of Barbara Milewski, who has shown that the familiar image of the composer mining authentic Polish folk traditions for his mazurkas is idealized, because the musical evidence suggests that he and other Polish composers relied more on published collections of the Polish folk songs (which included popularized urban products), nationalistic theater music, and amateur music.[9] Most recently, Halina Goldberg has demonstrated Chopin's indebtedness to the full spectrum of the Polish consumer music of his youth: dance music (including the nationalistic, non-salon krakowiak), vocal serenades and nocturnes, and fantasies.[10] In general, Chopin's relationship to the great body of this "lost" middlebrow repertoire is only beginning to be examined, and our understanding of the composer in his own immediate musical culture may require radical rewriting.[11]

It is in this middlebrow repertoire that we encounter the genre of amateur programmatic music for piano. Examples are sometimes aesthetically naive enough to make us uncomfortable, particularly given the ubiquity of depictive approaches to nationalistic, funereal, and military content. Such pieces are of particular interest, though, because in the decades preceding Chopin's piano ballades, increasingly artful and sophisticated narrative strategies were being worked out in this repertoire by composers ranging from dilettante to piano virtuoso, and the music was commercially successful. So although the music is long forgotten and tends to be overlooked by historians, these marches and fantasies shared parlor time with piano-vocal scores of operas, suites of dances, and similar repertoire. For these reasons, a brief look at several such works will point up some of the narrative strategies that were being practiced at the time Chopin composed his first ballades. There is no indication that

---

8. Ralph P. Locke, "Quantity, Quality, Qualities," *Nineteenth-Century Music Review* 1/1 (2004), 3–41.

9. Barbara Milewski, "Chopin's Mazurkas and the Myth of the Folk," *Nineteenth-Century Music* 23/2 (Fall 1999), 113–35.

10. Halina Goldberg, *Music in Chopin's Warsaw* (New York: Oxford University Press, 2008), 62–85.

11. One important recent study is David Kasunic, "Chopin and the Singing Voice: From the Romantic to the Real" (Ph.D. diss., Princeton University, 2004).

Chopin knew any of these specific works, of course, but given his piano-centered existence it is impossible to imagine that he was unfamiliar with works *like* these, and perhaps including them.

One of the earliest and most famous examples, *The Battle of Prague*, was composed by Franz Kotzwara, a Bohemian living in the British Isles. The piece appeared about 1788 and was most widely disseminated in its piano version, though the original was for piano or harpsichord, violin, cello, and drum *ad libitum* and is reminiscent in certain ways of Byrd's *Battell*. In contrast to Byrd's music-centered evocation, Kotzwara took more interest in depicting the actual sounds of battle. Based presumably on one of two Battles of Prague (either an episode from the Thirty Years' War or, more likely, one from 1757 involving Frederick the Great of Prussia), his piece has subsections titled "Slow March," "Word of Command," "Trumpet Call and Attack," "Grave: Cries of the Wounded," "Trumpet of Victory'/God Save the King," "Quick Step," and "Finale: Allegro—Go to Bed Tom—Tempo Primo."[12] (It is not clear what "God Save the King" is doing there, given that the English were involved in neither Battle of Prague, but 'twere to consider too curiously.) There is no indication that Chopin, born more than twenty years later, knew the work, but it exercised a strong influence on the entire early Romantic genre, which might even have been born in part out of attempts to capitalize on Kotzwara's success. The gestures from Kotzwara's piece show up repeatedly in later works—meaning not just generic march and quickstep, but also the stentorian recitative of the "Word of Command" and the anguished two-note slurs of the "Cries of the Wounded"—and also in the works of much more famous composers.

The Sufferings of the Queen of France, op. 23, was by Jan Ladislav Dussek, who had been part of the French royal circle, patronized by Marie Antoinette herself.[13] He composed and published the piece shortly after her death in 1793, but (significantly) he did so in London, where he had rather hurriedly resettled just before the Revolution in 1789, and where *The Battle of Prague* had already found an eager market. Among other points of similarity, the fiercely declamatory dotted-rhythm staccatos under "They pronounce the sentence of death" recall Kotzwara's

---

12. A wonderfully entertaining performance of this piece and other parlor favorites, with notes by John Michael Cooper, was released on a CD in 1997 by Illinois Wesleyan University: Susan Brandon and R. Dwight Drexler, One Piano, Four Hands, *The* Battle of Prague *and Other Parlor Delights* (Bloomington: Illinois Wesleyan University, 1997). A rather supercilious discussion of the piece appears in Arthur Loesser, *Men, Women, and Pianos* (New York: Simon and Schuster, 1954), 243–44.

13. A recent edition of this work, ed. Igor Kipnis (Van Nuys, CA: Alfred Publishing Company, 1975), is readily available in libraries.

"Word of Command," but also prefigure such Chopinesque piano recitatives as the closing passage of the Nocturne op. 32 no. 1 and the middle section of the Nocturne op. 48 no. 2. (According to Chopin's student Adolph Gutmann, Chopin's description of the latter passage was "A tyrant commands."[14]) Dussek's closing section, "Apotheosis," consists of fairly typical, pseudo-orchestral French Baroque ceremonial pomp but also features an upward-reaching passage suggestive of what will later become the "angelic" or "prayer" topic, which Chopin would also later use in the middle section of the third movement of his Second Piano Sonata, op. 35 ("Funeral March").

Significant to our inquiry for different reasons is *La journée d'Ulm* (*The Battle of Ulm*, 1805–9?) by the popular and celebrated pianist-composer Daniel Steibelt. The piece is a musical description of Napoleon's victory over the Austrians in 1805, and one of its innovations is the quotation throughout of well-known melodies in dramatically appropriate places, sometimes in elaborated form. When those tunes were originally vocal, the texts are included between the staves, though their relationship to the performance of the piece is not entirely clear.[15]

The words to the melodies account for an important part of the narrative, which now does not rely on styles and figuration alone, as Kotzwara's piece did (not counting "God Save the Queen" and "Go to Bed, Tom"). The French troops march off to battle to "A March from Grétry," and under the section labeled "Indignation upon Learning of the Invasion of Bavaria," an air from Gluck's 1777 opera *Armide* (act 2, scene 1) appears with its text: "La seule gloire a pour moi des appas; Je prétends adresser mes pas où la justice et l'innocence auront besoin de secours de mon bras" (Glory alone holds charms for me; I intend to direct my steps to where innocence and justice will need the help of my arms). For the section "Muster of the Fighting Men," which presumably would take place under the supervision of the commander (Napoleon), Steibelt interpolates a chorus from Nicolò Piccinni's 1783 opera *Didon* (act 2, scene 6) in which honor is rendered to Énée (Aeneas): "au fils d'une grande Déesse rendons un hommage éclatant, rendons un hommage

---

14. Quoted, via the Chopin biographer Niecks, in Eigeldinger, *Chopin: Pianist and Teacher*, 81.

15. Since the piece was subtitled "Fantasy for Pianoforte," actually singing the words seems to be at best optional; it is bit like Liszt's song transcriptions, which sometimes also include the texts. Another apparent imitation of *The Battle of Prague* was the 1795 piece *The Capture of the Cape of Good Hope* by Cecilia Maria Barthélmon, published "for Piano or Harpsichord, Concluding with a Song & Chorus." This piece, edited by Deborah Hayes, may be found in the anthology *Women Composers: Music through the Ages*, vol. 3, *Composers Born 1700–1799: Keyboard Music*, ed. Sylvia Glickman and Martha Furman Schleifer (New York: G. K. Hall, 1998), 213–32.

éclatant a la victoire qui l'attend" (To the son of the great goddess, let us render ringing homage, and also to the victory that awaits him). A victory is celebrated with a melody ("Victory is ours!") from Grétry's 1783 opera *La caravane de Caire* (act 1, scene 5), and the vanquished Austrians sing a lament originally given to a chorus of slaves from the same opera (act 1, scene 1), "Sur cet triste rivage, Hélas! Versons des pleurs livrés à l'ésclavage, deplorons nos malheurs" (On this grim riverbank, Alas! Let us pour out the laments of our enslavement, deploring our griefs—an obvious reference to Psalm 137, "By the Waters of Babylon"). The triumphal march at the end is the theme from the second movement of Haydn's "Military" Symphony (1794), and with a delicious irony that spans centuries in both directions the defeated Austrians are given the minor variation—Haydn's "Turkish" music—from the same movement.

Steibelt's *Journée d'Ulm* is truly intertextual, with the piece itself serving as a "web of allusion" (in Julia Kristeva's phrase) to other works and contexts. To be sure, there is plenty of familiar topical content in Steibelt's piece; the "cries of the wounded" section shares certain elements with a corresponding section in Kotzwara, and the words of command, fanfares, and drum tattoos likewise. But the intertextual allusions allow for a kind of thick-context hearing, in which the significant plot elements or character qualities of Steibelt's story gain an emotional or dramatic profile, via the original contexts of the quotations, that mere figuration or clichéd musical formula could not provide. What results is a kind of keyboard opera, wherein a story is told not only with subtitles and familiar musical gestures that depict them, but, more important, by reminiscences of well-known (especially operatic) works, the knowledge of which enables the listener both to follow the unfolding action and also to apprehend the composer-narrator's commentary upon it. This strategy is actually more sophisticated than the later ones of Weber and Berlioz, and we will see something strikingly similar to it in Chopin's Second Ballade.

There are some interesting operatic sidelights to be found here. Because all the pieces to which Steibelt alluded were more than ten years old when *La journée d'Ulm* was composed, and some more than twenty, it seems that there must have been a kind of semi-stable French operatic canon, a repertoire that a certain kind of educated listener could be expected to know. As targeted by a piece such as Steibelt's, this informed listener was one who would recognize and understand all the musical references, even when they were dressed up and expanded and put through a variety of different textures. It is also very possible that Steibelt's versions of the melodies, which differ in certain ways from the way they appear in the operatic piano-vocal scores, reflect more closely the way they were known and sung, which would in turn mean that works such as this represent an untapped resource in the study of vocal performance practices.

One programmatic work Chopin must have known is the *Grande fantaisie lugubre au souvenir des trois héros Prince Joseph Poniatowski, Kościuszko, et Dąbrowski, composé et dediée à la nation polonaise* (Warsaw: Fuss, 1818), by W. W. Würfel. Wilhelm (Vaclav) Würfel was, like Chopin's piano teacher Wojciech Żywny, a Czech transplant, working in Warsaw and teaching on Józef Elsner's staff at the High School of Music. This school was where Chopin would later study formally, and where he was Würfel's private student of organ and thoroughbass between the years of about 1823 and 1826. Here are Würfel's section headings:

Fateful night.
The sounds of the bells of the three towers. [These are the three towers of cathedral in the Wawel Castle in Krákow, where the three heroes would be buried.]
Gloomy presentiments.
Death proclaims the end of the three heroes.
Terror.
Acute suffering of the nation.
Memory of their self-sacrifice for the county.
They are no more.
The sound of the funeral bell from the cathedral announces the funeral ceremony.
Funeral March.
Grateful sentiments of the nation.

Again, superficial points of familiarity with earlier works may be found. Stately horn fifths for the funeral service seem to echo Dussek's apotheosis of Marie Antoinette, and the similarity between Würfel's "Funeral March" section and Chopin's C Minor Funeral March (c. 1826) reiterates the idea that the funeral topic and all its associated musical styles were well understood, probably thanks to the vocabulary of French post-Revolutionary music. Certainly, Chopin did not need to go to Paris to encounter this vocabulary or to become thoroughly conversant with it and its nationalistic associations.[16]

There is more, though. Steibelt's sections had been longer and the transitions more artful by far than the stop-and-start of the Kotzwara and similar works. The result is an expanded sense of the passage of time, a longer story in which we would linger at a few significant episodes. Würfel's piece seems to continue this trend, and also to accentuate the individuality of each

---

16. In fact, Würfel's piece is only one example from a flourishing Polish genre of fantasias that used quotation and narrative elements in the service of Polish nationalism. Halina Goldberg provides an overview of these works in *Music in Chopin's Warsaw*, 87–95.

section by setting it in an appropriate key. The piece begins in C minor and ends in C major —itself not that surprising—but the section of the bells tolling is in what must have been an agonized, borderline-dissonant E-flat minor, national grief is given voice in a tragic G minor, and the memory of the heroes' devotion to their homeland is in a sweet B-flat major. This is not the place for a discussion of key characteristics in nineteenth-century unequal temperaments,[17] but it is nonetheless worth noticing that the keys Würfel chose reflected traditional associations, appropriate to the kinds of mood and figuration he used (in view of cognate pieces of similar affects), but not really part of a trajectory at all, a there-and-back-again sonata form or anything else so easily codified. This, too, will be significant later, because the temptation for analysts is to view all harmonic plans as teleological: absolutely necessary, following an inexorable progression, coherent from first to last. A piece such as Würfel's demonstrates that the operative harmonic principles and effects can be far more local in nature and do not have to be subservient at every moment to a grand harmonic plan.

Halina Goldberg has, moreover, pointed out that the three tunes in the closing section of Würfel's piece were associated with the three departed heroes and thus had patriotic associations: *Prince Poniatowski's Favorite March*, the Trio of *Kościuszko's Polonaise* ("And When You Depart, Fare Well"), and the *Dąbrowski Mazurka* ("Poland Has Not Yet Perished").[18] The melodies play no rhetorical part in the unfolding action, as the quotations in Steibelt's piece had done, but rather serve as grand perorations after the series of dramatic images (bells, national grief, and so on) has been presented. This approach to musical narrative goes beyond the others in that it ties its narrative to the greater story—that of Poland and its national aspirations (which will receive more attention in chapter 5)— rather than remaining a self-contained memorial account. Significant here is that in 1818 there is already an example of a piano piece, by Chopin's own teacher, that sought to give expression not only to nationalism, but specifically to nationalism under oppression, and among the strategies used is the quotation of particular melodies.

Although the depth and character of the Paris-dwelling Chopin's relationship to Polish cultural consciousness and national aspirations in the

---

17. The best systematic treatment of the *Tonarten* or key characteristics is Rita Steblin, *A History of Key Characteristics of the Eighteenth and Nineteenth Centuries* [1983], 2nd ed. (Rochester, NY: University of Rochester Press, 2002). A preliminary look at the way Chopin's awareness of the key characteristics and qualities of unequal temperament may be seen in his music will be found in Jonathan Bellman, "Toward a Well-Tempered Chopin," in *Chopin in Performance: History, Theory, Practice*, ed. Artur Szklener (Warsaw: Narodowy Instytut Fryderyka Chopina, 2005), 25–38.

18. Goldberg, *Music in Chopin's Warsaw*, 91–92.

1830s and 1840s is a matter of some disagreement, there is no question that he associated with exiled Poles, including members of the nobility, and that he played these nationalistic tunes (his fragmentary arrangement of the *Dąbrowski Mazurka* survives on a leaf of manuscript paper)[19] to the great appreciation of the Polish community. Consider the poet Bohdan Zaleski's description of one of his improvisations:

> Finally, in my honor, [he played] an improvisation in which he evoked all the sweet and sorrowful voices of the past. He sang the tears of the *dumkas* and finished with the national anthem, "Poland is not [yet] dead" in a whole gamut of different forms and voices, from that of the warrior to those of children and angels. I could have written a whole book about this improvisation.[20]

Such a passage may strike the modern reader as a tad purple, but it describes an entirely typical way of hearing music. Later, we will see the writer Félicien Mallefille having a similar reaction to the composer's performance of the Second Ballade, which suggests that the musical gestures employed in that work were comprehensible to him—that he felt that he understood the story being told. Such programmatic conceptions, both for listeners and composers, suggest that our more modern view of absolute music in a pure, entirely nonassociative sense may not even have been imaginable at that time. Above and beyond the stories told in opera and song, numerous readily playable piano works of the kind just described conditioned listeners to think in a programmatic way, whether they were listening to *The Battle of Prague* or Beethoven's Sixth Symphony. Because of the popularity of such works, both their topical gestures (funerals, battles, grieving, angels, bells tolling, etc.) and the narrative strategies (e.g., allusions, transitions, approaches to the passage of time) became thoroughly familiar to the musical public, their vocabulary and syntax to be readily apprehended when encountered in other music. I would add that it is quite likely that talented improvisors would have produced such pieces at will to general listener delight, as suggested by both Zaleski's quote above and Elsner's admiring recollection of how Chopin, as a student, transformed a "Chorus of Devils" into an "Angelic Chorus."[21] The indications are that this sort of off-the-cuff keyboard storytelling, formalized in programmatic piano pieces but probably far

---

19. Józef Michał Chomiński and Teresa Dalila Turło, *A Catalogue of the Works of Frederick Chopin* (Kraków: Polskie Wydawnictwo Muzyczne, 1960), 239.
20. Quoted in Eigeldinger, *Chopin: Pianist and Teacher*, 283–84.
21. Józef Elsner, letter to Chopin of 13 November 1832, in Hedley, *Selected Correspondence*, 114.

more widespread in unwritten form, was much enjoyed when expertly done.

Beyond actual contemporary practice, which for us is in large part conjectural, it is important to know that there was a specifically Polish aesthetic and philosophical context for conceiving music this way. Goldberg, in her crucially important study "'Remembering that tale of grief': The Prophetic Voice in Chopin's Music," quotes two highly relevant Polish figures on the subject of how music could be composed to be understood in an allusive fashion. Józef Sikorski, a younger contemporary of Chopin's and a fellow composition student of Józef Elsner at the Warsaw Conservatory, wrote in an 1843 essay that "the musician can arrange sounds at will, but very few will understand him, unless he employs supporting gestures, or even expressions, that mentally mark the kind and degree of emotion. In such a state, it is difficult for music to be national; it is even more difficult to tangibly, so to speak, present this nationality." Moving beyond the difficulty, he then observes that the essential Polish melodic character as found in religious music—chant and chorale—is able to "enliven" larger forms, above and beyond the more generally understood Polish dances polonaise, mazurka, and krakowiak, and asserts that this character is to be found "in all works of Chopin."[22]

So supporting gestures and even "expressions," which presumably meant descriptive phrases and performance indications, are required to mark the kind of emotion the audience needs to understand. (Interestingly, years later Sikorski identified at least one work of Chopin's that did not seem essentially Polish—the Second Ballade, op. 38,[23] of all things—but, as will be seen, there is a reasonable musical explanation for that opinion.) Even more explicitly relevant to the genre of narrative piano works and the ballades are the remarks of Karol Kurpiński, a visible and influential figure in the Warsaw musical world: composer, director of the opera theater, conservatory professor at the time Chopin studied there, and even the conductor at his debut. In an article of 1821, Kurpiński stressed the value of melodic reminiscence—the quotation or less direct evocation of a well-known melody—as a way to communicate to the listener for whom the tune already had meaning. Music for the stage was

---

22. Józef Sikorski, "O muzyce" [On Music], *Biblioteka warszawska* 2 (1843): 665–73, quoted in Halina Goldberg, "'Remembering That Tale of Grief': The Prophetic Voice in Chopin's Music," in *The Age of Chopin*, ed. Goldberg (Bloomington: Indiana University Press, 2004), 64. The Polish translations are all by Goldberg.

23. Zofia Chechlińska, "Chopin's Reception as Reflected in Nineteenth-Century Polish Periodicals: General Remarks," in Goldberg, ed., *The Age of Chopin*, 250. Sikorski wrote this in 1848, but when he wrote his earlier article the Second Ballade had been in print for two years already. It is hard to know whether he did not yet know op. 38 when he wrote the first article, or if he did and just changed his mind later.

a natural venue for this approach, but it was also possible in instrumental works, expecially through the use of "arias, which—nested in everyone's memory through frequent repetitions—allow diverse allusions," and though "these are only reminiscences, they therefore speak stronger to the heart."[24]

It is hard to shake the feeling that Kurpiński was thinking of something very much like Steibelt's *Journée d'Ulm*, particularly when he gives the example of a march tune suggesting "national troops" to the listener, because his description—down to the aria allusions, march, and national significance—fits that particular piece like a glove. Goldberg further points out that Kurpiński later used precisely this method in his 1831 patriotic song "Litwinka" ("Lithuanian Song"), which contains a clear allusion to the *Dąbrowski Mazurka* (though in duple meter rather than the original triple), the melody which was to become the Polish national anthem. In the first publication of the song, Kurpiński explained himself: an annotation to stanza 4, line 5 of "Litwinka" ("The joyful sound penetrated a thousand hearts") explains that "this line became the reason for the composer to recall the tune of the *Dąbrowski Mazurka* in this spot."[25]

Sikorski and Kurpiński thus demonstrate that music with clear meanings and associations—national topics, patriotic sentiments—was, by the time Chopin was cutting his compositional teeth, not only heard and understood but also theorized in the Polish musical environment. The programmatic repertoire that had been published from the late eighteenth century onward provided a variety of models for both appropriate sorts of stories and techniques for conveying meaning. The significance of this strain of thinking for someone like Chopin, who (as we will see) was devoted to opera and had a lively dramatic imagination, can scarcely be overstated.

A key point about narrative music and its strategies is that it was always the composer who chose which episodes of a particular narrative were to be evoked. Just as an opera composer would add, delete, and recast episodes of a particular story (the Don Juan story, for example, or a pseudo-historical tale such as Daniel Auber's opera *La muette de Portici* [*The Mute Girl of Portici*]), so a piano composer would, via such choices, refashion the story in its retelling. In the aforementioned piano pieces, Kotzwara and Steibelt avoided anything explicitly dealing with death, and Würfel opted not to have any musical depictions of the Polish

---

24. Karol Kurpiński, "O expresji muzycznej i naśladowaniu," *Tygodnik muzyczny I dramatyczny* 6 (16 May 1821), 21–22, quoted and discussed in Goldberg, "'Remembering That Tale of Grief,'" 64–65.

25. Kurpiński, "The Hymn of the Lithuanian Legions" (Warsaw: Brzezina, 1831), quoted and discussed in Goldberg, "'Remembering That Tale of Grief,'" 65.

heroes' actual interment. Perhaps these choices are self-explanatory; rubbing listeners' noses in the grotesque would not have contributed to commercial success and wide dissemination, and so the composers chose to do otherwise. Yet it bears risking a statement of the obvious to stress that because narratives amount to the sum of narrative choices, they are more retelling than telling, particularly when the story is already known. It is too easy to criticize a narrative musical work associated with a specific poem or story for omitting key episodes that "should" be included but are not, and to imply that a narrative analysis is compromised thereby. Such criticism betrays a two-dimensional conception of storytelling. When bardic mastery is being evoked, for example, the ownership of the story transfers to the poet and does not remain with the ancient originator of the legend or even the "real" characters to whom the events of the story all supposedly happened. Choosing which episodes of a greater story to skip or highlight has always been the poet's responsibility, inherent in the act of storytelling itself.

Ballad Poetry and Musical Form

Storytelling as a cultivated art form—not just the traditional stories themselves but the recounting of them—experienced a kind of cultural rebirth in the late eighteenth and early nineteenth centuries in the form of a resurgent interest in ballads and the lengthier epics, the traditional narrative poems of many European cultures. This interest manifested itself both in the resurrection and translation of traditional ballads and epics and in the composition of new, pseudo-traditional works that drew on ancient styles and motifs. This taste for the archaic had musical manifestations also; ballad settings were popular in the vocal literature, whether as numbers within operas or in the piano-accompanied settings of ballad poetry for domestic use by such composers as Johan Rudolf Zumsteeg (1760–1802) and Carl Loewe (1796–1869).

Beyond the simple setting of narrative texts, specific musical strategies were evolving to meet the needs of the poetic form. Such strategies might include type of accompaniment or melodic material, as for example when a brisk 6/8 meter might evoke a galloping horse, or when horn fifths were used to suggest not only the hunter and hunt but, more broadly, the outdoors in general. Changes of mode or key could provide another instantly recognizable dramatic shift: a sudden introduction of minor mode might suggest a sense of foreboding, and major could signify love or triumph. More subtle was the way that variations of texture or range, particularly when used with previously introduced melodic material, could evoke changes of action and scene over elapsing time, or even character development. That such musical devices were already associated with vocal narratives meant, of course, that a ballade for piano did not appear in a vacuum: the generic title already bore certain associations, and a listener would have certain expectations, some musical but most probably otherwise, against which something called "Ballade" might be measured.

Chopin's use of the title "Ballade" virtually insists upon this association with narrative poetry, so a glance at the poetic tradition will give some idea of what, from the dramatic perspective, these expectations might have been. In his superb 1992 study of the Chopin ballades and their generic offspring,[26] James Parakilas offered a deft treatment of the mechanics and cultural background of ballad poetry, demonstrating that the content and structure of this poetry informed the Chopin ballades in ways not usually acknowledged in musical analyses. Because the narrator's presence is central to the entire genre of ballad poetry, he must appear at least at the beginning and end of the story, and often at points in between also. This means there is a constant, though sometimes implied, counterpoint of voice: sometimes the narrator is telling the story, and sometimes the listener is immersed in the story itself, hearing the characters and witnessing the action, seemingly without narratorial mediation. (The strategies Chopin used to meet these compositional challenges account, in large part, for the radically new approaches to form found in these works.)

Ballads tended to be lengthy stories put in motion by a character's fateful choice or violation of a taboo. Once the wheels are put in motion, there is no turning back: ballads mostly end tragically, and the closing scene—which Parakilas calls the "reckoning"—was where the forces put in play at the outset reached their grim conclusion,[27] as inexorable as fate itself. Between the opening narrative frame and the reckoning is the tale itself, and as with any other story the passage of time is inconsistent. Some ballad episodes are treated in detail (perhaps a battle scene or conversation between lovers), while in other cases a period of years might be glossed over in a stanza or even a few lines ("time passed, and the boy grew to be a man"). This narrative feature has aptly been called "leaping and lingering,"[28] and it is crucial to understanding the real-time strategies of both poetic ballads and their musical analogs. Today we might think of cinematic treatments of books or plays: the narrator is more or less in

---

26. James Parakilas, *Ballads without Words: Chopin and the Tradition of the Instrumental "Ballade"* (Portland, OR: Amadeus Press, 1992).
27. Ibid., 74–76.
28. Ibid., 45–46 ff.

charge, some of a story's episodes are dwelt upon while others are skimmed over or skipped, and the passage of time is accelerated or slowed in order to best suit the dramatic trajectory and the relative importance of the various scenes and transitions.

The cultural significance of the ballad was twofold. It could sing of universal experience such as lost love or heroic defeat, something every listener understood, but it could do so with a particularistic tone: the betrayal of the naive peasant girl by the landowner's son, or the defeat of a beloved homeland by a cruel and distant imperial power. This could have the function of solidifying national or cultural or even tribal stories into myths while maintaining their relevance and appeal on the personal level. Especially important in an era of emergent nationalism was that this process could confer a status of greater nationhood onto a nation or group that was under stress, politically disadvantaged, or in (perceived) danger of fragmenting or disappearing. Ballads old and new thus worked on at least two levels: they entertained with tales of love, betrayal, heroism, and vengeance, and they spoke to a deeper, almost tribal sense of shared group experience. Reflecting this dual character, they both fed a popular taste with a canny blend of novelty and nostalgia and reinforced—through a sense of tradition and timelessness—the growing national or ethnic consciousness within the changing European political landscape.

Symbolic of the poetry was the iconic figure of the bard—teller of tales, repository of ancient lore, memory incarnate—and the most famous bard was Ossian, an elusive, putatively second-century figure, "translations" of whose works had been published by the Scot James MacPherson in the 1780s.[29] Ossian's authenticity had been questioned from the beginning, but that did not seem to matter to the greater public; "his" poems about Fingal the Giant and other mythical figures gained a wide readership, and the bardic topic—the suggestion of a grizzled ancient recounting a momentous historic tale to his own accompaniment, often with harplike arpeggiations to introduce and finish and occasional plucked chords to punctuate—became a standard feature of the Romantic musical vocabulary. Bardic archaism is a noteworthy aspect of Lesueur's 1804 opera *Ossian, ou les bardes*, and harplike arpeggios and punctuation figures are common in operatic and song literature starting with the first third of the nineteenth century. (Later examples include the understated harplike arpeggios that open and close Mendelssohn's 1837 Song without Words in E Major, op. 30 no. 3, and the more elaborate cadenzas that frame the

---

29. An excellent treatment of the Ossianic craze in music can be found in John Daverio, "Schumann's Ossianic Manner," *Nineteenth-Century Music* 21/3 (Spring 1998), 247–73.

sonata-allegro finale of Brahms's 1852 Piano Sonata no. 2 in F-sharp Minor, op. 2.)

In the chapters that follow, we will see that Chopin's First Ballade evidences a good deal of underlying poetic thought, while in the Second Ballade a variety of more specifically operatic strategies are used. There is no contradiction in this; Parakilas and others have shown that by the 1830s the ballade encompassed several different traditions, and for Chopin to avail himself of more than one of them simply demonstrates how a new musical genre could develop variant forms entirely appropriate to itself. The beauty of Parakilas's formulation of the ballade genre is that it illuminates the close correspondences between the instrumental ballade, the poetic genre that gave it its name, and the vocal settings of ballade and ballade-like poetry that belong to the same genre. For Chopin's pieces, discussions of themes, motives, harmonies, textures, topics and so forth make more sense when placed in a context of narrative concerns—framing, dramatis personae, the leaping and lingering of the plot, and a reckoning—than when (as is more common) a rhetorical form such as sonata-allegro is insistently mapped onto musical content for which it has little relevance. The terminology derived from the poetic ballad refocuses analytical and interpretive attention on the narrative impulse, which offers, for Chopin's ballades especially, a much better fit.

Chopin's choice of a nonspecific but clearly narrative title such as "Ballade" for an instrumental piece is something of a watershed; it acknowledges a change of paradigm in the way that stories in tones could be told. In the early history of programmatic music—say, up to the mid-1830s—the dominant approach was the sectional form, in which separate movements or sections could depict discrete episodes of a particular story. Real storytelling was most commonly associated with vocal music, where composers could rely on the text. Because of the narrative strategies that had begun to evolve in the programmatic piano repertoire, though, composers had more resources at their disposal: a series of depictive episodes could now be joined without breaks, neutral and more characteristic musical material could be juxtaposed to highlight important episodes in the greater narrative, quotations of or allusions to better-known music could access preexistent associations in the new narrative context, personages could be signified with particular songs or motives, and so on. These devices contributed to the musical solutions for the most pressing compositional challenges that piano ballades inherited from their poetic models: elapsing time, dramatic "leaping and lingering," and character development and transformation.

Beyond these procedural issues, the use of a poetic genre title such as "Ballade" for a musical work suggests something about tone and posture.

An instrumental ballade implies both the epic, perhaps mythical story and the narrative presentation of it, which is where it differs from a "legend" or "poem" (which in any case did not yet exist as musical genres in the 1830s). These latter two are character pieces, but "Ballade" implies a tale of moment and significance and a narrative process worthy of it. A ballade's musical materials and their deployment both have to be appropriate to such a tale, and the success of any particular work depends on how well the tone and narrative are projected.

In certain ways, this chapter is a gloss on what may be informally called the "in the air" principle, which holds that if certain styles, ideas, or principles were present and well understood in a particular musical environment, it is safe to assume that an accomplished musical mind such as Chopin's was aware of that cultural currency and was far more likely to be partaking of it than than ignoring or flouting it. It is not necessary to demonstrate that Chopin knew a specific piece, in other words, or a certain kind of harp imitation, or a particular kind of poem. If the principles under discussion were not only present but widespread in his musical environment, then it is fair to surmise that he was at the very least unconsciously aware of them. It is true that this is an assumption, but the counter-assumption—that Chopin was somehow sealed off from his contemporary musical environment, that he did not fully understand and participate in it, and that he must be understood only in terms of the music he composed, the music he is known to have studied or been exposed to, or (more preposterously) the music of his time that *we* have decided is important—is far harder to defend.

The genre of programmatic piano works provides a variety of non-sonata-allegro models for larger-scale pieces, and it is worth noting that these pieces often had specifically nationalistic associations (as did, it seems, Chopin's ballades). Such works have been hiding in plain sight for a long time. Surely their existence is part of the reason that the ballades were heard in their own time in ways so utterly different from modern motive- and form-based hearings today. It also means that our primary task is to parse the musical styles and compositional strategies found in Chopin's Second Ballade, op. 38, to understand what they meant to contemporary listeners, and how the piece, to our best conjecture, would have been heard. First, however, we need to address Chopin's first work in the ballade genre, a work that has its own mythology, before we concentrate on the second. We will take up this task in chapter 3. The external evidence associated with the First Ballade is fragmentary to the point of nonexistence, yet when viewed in light of the musical content and organization of the ballade, it begins to hint at a very interesting story.

3

HEARING *KONRAD WALLENROD*

The First Ballade, Op. 23

> If [Huneker] had ever read *Konrad Wallenrod*, he would have known that there is about as much connection between the G Minor Ballade and Mickiewicz's grim narrative poem, with its exceedingly tough and unpleasant hero, as between *Macbeth* and Chopin's Barcarolle.
>
> Gerald Abraham

Overview and Stylistic Summary of the First Ballade

The issue of form in the Chopin ballades has been a matter of debate for over a hundred years.[1] After the general poetical appreciations of the nineteenth century, the tendency after the turn of the twentieth was for individual ballades to be identified with specific Mickiewicz poems—the approach discussed in chapter 1—and the poems then could govern the evaluation or analysis of the pieces. After about the mid-1930s, the Mickiewicz-based approaches gradually gave way to increasingly rigorous formal and motivic studies.[2] These approaches share little common

---

1. John Rink's 1994 overview of the different analytical perspectives on these pieces is an especially useful resource for charting changes in the way these pieces have been understood. See Rink, "Chopin's Ballades and the Dialectic."

2. The passage quoted as the epigraph to this chapter exemplifies the growing discomfort with literary or programmatic readings. Gerald Abraham, *Chopin's Musical Style* [1939] (London: Oxford University Press, 1968), 57–58.

ground; narrative discussions spend little time with actual musical content and purely musical studies often scant narrative or poetic ideas. The general result has been that no analytical perspective on these pieces has been persuasive enough to gain wide acceptance.

In 1992, James Parakilas advanced his poetry-based approach to the genre of the instrumental ballade (outlined in chapter 2), which was a major analytical departure.[3] Parakilas spent a good deal of time with op. 23, identifying strategies that evoke the narrative process, the passage of time, distinctions between characters, and other elements that, taken together, amount to a kind of ballade paradigm, a paradigm that enables one to read the narrative protocols of ballade poetry into the instrumental works that purposely evoke it. His innovation was to pinpoint and stress the poetic basis of these pieces, and his admirably flexible model requires no major qualifications or adjustments to be applied to widely differing pieces. Parakilas's approach to the analysis of these works is, to my knowledge, the first to take Chopin's choice of the genre designation "ballade" seriously, and therefore the first to develop an analytical conception consistent with it. But because he sought to tease out the greater formal patterns and compositional strategies in the interlinked subcategories that make up the instrumental ballade, Parakilas did not spend a lot of time with constituent styles and the identification of musical topics in individual pieces. This aside, the few early reactions to these works that do survive validate his approach by stressing the storytelling component more than the strictly musical considerations—keys, modulations, themes—favored by later analysts.

The first recorded reaction to the piece, in a review of new music by G. W. Fink, the editor of the Leipzig *Allgemeine musikalische Zeitung* (January 1837), speaks only of the narrative and poetic aspects. Here is the passage in full:

> The first instrumental piece is a "Ballade without Words" by Chopin, for the pianoforte. As there are Songs without Words, why shouldn't there also be Ballads without words? In general, modern music loves to compose stories in sounds. To involve myself in the pedantic question of whether people go too far in this Romanticism would lead too far afield and be out of place here; it is more appropriate to speak of the impression that this Ballad produces in me and several [others] of those who listen to the strains of this nocturnal stargazer [i.e., Chopin]. At first, it was not a promising

---

3. David Kasunic declares that Parakilas's work is in the tradition of associating a specific Mickiewicz poem with each of Chopin's ballades, which it actually is not. David Kasunic, "Chopin's Operas," in *Chopin and His Work in the Context of Culture*, ed. Irena Poniatowska (Kraków: Musica Iagellonica, 2003), 390 and n. 12.

impression at all; parts of it struck me as so harsh and peculiar, and if I had had to offer judgment after but one listening, I would, with a shrug, have commented in all honesty: to me, this story seems so fantastical! But whenever critical judgment is concerned, I never do that: I would take it for a breach of duty and honor. By now, I have heard this ballad five times, and every time I have liked it better. Perhaps others experience it the same way. It is too characteristic [in the sense of being singular] and needs to be well comprehended; even when it is performed well, most listeners would do better to pass judgment only after further listenings. The piece is not easy; it requires players who are familiar with Chopin's compositions, which I have already described several times. There remains nothing to say other than to give a poetic interpretation of the poem, which is not difficult; each is best able to do so for himself.[4]

Obviously, in its own time this piece presented listeners with a real challenge, a fact noted by Georges Mathias, one of Chopin's most accomplished students. The ten- or eleven-year-old Mathias and his father ("a very good musician") understood little of the First Ballade when it came out: "at that time it was music of the future."[5] Perhaps so, but it was likewise music of the common practice, and as such it drew on a shared stylistic vocabulary to tell its story. Style analysis will explain a good deal

---

4. "Das erste musikalische Stück ist eine Ballade ohne Worte für's Pianof. von Chopin. Hat man Lieder ohne Worte, warum soll man nicht auch Balladen ohne Worte haben? Ueberhaupt liebt es die neuere Musik, Geschichten in Tönen zu dichten. Es würde zu weit führen und hier nicht am Orte sein, wollte ich mich auf die pedantische Frage einlassen, ob man in dieser Romantik zu weit gehe: angemessener wird es sein, von dem Eindrucke zu sprechen, den diese Ballade auf mich und mehre Hörer der Töne dieses Sternbeschauers der Nacht hervorbrachte. Anfangs war es durchaus kein günstiger; zu schroff und seltsam trat mir Manches entgegen und hätte ich nach dem ersten Anhören mein Urtheil abzugeben gehabt, hätte ich nur achselzuckend ehrlich herausgesagt: Mir ist diese Geschichte so wunderlich! Das thue ich aber nie, halte es vielmehr für pflicht- und ehrvergessen, sobald von einem kritischen Urtheile die Rede ist. Ich habe nun diese Ballade 5mal gehört und sie hat mir immer besser gefallen. Vielleicht ergeht es Andern eben so. Sie ist zu eigentümlich und will aufgefasst sein; selbst wenn sie gut vorgetragen wird, werden dennoch die Meisten wohlthun, wenn sie ihr Urtheil erst nach öfterm Hören abgeben. Der Vortrag derselben ist nicht leicht; sie verlangt Spieler, die mit Chopin's Compositionen vertraut sind, die ich öfter geschildert habe. Es bliebe nichts übrig, als eine dichterische Auslegung des Gedichts zu geben, die, nicht schwierig, Jeder sich selbst am Besten gibt." G[ottfried] W[ilhelm] Fink, "Musikalisches Album," *Allgemeine musikalische Zeitung* (January 1837, no. 2), cols. 25–26.

5. The comment is taken from Mathias's preface to Isidore Philipp's *Exercices quotidiens tirés des œuvres de Chopin* (Paris: J. Hamelle, [c. 1897]), vol. 1, vi., quoted in Sandra P. Rosenblum, "'Effusions of a Master Mind': The Reception of Chopin's Music in Nineteenth-Century America," *Polish Music Journal*, 3/2 (Winter 2000), note 68; http://www.usc.edu/dept/polish_music/PMJ/issue/3.2.00/rosenblum.html.

about op. 23 and will demonstrate how general narrative strategies can gain specific meanings in the course of their interactions with musical content. As Chopin's first effort in the genre, the First Ballade is crucial to understanding the Second, although in some respects they differ greatly; the influence of opera, for example, is negligible in the First and pervasive in the Second. But if we fail to scrutinize the musical gestures of which Chopin made up his ballades and how they might have been understood by his contemporaries, we deprive ourselves of key insights into his musical language and make it all but impossible to glean any information about what these works might have been heard to express.

The way the First Ballade is organized represents a radical departure from the piano literature of the time, yet it is completely coherent. Setting a pattern that will be continued in his other three ballades, it offers a sense of dramatic progression through an unfolding sequence of musical events, events that build to a clear climax at the end of the work. This is something quite different from the measured rhetoric and logical presentation of a well-constructed sonata-allegro form, in which recapitulation and coda provide closure of a less dramatic kind, with final workings-out of material that had already been presented toward the beginning of the work. One result of the constant forward motion in op. 23 is that the work seems shorter than it is; it is a bona fide large form with more musical content than many sonata-allegro movements, yet the listener is swept through it without the mental repose that even a minuet's repeated A section would provide. We hang on, so to speak, to every word. Unfortunately, aside from Fink's review and Schumann's endorsement ("His *Ballade* I like best of all"), very little survives about the work's initial reception. The following capsule summary of op. 23 from a style perspective will enable us to examine the drama in some detail, and will be most useful if the reader is familiar with the work or has a score to hand (and ideally both).

One apparent oddity is Chopin's metrical plan for this piece, which consists of an even 200 measures in 6/4 time framed by seven bars of largo common time at the beginning and 57 bars of presto con fuoco cut time to finish. The opening 7 measures are clearly introductory: upward-reaching *unisono* arpeggios outlining an A-flat major harmony are followed by an incomplete half cadence, almost bursting with significance, and end with a strummed dissonant chord (D–G–E-flat–B-flat) that sets the 6/4 meter—and the story proper—in motion (see ex. 3.1). I am not alone in finding this introduction bardic in character, pregnant with narrative expectation;[6] the meandering improvisation culminates in a nobly

---

6. Carl Dahlhaus called it "immediately recognizable as a musical rendering of a 'narrative posture.'" *Nineteenth-Century Music* [1980], trans. J. Bradford Robinson (Berkeley: University of California Press, 1989), 105. See also Parakilas, *Ballads without*

Ex. 3.1. Chopin, Ballade no. 1, op. 23, mm. 1–7.

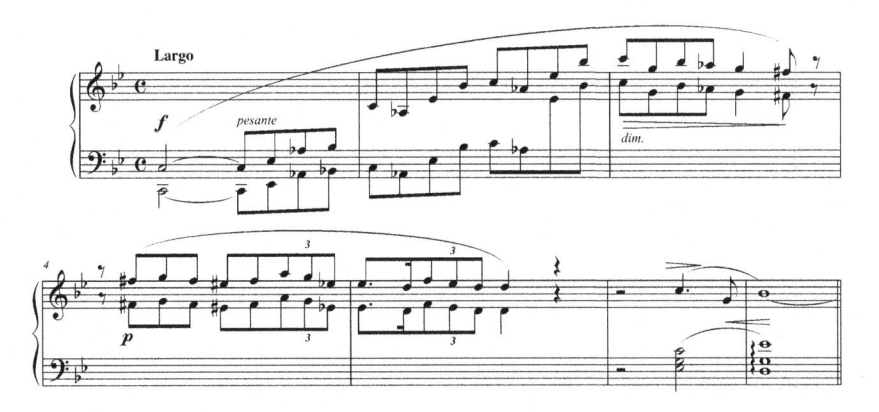

plangent melodic cell (C–G–B-flat; descending fourth and ascending minor third) that seems from the very outset to promise a grand but tragic tale.

The musical paragraph that follows comprises the first theme, the opening of which is found in example 3.2, and a meditation upon it. Made up of a four-bar antecedent and a much more extended, rhapsodic consequent, the melody is usually called "waltzlike," which—in the course of further discussion—too often becomes "waltz." Waltz is actually an improbable topic, given the meter (waltzes are in 3/4, not 6/4 time), the uneven phrases, the absence of bass notes to mark strong beats, and the singular melodic character. It is unquestionably a song—the phrases carefully notated, the punctuating accompaniment plain and sparse—but what kind of song alternates melodic flourishes that lead to phrase-ending downbeats with two-note sighing figures?

Among pianists especially, it is all but impossible to hear the First Ballade as anything but a beloved warhorse, familiar and inevitable from the first note to the last. This masks the fact that, as Fink noted, the piece is actually quite strange, even radical (Schumann called it "one of [Chopin's] wildest and most original compositions"), and the first theme exemplifies this strangeness. I know of no relatives of this theme in Chopin's other music; it seems to be composed almost entirely of sighs, requiring more than a dozen bars before the "singer" is sufficiently calmed to take a deeper breath. The upbeat flourishes almost always stop dead on the following downbeats, and the answering slurs—those phrase cells without the decorated upbeat—seem to evoke a lamenting

---

Words, 57, and Frederick Niecks, *Frederick Chopin as a Man and Musician*, 2 vols. (New York: Cooper Square, 1973), 2:268.

Ex. 3.2. Chopin, Ballade no. 1, op. 23, mm. 8–16.

refrain, as if every few painful words required assent or at least verbal punctuation. Edward Perry sensed an archaic tone: "I think no one ever played this composition, or listened to it attentively, without feeling that its mood was not of our day and land. The time it represents is the middle ages."[7] The important melodic notes tend to be the first and fifth scale degrees of the prevailing chord, while the third and more piquant non-harmonic tones are avoided, especially in the long-breathed passage in mm. 21–26, so the net effect is one of antique sternness and sobriety.

There is more than the archaic at work here, however. Chopin's careful phrasing and articulation cast further doubt on the waltz topic: the lack of accompaniment on beats 1 and 4 and the connection, via slurs, of the portato-dotted beats 2–3 and 5–6 hint at an atypically characteristic rhythmic inflection, perhaps something like Chopin's famous four-beats-in-three Polish rubato[8]—an agogically irregular effect that eludes traditional notation.

---

7. Perry, *Descriptive Analyses*, 128. Of course, Perry proceeds from the assumption that Chopin was musically narrating *Konrad Wallenrod*, and so he continues, "its scene is laid in stern and rugged Lithuania, among warlike knights and resentful rebels, and its whole spirit is therefore medieval and military."

8. See, for example, the accompanimental figures in the Mazurka in A Minor, op. 7 no. 2. Chopin's Polish rubato is certainly a matter of ongoing debate, and both contemporary descriptions and early recordings suggest that precisely which of the three beats received an agogic accent depended on which type of mazurka one was playing. Charles Hallé, who was a student of Chopin's in the mid-1840s, described the inflection this way: "It must have been in 1845 or 1846 that I once ventured to observe to him that most of his mazurkas (those dainty jewels), when played by himself, appeared to be written, not in 3/4, but in 4/4 time, the result of his dwelling so much longer on the first note in the bar." Charles Hallé, *The Autobiography of Charles Hallé, with Correspondence and Diaries*, ed. Michael Kennedy (London: Elek, 1972), 54. A helpful explanation of Chopin's "Polish" rubato can be found

Thus, although Chopin does not use the same formulas that (for example) German composers did to evoke either the archaic or the exotic, this thematic paragraph is still surpassingly strange, of almost Attic starkness.

A dramatic change occurs in m. 44, where the long line is suddenly cut off by a couple of brusque, accented, offbeat figures that lead to a furious series of arpeggio-based passages that modulate to E-flat via some faraway, echoing horn calls on the secondary dominant, and then the second theme (see ex. 3.3). Let us pause to observe that this might be just the sort of passage to evoke, for the Polish listener familiar with both artists, the general affinity between Chopin and Mickiewicz that many noticed. Consider how Chopin's horn-call passage, emerging as it does from a previous accompanimental figure, resonates with this excerpt from book 4 of Mickiewicz's *Pan Tadeusz*, first published in 1834:

> Until at last he raised his horn on high,
> And with a hymn of triumph smote the sky.
> He ceased, but held the horn. The Seneschal
> Still seemed to play—but 'twas the echo's call.
> In every tree there seemed to be a horn,
> From each to each like choirs the song was borne,
> So far and wide the music onward flew,
> And gentler and more pure and perfect grew,
> Until it died somewhere at heaven's door.[9]

No connection between the First Ballade and *Pan Tadeusz* is necessary (and to my knowledge none was ever made) for Chopin's musical idiom to echo Mickiewicz's poetic voice, or vice versa. The two artists were paired constantly in Polish writings, though in this latter day attempts to connect their aesthetics will have to remain speculative. "Speculative" does not, however, mean "baseless and untrue," and the fact that many Polish contemporaries perceived a strong affinity between the two counts for a good deal.

To return to the ballade: the new theme in E-flat is also a song, a longer-breathed one in major mode, and like the first theme it is vocal rather than

---

in Richard Hudson, *Stolen Time: The History of Tempo Rubato* (Oxford: Oxford University Press, 1994), 184–89.

9. "Strzelców, psiarni i zwierząt; aż Wojski do góry / Podniósł róg, i tryumfu hymn uderzył w chmury. Tu przerwał, lecz róg trzymał; wszystkim się zdawało, / Że Wojski wciąż gra jeszcze, a to echo grało. / Ile drzew, tyle rogów znalazło się w boru, / Jedne drugim pieśń niosą jak z choru do choru. I szła muzyka coraz szersza, coraz dalsza, / Coraz cichsza i coraz czystsza, doskonalsza, / Aż znikła gdzieś daleko, gdzieś na niebios progu!" Adam Mickiewicz, *Pan Tadeusz* [1834], trans. Kenneth R. Mackenzie (New York: Hippocrene Books, 1986), 188 (lines 697–705).

Ex. 3.3. Chopin, Ballade no. 1, op. 23, mm. 66–76.

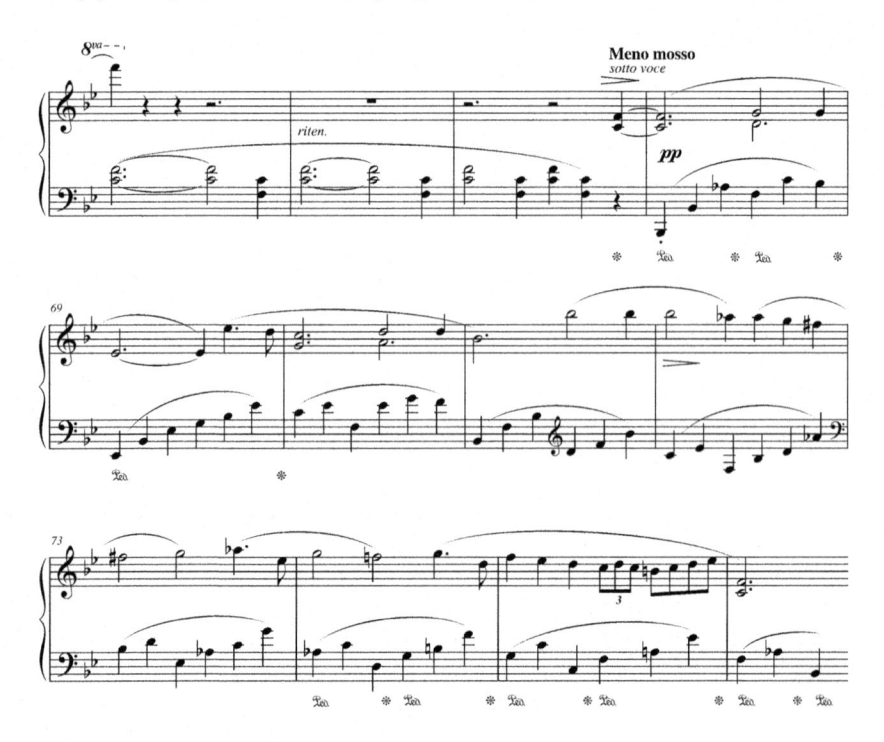

rhetorical, seemingly more song than theme. Also like the first theme, both antecedent and consequent are composed of short subphrases. These do not follow the usual melodic rise and fall; rather, each starts on a high note and descends from there—which, were it being sung, would be more difficult. It is as if the singer is wrought up, perhaps trying not to weep, and able to force out passionate words only in short bursts.

More subtle connections between the themes may be identified. Like the first, the second also comes to rest on the prime after the shortest of upbeat phrases, seeming almost to end before it begins. Also, both themes are linked to the bardic introduction via the descending fourth–ascending minor third melodic figure first heard in mm. 6–7; the first theme closes with it in mm. 34–35, and it appears twice in the second theme, in mm. 73–75. It is a striking musical figure, not a neutral one, and the way it stands out ties the first three sections together in a subtle, almost subliminal way: "The tragic fate connecting the first character and the second was foreseen from the moment I began with 'Long, long ago...'"[10]

---

10. Other potential connections between the two principal themes are posited by Alan Rawsthorne in his chapter "Ballades, Fantasy, and Scherzos," in *The Chopin Companion:*

Ex. 3.4. Chopin, Ballade no. 1, op. 23, mm. 106–114.

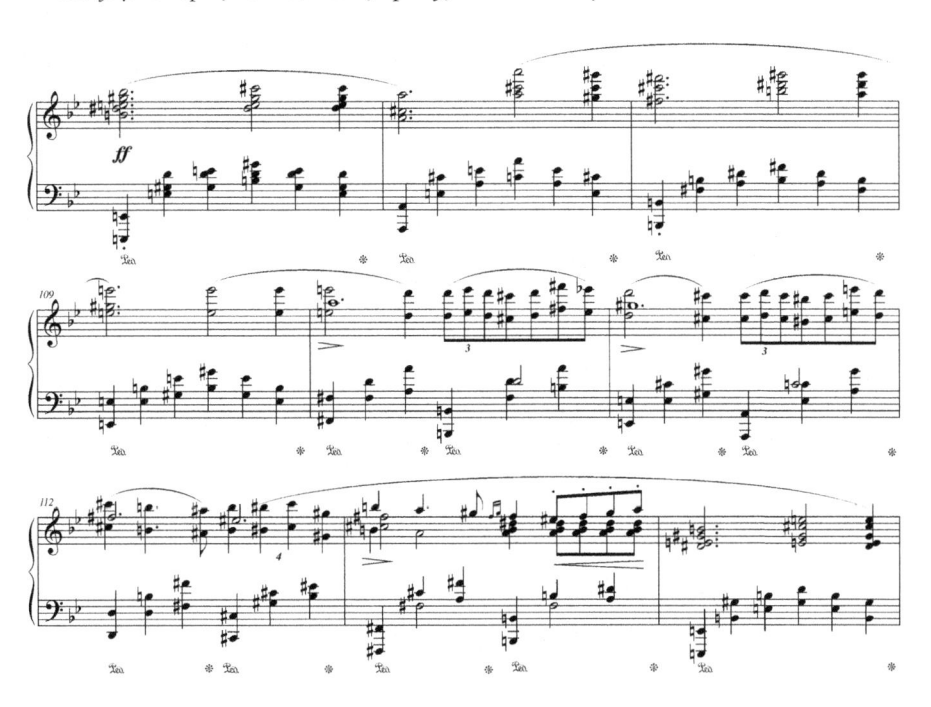

An idyllic section over an E-flat pedal, hinting at blissful memories of times past (mm. 82–94), follows. Sonata-allegro advocates might expect, after these two themes, that the work would proceed to the "development"; yet what happens next is not developmental, but rather dramatic. The pedal passage leads directly back to a fragmentary reminiscence of the first theme (94–105), starting softly but becoming increasingly anguished and agitated, now on the dominant of A major. Finally the suppressed rage explodes into an epic statement of the second theme, this time in A major, with the melody stated in chords and octaves and the accompaniment spanning half the keyboard (see ex. 3.4). Three fanfare figures (long-short-long, mm. 117–118, 120–121, and 122–123) serve to halt this section on a stark fortississimo tritone at the extremes of the keyboard in m. 124 of the ballade ("essentially its midpoint," says Parakilas[11]), at which point the there is a drastic change of character, the balance having tipped once and for all. Surface movement is now

---

Profiles of the Man and the Musician, ed. Alan Walker [1966] (New York: W. W. Norton, 1973), 46–47.
  11. Parakilas, *Ballads without Words*, 74.

Ex. 3.5. Chopin, Ballade no. 1, op. 23, mm. 138–141.

consistently in eighth notes, not quarters as before, and the figuration is based on the tritone, so there is a noticeable sense of increasing urgency.

Following a turbulent transitional passage, a short scherzando seems to hint at frivolity, with almost whimsical changes of direction and even a polymeter in m. 141 (see ex. 3.5). It soon turns deadly serious, though, stormily traversing the keyboard a couple of different times before resolving into the second theme, which is given a full statement in its original key of E-flat major but now has a rolling eighth-note accompaniment and impassioned quintuplet elaborations (mm. 166–192). This statement is another one of those passages that might be interpreted as a marker of sonata form, insofar as the theme returns in its original key, but of course this key is not the tonic of the piece, nor was the theme ever really developed; it was simply stated again in the middle section, arguably even more commandingly, in the distant key of A major. The return of the E-flat pedal section is now less nostalgic and more insistent and leads to another reminiscence of the first theme, in mm. 194–205, which is analogous to the tormented and unresolved passage in mm. 94–105 and now on the dominant of G minor. When the energy can no longer be suppressed, the meter snaps into cut time, and the dramatic reckoning (usually, and misleadingly, called the "coda") bursts forth, a presto con fuoco krakowiak of virtuosic difficulty (see ex. 3.6), which culminates in a blistering chromatic scale accompanied by a yelping chordal passage (see ex. 3.7) that, oddly, does not really resolve. Following the scale's final arrival on a low G, a couple of declamatory scale passages, funereal tattoos, and a last agonized octave paroxysm bring the work to a close.

A few more words on this closing section are in order. The choice of a krakowiak, a quick and highly syncopated duple-meter dance (originally

Ex. 3.6. Chopin, Ballade no. 1, op. 23, mm. 208–212.

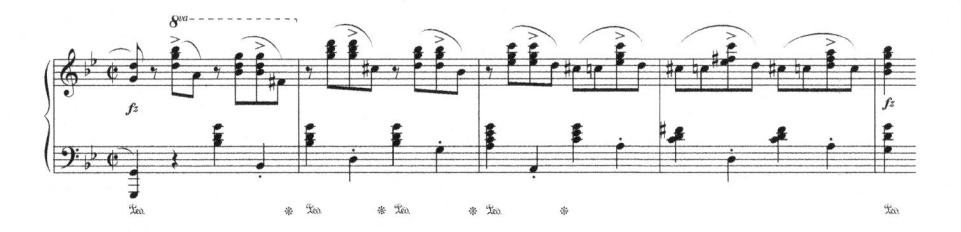

Ex. 3.7. Chopin, Ballade no. 1, op. 23, mm. 242–250.

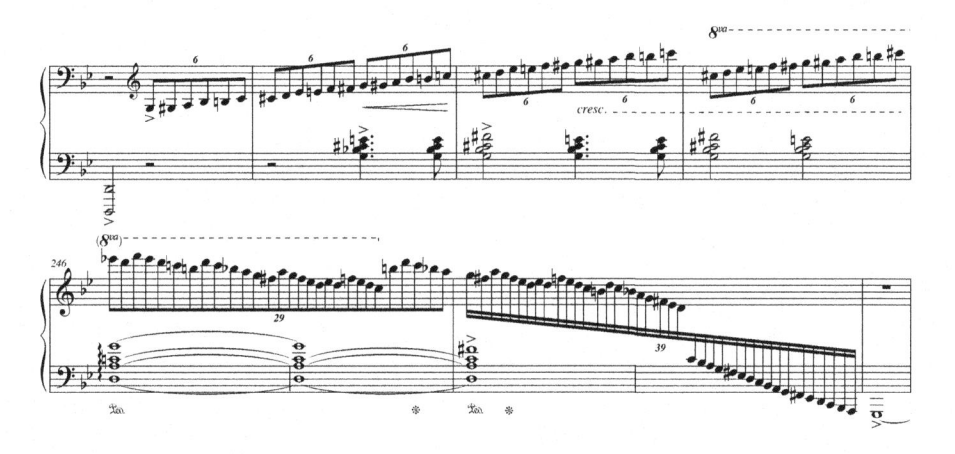

from the Kraków region), is a striking one, particularly given that almost the whole of the rest of the piece was in 6/4 time. Although both the krakowiak and the mazurka signified Polish nationalist feeling (as opposed to the polonaise, which specifically evoked Poland's aristocracy and the idealized past, before the partitions), the krakowiak never achieved the salon popularity of other dances, either native Polish or otherwise.[12] Chopin used it only infrequently; besides this vivid example from op. 23, there is the *Rondo à la krakowiak*, op. 14 (1828, although not published until 1834 and dedicated to the wife of Adam Czartoryski, the exiled Polish prince and "uncrowned king" of the no-longer-extant Polish nation), and the more distant and abstract krakowiak elements in the vocalistic middle section of the nocturne op. 62 no. 1. The right-hand passagework of mm. 92–111 of the op. 14 *Rondo* makes for an especially good comparison with the closing section of op. 23 for reasons including

12. Goldberg, *Music in Chopin's Warsaw*, 63, 65.

the same G minor tonality, similar strong syncopations on the second eighth note, and similar arpeggio-based figurations.[13]

The sudden appearance of this dance topic to close the work means that the musical material of the ballade's last section is new for the piece, atypical for Chopin, and clearly climactic: it is technically the most challenging to play, signals the long-deferred return to the tonic, and finally releases the titanic energy that has built up over the course of the work. For all these reasons, this closing section is clearly not a mere coda, though it is often called one; it is not appended at the end as a postscript, carrying no more or less than a coda's structural semi-significance.[14] Instead, this final section of op. 23 is the dramatic episode to which the entire story has been building, and without this musical reckoning, there is no ballade at all.

As we saw in chapter 1, the usual association made with this ballade (beginning with Huneker in 1900) is Mickiewicz's lengthy poem *Konrad Wallenrod*, which the poet did not actually designate a "ballad" but which does meet a variety of other ballad criteria: a momentous, nationalistic tale of doomed heroism and sacrifice, a discrete narratorial voice, chronological leaping and lingering, and so on. It is true that there is virtually no external evidence—such as attestations by other people or mentions in the Chopin correspondence—"proving" that Mickiewicz's poem was the model for Chopin's op. 23, but there are enough congruencies between the two that it is worth asking how knowledgeable listeners might have made the connection, and what they heard in the ballade that recalled the poem.

---

13. There is, unfortunately, a widespread practice of playing the opening eight measures of the ballade's presto con fuoco section (mm. 208–215) with a beat displaced, which makes the underlying krakowiak impossible to hear. In such readings, the pianist hesitates so long after the downbeat of m. 208 that its rhythmic connection to what follows is lost, with the result that he or she suddenly begins playing measures composed of beats 2–3–4–1, 2–3–4–1 (rather than 1–2–3–4, 1–2–3–4), which eliminates any feeling of syncopation. Because the right-hand leaps to the high register of the piano are now done between phrases, rather than after the first beat of the phrase (as they would be if the krakowiak's rhythmic integrity were maintained), the passage is somewhat easier to play in this distorted fashion than it is when the dance rhythm is retained. It can also be played at a faster tempo, with more virtuosic élan, a temptation few pianists can resist. Following this practice necessitates what is usually an awkward return to the proper meter in m. 216. The Vladimir Horowitz recording of 19 May 1947 is one influential example of this common metric distortion.

14. The articles s.v. "coda" in *Grove Music Online*, the *Oxford Companion to Music*, and *The Oxford Dictionary of Music* are all in agreement on the added-on, secondary nature of a musical coda. And even with Beethoven's expanded and increasingly weighty codas, energy is diffused throughout the earlier parts of the movement in accordance with the protocols of sonata-allegro form.

Konrad Wallenrod: Plot and Structure

Mickiewicz's *Konrad Wallenrod* first appeared in 1828, during the poet's exile in Russia, which was his (relatively lenient) punishment for affiliation with the Philomats, a student organization at the University of Wilno with revolutionary ties and sympathies.[15] The setting of the poem is medieval, and its historical context is the ongoing struggle between the pagan Lithuanians and Christian Germans. The poem chronicles the tribulations of Konrad, leader of the Teutonic Order of Knights, though we later discover (after much foreshadowing) that he had originally been Lithuanian, kidnapped as a boy when the Teutonic Order ravaged his city, then baptized and raised lovingly among them. The traditional interpretation of *Konrad Wallenrod* is a nationalistic one, with the exiled Mickiewicz carefully disguising his martyred Polish nation in Lithuanian garb and casting the threatening Russians—in whose country he was still resident—as German knights (though other interpretations have been suggested[16]). The tone is remote, as befits a grandly historical tragedy; the poet evokes the distant past not only with the historical setting and purposely rough-hewn plot, but also with the two-dimensionality of the characters: the three main figures are more symbolic than human, possessing two or three emotions at most, and the other knights are not characters but props, the dramatic equivalent of toy soldiers, trusting, believing, and misinterpreting in dramatically convenient but wholly implausible ways.

In a brief preface, Mickiewicz outlines the place of the medieval Lithuanian nation (Lithuanians, Prussians, and Slavs) among such other groups as the Russian tribes and Poles.[17] The Lithuanians had initially been dominant, but as Christians the other nations "stood on a higher rung of civilization" and eventually either absorbed the pagan Lithuanians or conquered them. As the poem begins, the poet—now in character, setting the stage—explains that the Teutonic Order is killing Lithuanians, that Prussia is a vassal state to the Teutons, and that the Niemen (Neman) River separates the Lithuanians from their enemies. There follow six rather polygeneric cantos, which include—in addition to the narrative itself—a hymn, dialogues, and bardic lays.

---

15. The city of Wilno is called Vilnius in Lithuanian and Vilna in Yiddish.

16. Some of the different perspectives are summarized in Kenneth Lewalski, "Mickiewicz'[s] *Konrad Wallenrod*: An Allegory of the Conflict between Politics and Art," *American Slavic and East European Review* 19/3 (October 1960), 423–41.

17. I am working from the Irene Suboczewski translation of *Konrad Wallenrod* (Lanham, MD: University Press of America, 1989), with reference to the Polish original, http://www.oss.wroc.pl/mickiewicz/konrad/konrad_ramka.htm, accessed 13 June 2007. Line numbers refer to the Polish version.

Canto 1 is titled "The Elections." Konrad Wallenrod, a member of the Teutonic Knights, is named Head of the Order of the Cross. He is an odd hero: a foreigner among the other knights, yet in the Crusades he established himself as the bravest and most daring among them. He is prematurely aged, stern, and remote, and since his youth has possessed the Christian virtues of poverty, modesty, and unworldliness, which makes him uninterested in courtly trivialities; he is only interested in, and troubled by, such ideas as homeland and Crusade. Drink is his chief vice—he usually drinks alone, and excessively—and we first encounter him in its grips, taking comfort in music: "He gropes for the lute and pours out a song, the words of which are in a strange tongue" (lines 143–44). Upon being interrupted by some brother knights, he flies into a rage, only to be calmed by Halban, an older friend and father-confessor who stares him in the face much as an animal tamer would, whispering softly.

Canto 2 opens with a vespers hymn and relaxing stroll in the garden, but Konrad takes Halban and a few others on a longer trip out to the plain. After a night's wandering they head back, only to be stopped at dawn by a voice from the tower that houses a famous anchoress who has settled in Marienburg. She sees no one but occasionally blesses little children as they play nearby. To the knights' surprise, she calls to Konrad (by that name, line 294 and ff.), alluding to his "hiding in vain" because his soul still contains much of the past: "They are bound to recognize you!" Halban immediately interprets this as a prophecy that Wallenrod is to be recognized as Master, and the other knights all assent. While they celebrate, though, Halban stands apart, singing an allegorical song about the Wilija (Vilja) and Niemen Rivers, which join together but then disappear in oblivion, and the canto closes (line 352) with "And the maiden weeps in the anchoress's cell."

As canto 3 begins, Konrad has accepted the honor of being named Master (how much better this is than Head is not really clear), and the other knights impatiently anticipate overrunning the Lithuanian capital, Wilno, and slaughtering pagans. Things have changed since former times, when the Teutonic Order ensured that Lithuanians lived in fear; now the Lithuanians terrorize the inhabitants of German lands, and the knights thirst for revenge. Instead of giving the order, though, Konrad prescribes fasts, forbids pleasures, punishes, and at last goes missing—even Halban can't find him. He is observed roaming the riverbank at night, and finally we encounter him outside the tower, in tortured dialogue with the recluse within. The voice from the tower is stronger, more accusatory, and very different from the first time we heard her: "Handsome young man, why did you tell me things no Lithuanian had heard previously?" she demands. She means Christianity: churches, afterlife, courtly love, holy faith, God, angels—but after her introduction to these ideas, she says, the world around her grew warlike, and she was confused and alone.

There follows a stylized dialogue in which she laments the past, and Konrad, the former "young man," mocks his own role with cruel irony and demands to know why she left her country for "this land of rogues and lies." She says she only wanted to be near him, but then tries to say farewell; this causes him to threaten suicide, which forces her admission that they must have pity on each other. Konrad is miserable; time is short and he must go to war, but he lives every day only to be near her and hear her voice. The canto ends with his indecisiveness and her grief.

In canto 4, "The Banquet," the action pauses. Konrad, as Master, is an unwilling participant in the huge celebratory banquet for the patron's day; present are both the knights of the order and the Lithuanian leader Witold, who has come over to the German side. The knights celebrate coarsely, whetting their appetite for pillage, but the hard-drinking and dissatisfied Konrad calls for entertainment. First, an Italian "with a voice like a nightingale" lauds Konrad's valor and piety; a troubadour "from Garonne's banks" sings of lovelorn shepherds, bewitched maidens, and knights errant. Konrad pays the Italian and offers kind words to the other (though no money, because he wasn't himself praised), but requires another kind of song for such warlike revelry.

An old bard, wizened, scarred, and sitting with the grooms, volunteers; he speaks of having sung for Lithuanians and Russians and of the bravery of those who fight on. He calls Witold a traitor and then, with growing bitterness, calls shame on the Lithuanians who didn't interfere when he was dragged away, since he has now grown old under alien skies. Finally, resentfully, he stands to sing. The Teutons mock and contest his participation because Lithuanian music and language are laughable. Konrad silences them (the reader remembers that his song at the beginning of the poem was "in a strange tongue"), telling them to listen out of courtesy. The old bard begins by singing of old Lithuania, of having respect for the dead, and of treasuring the folklore, their "ark of the covenant."

The bard's tale, the first of this canto's two major digressions from the narrative, begins with two Lithuanians returning to Lithuania from battle. Though they are on the German side, they abandon the Germans in the middle of battle and flee to be received at the castle of the Lithuanian Duke Kiejstut. The younger explains: he was born and raised in a large Lithuanian city until the Germans invaded his home. His final memories of his parents consisted of his father's arming himself and disappearing— forever—and his mother's sustained scream, which still haunts him. He fled but was captured and subsequently baptized by the Master of the Teutonic Order, who raised him as his own son, now called Walter Alf. In his youthful loneliness, the boy befriended an old Lithuanian bard, long a captive servant of the Teutons, who spoke his language, sang old songs, and cultivated his memories—and this is the old bard he has brought with him back to Lithuania. Kiejstut welcomes them, and soon his "divinely beauteous" daughter Aldona is attracted to the young knight and spends increasing amounts of time with him. He woos her, telling her of the castles and cities he's seen, and eventually converts her to Christianity. With Kiejstut's blessing, they are wed.

However, the Lithuanians' war with the Teutons goes ill, and Walter—because he lived among the Teutonic Order and knows of their pan-European support—understands that a desperate measure is called for, and that there is only one possible course of action, which requires his immediate departure. There is a grim meeting with Aldona, who doesn't understand the sudden need for a permanent farewell. She spies a convent; he takes her meaning and "in silent understanding Walter nods agreement"... and the bard's song is done. Though the assembled knights call for the end of the song, the bard won't sing it. Konrad, continuing to consume heroic amounts of wine, grabs the lute himself and elects to sing a song of old Spain.

This lay, "The Ballad of Alpuhara," recounts an episode in the Muslim-Christian struggle for Spain. Moorish Granada is barely holding on but has been ravaged by both war and plague, and the end is clearly near. Alpuhara is a shelter for the Arab King Almanzor and his fellow knights, who are facing defeat. Almanzor sues for peace and surrenders to the Spaniards, agreeing to serve their God. They embrace him, and—with the chivalric behavior honored even by military opponents—he kisses the leader on the lips. Only then does Almanzor confess: he has the plague. His eyes are bloodshot, he is pale and bluish, and he dies in convulsions with a horrible grin—both a symptom and the poetic proof of his knowledge that he has just given them all a death sentence. The Spaniards flee Alpuhara's hills to die alone, in horrible torment. Konrad then moralizes that the Moors practiced vengeance in this way, but do the Lithuanians? No longer; they betray their own instead (seemingly a contemptuous reference to Witold). Though he intends to sing further, he is too drunk; he sets the lute aside, overturns the table, and falls asleep. The knights, aware of his alcohol problem, still can make no sense of his behavior.

In canto 5, "The War," the action accelerates. Following the banquet and the incendiary bardic lays, Witold has abandoned the Teutons and led his knights back to Lithuania. The vengeful Teutons, Konrad at their head, lay waste to the Lithuanian landscape, though the resultant gore, blood, fire, and the plans to besiege Kovno [Kaunas in Lithuanian] and Wilno do not produce the expected victory. Desperate for updates, their Prussian vassals send off scouts, who don't return, and the early spring finds the German populace emerging from their dwellings, wondering what went wrong. Finally the knights return, ragtag, broken, while the ravens circle overhead: the sieges were a disastrous failure. Witold's trap had been to let the brutal winter finish the soldiers off while the Lithuanians intercepted their supplies. In response to these developments, however, Konrad did not alter his apparent plan at all; eschewing the possibly decisive battle, he instead conferred endlessly with Halban while the Teutonic forces starved. The returning Konrad is unfazed. No one knows if he is satisfied or insane, but the magnitude of the military failure requires a trial, and he is accused of having secretly plotted with Witold, deep in the forest, in the Lithuanian language. The judgment of guilt for "falsehood, heresy, and treason" falls upon him.

As the forces of justice close in, canto 6, "The Farewell," opens with Konrad riding to see the anchoress one final time. The reader understands, by now, that the bard's tale in the previous canto was about Konrad and his then-young wife Aldona, who is now the anchoress in the tower. He tells her that all is accomplished, that the Lithuanians are rampaging over Teutonic land, but she just asks naively how he is and if now he will finally be able to stay. Konrad is soured on war and vengeance both; Kovno Castle is destroyed, and memories of the Lithuanian fields and forests obsess him. He asks Aldona to leave her tower and run off with him, but she says no, it is too late; she does not want him to see her; she has aged, is no longer beautiful, and has sworn an oath to God. Despondent, Konrad wanders by the river, returning to her at daybreak to say farewell. He requests a memento but does not receive one and leaves her behind, her arms stretching out to him.

Nothing remains but the suicide pyre. Konrad, locked in a chamber with Halban, poisons himself and then, collapsing, yanks down an oil lamp, which shatters and ignites while Halban looks on, horrified. There is a scream from the distant tower—"sudden, prolonged, intermittent, and strong" (Krzyk nagły, mocny, przeciągły, urwany; line 1930)—and, in the poet's final words, "Such is my lay of Aldona's fate" (Taka pieśń moja o Aldony losach; line 1940).

A story of such fatalism and vengeance resonated deeply with the Poles of the 1820s and 1830s (and, in fact, ever after), who were chafing under ever-tightening Russian control. (The Polish political situation will be presented in more detail in chapter 5.) Canto 4 includes not one but two clear foreshadowings of revenge, the tale of the bard and that of Konrad himself. The bard's tale both provides the crucial history of Walter Alf/Konrad and hints at the dire outcome of the forthcoming battle against the Lithuanians, yet it stops before the festive and rather unperceptive knights can realize what is being said to them. As for Konrad's Ballad of Alpuhara, the Christians would of course ultimately be victorious in Spain, which was certainly known to Mickiewicz's Polish readers; it is implied that it would have been known to the Teutonic Knights,[18] and the Moorish king Almanzor

---

18. This episode represents poetic license on Mickiewicz's part. The historic Konrad died in 1394 (Mickiewicz, notes to *Konrad Wallenrod*, Suboczewski edition, 70). Granada

would certainly have realized as much—yet vengeance was nonetheless to be his. Neither Konrad nor the reader is under any illusions regarding the ultimate victory of the Teutonic Knights over the Lithuanians, regardless of his actions, because Mickiewicz explained it all in his introduction to the poem. Still, a lifetime's worth of resentment is visited upon Teutonic heads as Konrad makes his fiery exit. It is clear, in this poem, what proper action is: cherish the nation and wreak justice, no matter how hopeless the odds, even if it involves duplicity. *Konrad Wallenrod* is therefore a paean to revenge, a song of the vanquished but unhumbled, couched by Mickiewicz in superficially unobjectionable terms, and it soon became part of the Polish national narrative, its myth. There is even a Polish term, "Wallenrodism," to describe this strategy of placing a subversive, sacrificial mole within the power structure of the ruling nation to which he supposedly owes loyalty.[19]

Konrad Wallenrod as Ballade Scenario

As discussed in chapter 1, several commentators associated Chopin's First Ballade with this poem, beginning with Huneker's simple phrase, "after *Konrad Wallenrod*."[20] The temptation is to write Huneker off as a journalistic fabulist, given his habitual style and because he provides no source for the attribution. His connection with Chopin's longtime student Georges Mathias, however, cannot simply be written off; Huneker audited Mathias's master classes at the Paris Conservatory in 1878–79, as pointed out in chapter 1. For that reason, I would argue that unless contradicted by other proof, his statements about Chopin should at least be treated as a student's account of statements by his teacher: credible, worth consideration, not necessarily true but privileged at least by proximity. Consider the conflicting statements about Beethoven by Carl Czerny and Anton Schindler: facts are uneasily mixed with personal bias (and some outright falsehood), but truth is still to be gleaned from both individuals. For me, the nonchalant certitude of Huneker's declaration (rather different from his more painstaking and self-conscious discussions of the Second and Third Ballades) hints that he may have been privy to some kind of general

---

fell in the second half of the fifteenth century, yet the tale of Alpuhara is presented as ancient history at this banquet.

19. Polish *Wallenrodyzm*. Patrice M. Dabrowski, "Russian-Polish Relations Revisited, or the ABC's of 'Treason' under Tsarist Rule," *Kritika: Explorations in Russian and Eurasian History* 4/1 (Winter 2003), 177–99. Wallenrodism is also mentioned in Stan, *Les ballades de Chopin*, 28.

20. Huneker, *Chopin: Man and Musician*, 156.

understanding about the First Ballade and *Konrad Wallenrod* among those close to Chopin. Nothing more than the identification seems to have been written down, though, and Huneker's ensuing explanation is unfortunately every bit as unconvincing as anyone else's.

For Edward Perry, the First Ballade was "founded upon one of the most able and forceful, as well as extended, patriotic historical poems by Mickiewicz... entitled *Konrad Wallenrod*," though Chopin was "not following literally its successive steps, but emphasizing to his utmost its spirit, character, and moral."[21] And so it was with all the writers identified in chapter 1: there was no disagreement about the actual identification, as there later would be with the poems linked to the Second and Third Ballades, just some predictable equivocation about how the piece actually told the story.[22] For the inventive Cellier/Cortot suggestion that the piece was based on the Alpuhara episode alone, we probably need only credit received knowledge about *Konrad Wallenrod*, along with an assumption based on the word "Ballad" in the title of Konrad's lay in canto 4. (Stan noted that, in addition to the complete absence of any Spanish character in Chopin's op. 23, "no document" links it solely to the Alpuhara story; he is still, however, willing to relax his documentary requirements enough to assert that "informed musicians all know that this Ballade was suggested to Chopin by the poem *Konrad Wallenrod* by his friend Mickiewicz.")[23] The evidence is far from incontrovertible (truly, it is not even "evidence" at all), but because the First Ballade has never had more than one Mickiewicz poem associated with it, it will be worth asking what precisely about Chopin's op. 23 enabled so many to hear Mickiewicz's bitter tale evoked in it.

In doing so, it will be necessary to ignore the various vague mappings of Mickiewicz's *Konrad* on Chopin's Ballade that have already been put forth in the literature, for the simple reason that they do not persuade. Once having asserted them, even sympathetic authors tend to elaborate briefly and awkwardly, avoiding analysis or detail, and to leave the subject—generally without progressing very far in either piece or poem—with all possible haste. Instead, before returning to the music, let us briefly assume the composer/narrator's desire to identify the aspects and episodes of the poem that would best lend themselves to a concise musical retelling—a necessary exercise, because the poem nears epic length and to include everything would make any artistic representation of it unmanageable. This scenario will be followed by a style analysis, the identification of the topics and styles of which Chopin makes up his piece and how they proceed one from another.

---

21. Perry, *Descriptive Analyses*, 123, 128.
22. The first identification for the Fourth Ballade, by Cellier/Cortot, is so late and implausible that it does not really bear discussion.
23. Stan, *Les ballades de Chopin*, 27, 28, 19.

Before I posit such a scenario, though, there is one more account of the ballade to consider. In 1855 the German pianist and composer Johanna Kinkel wrote a complete narrative description of the piece. It illustrates what one informed contemporary listener could hear in the piece—a listener unfamiliar with the putative Mickiewicz association and thus unspoiled by expectations born of knowledge of *Konrad Wallenrod*. Kinkel was an exact contemporary of Chopin and had been well acquainted with Felix Mendelssohn and Fanny Mendelssohn Hensel, and so (it goes without saying) she was well versed in the musical language of the time. At the time this was written, she was living in London and giving lectures to musical amateurs.

> Let us examine the Ballade, op. 23 (in G Minor) by sections; it was the first work in this form with which Chopin came before the public. The introduction puts us in a elegiac mood, and the main theme sings of lovesickness or solitary imprisonment. Storms and battles are depicted in the turbulent interludes that follow. In the passage that moves to E-flat (it is denoted *meno mosso* and *sotto voce*), distant tones of comfort whisper to us of a new hope. After a section whose strong dissonances sound like a voice begging for help, the magnificent section in A major enters, its chords sounding like a procession of knights in gleaming armor moving past. The following section (with the indication *più animato*) depicts the clash of swords and furious flight. Further and further the figures storm onward, now over serene meadows, now across dark abysses, and—after the mild, hopeful strains of an earlier section sound again and lead us to believe, momentarily, in a happy conclusion—the singer again steps to the fore and prepares us, with the mournful tones of the main theme, for the closing section, in which the demise of the characters is depicted. In the figures and rhythms of the whole work, as with a narration, colorful romantic adventures follow one after the other, to which the harmony of the spiritual temperament of the characters is joined.

Neither with this ballade nor those that follow should the statement that the composer had a certain specific text in mind and no other be allowed to stand. Besides that, the correspondences between poetry and music are too nebulous, and vary along contours much too dreamlike, for a slavish word-for-word connection with each note.[24]

---

24. "Wir wollen die Ballade Op. 23 (in G-moll) in ihren Teilen betrachten; sie war das erste Werk dieser Form, mit welchem Chopin vor das Publikum trat. Die Einleitung versetzt uns in eine elegische Stimmung, und das Thema erzählt von Liebesklage oder einsamer Gefangenschaft. Stürme und Kämpfe werden in den folgenden bewegten Zwischensätzen

As most musicians would be, Kinkel was uncomfortable with too literal a poetry-to-music equation, and certainly with the idea of a single poem leading to only one possible interpretation. This said, she still offers a rough program, from the introduction, to "solitary confinement," to "storms," "distant tones of comfort," a knightly procession, furious battles, and ultimately "the demise of the characters"; she stresses, moreover, the way "romantic adventures follow one after another," tied to the characters. This is a valuable document in that it does not seem to be colored by knowledge of Schumann's remark connecting the first two ballades with Mickiewicz's poetry, and it is an unaffected reaction, by a very competent listener, to the narrative and style content of the ballade. The key point is not just that imaginative stories represented a common way of hearing and describing music; it is—more important—that Kinkel's account testifies to the expressive content of particular themes and passages, and to the way this music, in its own time, was understood by an accomplished musician to speak. This is significant, because even if Chopin was reluctant to discuss specific meaning in his music (and he was), he still partook of the contemporary musical vocabulary, the gestures of which had meanings that were generally understood (horns and fanfares, stormy writing, lullabies, and so on). That Chopin chose not to broadcast the meanings or inspirations or hidden programs of his music is therefore really beside the point; he used the same idioms everyone else did. We should perhaps not be as confident as we usually are in brushing aside the possibility of (relatively) specific meanings, especially when they

---

geschildert. In dem Satz, der sich nach Es-dur wendet (er ist mit meno mosso und sotto voce bezeichnet), flüstern uns Trostesslaute von der Ferne eine neue Hoffnung zu. Nach einem Satz, dessen hohe dissonierende Noten wie eine um Hilfe flehende Stimme klingen, tritt der prächtige Satz in A-dur ein, dessen Accorde wie ein Zug stolzer Ritter in schimmernden Harnischen vorüberziehen. In dem hierauf folgenden (mit più animato bezeichneten) Satz wird von Schwertklirren und wilder Flucht erzählt. Dann über heitere Auen, dann über dunkle Abgründe stürmen die Gestalten weiter und weiter, und nachdem die milden Hoffnungsklänge einer früheren Strophe sich wiederholen und uns für einen Augenblick an eine heitere Lösung glauben liessen, nimmt der Sänger wieder das Wort und bereitet uns mit den klagenden Tönen des Themas auf die Schlußstrophe vor, die den Untergang der handelnden Personen schildert. In den Figuren und Rhythmen des Ganzen reihen sich, wie bei einer Erzählung, romantische Abenteuer von bunter Färbung aneinander, denen die Harmonie die Seelenstimmung der erlebenden Personen zugesellt.

"Weder in dieser Ballade noch in den folgenden würde sich die Behauptung durchführen lassen, dass der Komponist gerade einen bestimmten Text und keinen andern im Auge gehabt habe. Dazu sind die Analogien von Poesie und Musik zu ätherisch und schwanken in viel zu traumhaften Umrissen, als dass sich Wort auf Wort mit jeder Note sklavisch verknüpfen liesse." Johanna Kinkel, "Friedrich Chopin als Komponist" [1855], *Deutsche Revue* 27/1 (1902), 221–22; my translation.

are supported by the musical language—what Perry would later call "internal evidence." This language provides the clues to what people understood the music to mean.

The first memorable episode from *Konrad Wallenrod* is of course the bardic introduction, a culturally resonant image that both readies the reader for the conventions of a lengthy "oral" poem and establishes the long-vanished historical setting for the action. Konrad must be introduced first, but his election as Head of the order and the ensuing public acclaim would be less dramatically efficient than a fade-in on the essential character: Konrad in inebriated solitude, plucking his lute, singing a strange Lithuanian song, and, when interrupted, flying into an irrational rage. In fact, this scene was particularly important to the poet himself, as we learn from Kenneth Lewalski's summary of the correspondence between Mickiewicz and the artist Gotard Sobański, who was interested in illustrating the poem. Mickiewicz gave detailed directions about what Konrad's room should look like and told Sobański he wanted him "to show Konrad, transformed by liquor...taking up the lute and singing," then to "show how he stops singing suddenly as he sees several knights peering through the door," and finally "to capture the moment when Konrad throws his lute to the floor."[25] Konrad's troubled character—obviously a significant point—has been established, and what remains, in a plot treatment, is a segue and fade to the next episode.

In canto 2, such scenes as the vespers hymn in the church, the stroll in the garden, a longer trip to the plain, and (especially) the description of the anchoress are relatively static, in dramatic terms, and thus dispensable. The introduction of a new character and the obvious, though as yet unexplained, emotional charge in her relationship to Konrad make the first conversation between the two the heart of the canto, a highly dramatic, even pivotal moment that ends badly, with Aldona's lonely grief in her cell serving as backdrop to Konrad's heartsick withdrawal. So by the end of the second canto, we have a commanding but tortured protagonist and a mysterious female contrasting character—the voice from the tower—though whether it is a love interest or not is not yet clear (though no devotee of operas, novels, or poetry would have, even by this early point, any doubt at all).

As an aside, Halban's role is less dramatically necessary than those of Konrad and Aldona, and so a retelling of this poem might well omit him, perhaps on the three's-a-crowd principle. To Konrad he is something between a mentor and Rasputin, and regardless of his presence, Konrad's own history is the engine of his fateful actions. Halban's calming of

---

25. Lewalski, "Mickiewicz'[s] *Konrad Wallenrod*," 429–30.

Konrad in the first canto would be needlessly difficult to project (Perry's reading of Chopin's First Ballade to the contrary); "calming after rage" is simpler, more practical, and more effective. Similarly, Halban's song at the end of the second canto, as an oblique commentary on the story itself, is a stylishly digressive literary device (as are the lays of canto 4) in a leisurely paced epic poem but unnecessary to a more taut retelling. Finally, the natural musical contrast of themes for contrasting characters—minor versus major, fragmentary versus longer breathed and lyrical—would be needlessly complicated by the addition of a third theme or character, whose role would consist of goading the first character and providing occasional commentary.[26] Glossing the action is, after all, what the poet—the bardic narrator, the author—is for. Without Halban, we have doomed love set against the background of patriotism and treachery in an equally doomed struggle for national survival. That is just about ideal: mirrored conflicts with all the dramatic essentials, presented in the most economical way possible, unencumbered by excessive backstory.

Canto 3 finds Konrad back at Aldona's tower for the heartbreak and wild accusations of the second conversation between them. Again, the main characters and their as-yet-undisclosed relationship take the spotlight, while such ancillary plot elements as Konrad's election as Master and the knights' desire for Lithuanian bloodletting pale by comparison, little more than colorful scenery. This conversation ends with Konrad's grim certitude that it is time to go to war—for what purpose it is not yet clear—and his contradictory admission that he lives only to be near her. Thus the fateful end is again foreshadowed; if he must unavoidably forsake his only reason for remaining alive, then catastrophe is unavoidable.

Canto 4 is the feast, with the bard's lay of Walter/Konrad and Aldona and Konrad's Ballad of Alpuhara. Neither is necessary to the greater plot, and the narrative complexities of detailed songs within and epic and characters glossing their own biographies with poetic curlicues probably are compositionally insoluble; the idea of listeners somehow perceiving this episode, in proper dramatic context, in an instrumental treatment of *Konrad Wallenrod* is simply too far-fetched. The action returns in canto 5, which is the disastrous war—with the fragmentary references to combat, violence, initial success turning disastrous with the onset of winter, failed leadership, and betrayal—and the Teutons' judgment upon Konrad. The key images of canto 6 are Konrad's last desperate ride to Aldona, their final fateful conversation, his defiant and vengeful self-immolation, and her final scream.

---

26. Liszt's seventy-minute *Faust Symphony* (1857) is one example of how the interactions of a three-character drama might play out in music.

The Lay of Aldona's Fate

Mickiewicz's provocative final line, "Such is my lay of Aldona's fate," suggests that even to the poet himself, *Konrad Wallenrod* was more about her than about the forbidding title character. Contemporary operas such as Auber's *Muette de Portici* and Gioachino Rossini's *Guillaume Tell* (both well known to Chopin) suggest that a musicodramatic treatment of a historical story such as this would likely to focus on doomed love; the nationalist vengeance, however treacherous and/or justified, of the profoundly flawed but heroic Konrad works better as context for the desperate, suicidal intensity of the love story than vice versa. The poem as just summarized, perhaps titled *Aldona* or *The Lay of Aldona's Fate*, results in a plot outline very like those of the contemporary historical operas, and also very like the dramatic plan of Chopin's First Ballade, so it only remains to examine the musical styles of the piece in order to see which plot and character elements a literate Polish listener of the time might have heard in this piece.

Chopin's bardic opening musical gesture (in Kinkel's "elegiac mood") has already been discussed and was shown in example 3.1. Perhaps not entirely by coincidence, this gesture has a close cognate in the contemporary vocal repertoire. Will Crutchfield has pointed out that Vincenzo Bellini's romance for voice and piano "L'abbandono" (The Abandonment, a setting of a fairly conventional lament text), composed in the early 1830s though not published until 1836, is also in G minor and opens—like the ballade—with a sustained A-flat octave in the bass, an ascending arpeggio that ultimately reaches high C, and a turn figure on G that milks both the F-sharp below and A-natural above.[27] (Compare Bellini's opening in ex. 3.8 with Chopin's in ex. 3.1.) Beyond the musical correspondences, we know from the testimony of the pianist Ferdinand Hiller that Chopin and Bellini were friends at this time and shared musical ideas:

> I can never forget some evenings that I spent with [Bellini] and Chopin and a few other guests at Madame Freppa's.... There music was discussed, sung, and played, and then again discussed, played, and sung. Chopin and Madame Freppa seated themselves by turns at the pianoforte.... Bellini made remarks, and accompanied himself in one or other of his *cantilene*, rather in illustration of

---

27. Crutchfield shared this with me in conversation in April 2007, though he had been giving talks about it for years previous.

Ex. 3.8. Vincenzo Bellini, "L'Abbandono," piano introduction.

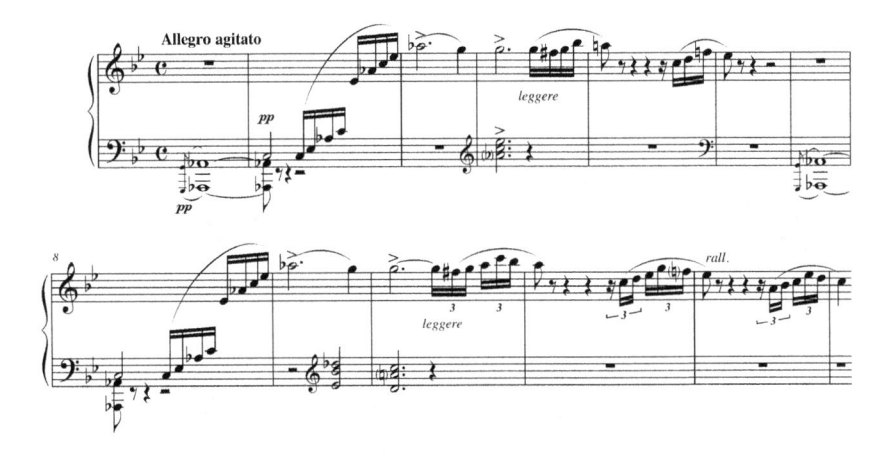

what he had been saying than for the purpose of giving a performance of them.[28]

It is not far-fetched, given the chronology, to suggest that "L'abbandono" might have been one of the vocal works Chopin heard and discussed on such an occasion, nor that he might have been sufficiently struck by Bellini's Neapolitan-degree introduction to the song of a bereft lover that he adopted the idea for an *abbandonata*-type work of his own.

In our posited *Lay of Aldona's Fate*, there are two main characters—Konrad and Aldona—and the more important is introduced second. Her theme is more commanding and memorable than the first theme, for her voice is the more compelling in the three conversations between the two, and she is also the more fully developed emotionally. The only real picture of Konrad we have is at the beginning; after his sorrowful song and ensuing drunken fury, he is presented only in relation to events: desperate for Aldona, still questioning yet separated from her by stone wall and vow, and later grimly bidding farewell before his suicide—always torn, insistent upon leaving, yet lingering and reluctant, having to violently wrench himself away. This summary of Mickiewicz's characters, as it happens, fits the arrangement of themes in op. 23 rather well.

Following the bardic introduction, the extraordinary opening songlike theme and its extensions are heard (see again ex. 3.2.) This theme, which as we saw had both archaic and nationalist elements (antecedent and half a consequent, mm. 8–20), is completely appropriate for the drunken and

---

28. Quoted in Niecks, *Chopin as a Man and Musician*, 1:287.

tormented Konrad, singing a lonely song—song, not dance—with strange words, far from his beloved Lithuania; the punctuating chords might well suggest a lute, as in Mickiewicz's poem, or perhaps even the *kanklės*, a traditional Lithuanian zither that was used to accompany singing. (Kinkel's association of this theme with "lovesickness or solitary confinement" is almost too convenient.) A rhapsodic extension in mm. 21–36 seems to hint at happier days, and the melody tries twice, unsuccessfully, to take wing and modulate to the relative major (mm. 26 and 33–34). A reverie follows, first gently sentimental, then increasingly agitato (mm. 36–44), as Konrad disappears into memories—comforting and agonizing both—that would be clearest to those familiar with the poem, but the door slams shut on it with finality in m. 44, an admirable depiction of the explosive rage of a proud man rudely interrupted in a moment of private grief. This is the beginning of the violent and stormy passage that leads to the horn introduction to the second theme in mm. 64–65 ff. A Polish listener might thus find the title character of *Konrad Wallenrod* suggested in perhaps four or five different ways by this theme, and its abrupt explosion into arpeggiated fury would probably suggest once and for all not only the character but the story itself: the character's first significant appearance and what happened immediately after.

To link the two themes, the mists clear and the repeated horn-call sounds, its first tones overlapping with the final notes of dispersing rage. Not only does it signal the new outdoor setting, but it also seems to recall distant memories of noble deeds and a sweet, cloudless past. Given the *Konrad-* related context, even before it sounded the second theme would have the expectation of somehow representing Aldona; that it likewise has alien melodic characteristics but is more expressive—in fact, it opens as an apotheosis of shy and hesitant or grief-laden song—strengthens the case (see again ex. 3.4; Kinkel responds to the change of mode and tone by saying of the theme that "distant tones of comfort whisper to us of a new hope"). As suggested earlier, both themes share a certain strangeness, since neither seems rooted in Chopin's more typical melodic vocabularies, and both begin with short-breathed pickups to the tonic note. Whether or not Chopin was evoking "Lithuanianness" with these themes is impossible to say, owing to the dearth of either authentic or pseudo-Lithuanian music from this period,[29] but elements of both the epic (thus ancient or timeless) and the alien do seem to be present.

---

29. For example, I found no more than a few very tenuous similarities in my examination of the more than 1800 Lithuanian melodies collected in Antanas Juszka, Oskar Kolberg, and Izydor Kopernicki, *Melodje ludowe litewskie* [*Lithuanian Folk Melodies*] (Kraków: Wydawnictwo Akademji Umiejętności, 1900).

The second theme—Aldona's, to pursue this line of speculation—is first stated completely, antecedent-consequent, and this is followed by an extension over an E-flat pedal point (mm. 88 ff., all moonlight and lingering nostalgia—we can almost hear Aldona's gentle reminder to Konrad that his soul contains much of the past in it). This seems to complete our introduction to the second character, and the scene fades away in a gentle passage that winds back to an isolated E in the bass, soon contextualized as the dominant pedal of A minor, and we hear the fitful, incomplete, and harmonically unmoored pieces of the first theme—the fitful Konrad, unredeemed, shackled by his memories and rage.

This is the first point where the proximity of the themes gives a sense of conversational exchange. Konrad's theme is now changed, as he himself is; he is now Master of the order of knights but (paradoxically) less himself than when we first encountered him, drinking alone. The time for war draws closer, and his knights are restive, but a year has passed and he still refuses to give the command. He again finds himself outside the tower, begging for a few more days so as to postpone the unavoidable heartache. Vacillating, he blames himself, then blames Aldona (for leaving the cloister and becoming a hermit); he knows what he has to do, but she doesn't really understand, and their conversations through the openings in the stone wall of her tower are equal parts lifeline and sheer torment for both characters. The stuttering, expostulatory fragments of his theme, mm. 95–105, are interrupted by the thunderous return of hers immediately following, now in A major, a change of mode implying that the situation he thought he was in—the conversation he prepared and thought he was having—has just been wrenched from his control by a more ardent spirit. The dam break of explosive passion ("Handsome young man, why did you tell me things no Lithuanian had heard previously?") is unmistakable; the self-devouring, ultimately ineffectual first character is swept away before the sheer emotional force and anguish of the second. Kinkel's image of a resplendent knightly procession does not seem out of place either: this is the point when the Teutons depart for war, with knightly pride and overconfidence, and the passage works well for either. It would work ideally for both, psychologically, if one interprets the fatal campaign as somehow being, in Konrad's mind, for Her and Lithuania, with her impassioned speech as a voice-over for, or segue to, the glorious departure. This time the consequent is not completed, and instead the second theme disintegrates into a series of contrasting stormy passages, including a kind of wild horseman figure (mm. 126–130) and the aforementioned scherzando (mm. 138 ff.) that, after feinting capriciously, begins to flicker between seeming hopefulness (mm. 146–153 and 158–162) and increasing threat (mm. 154–158 and 162–166). Kinkel sees in this section "the clash of swords and furious flight. Further and further the figures storm onward, now over serene meadows, now across dark abysses."

The whole section that follows the A major statement of the second theme functions well as a telescoped version of the war with the Lithuanians—and Kinkel's narrative shows that she heard something quite similar in the ballade, even while denying a relationship between it and any specific poem—moving from overconfidence, or even playfulness, to more frequent mood changes and increasing dread, and its closing prestissimo five-and-a-half-octave free-fall descent leads directly to the final statement of the second theme. This theme is back in its own key of E-flat, stable but also now wonderfully distorted by the 5:6 and 3:4:6:9 polyrhythms (mm. 169–173 and 179; Aldona has taken a vow, she won't leave; she is too old now and doesn't want Konrad to see her). Crippling reluctance and eleventh-hour doubt (Konrad's lingering on the bank near her tower until daybreak) characterize the final fragmentary appearance of the first theme, now over the dominant of G minor, but aside from tonality almost exactly like the previous reminiscence in mm. 94–105.

This time the second theme will provide no redemption, as it did after the other two statements of the first theme, because it has already been heard for the last time. The accrued tension and psychological agony are released—obliterated, really—by the closing krakowiak, which initiates the reckoning section and then gradually recedes behind flying chords and prestissimo scales. (This is Kinkel's "demise of the characters"; given the closing inferno of *Konrad Wallenrod*, both Chopin's performance indication of "presto con fuoco" and Karol Berger's description of this passage as the "final conflagration" seem almost mischievously apposite.[30]) The last gesture before the prolonged final cadence consists of two chordal expostulations in the left hand (mm. 243–248; see ex. 3.9). Remaining unresolved, it might easily be interpreted as a scream: "sudden, prolonged, intermittent, and strong." Three fitful gestures, each a combination of scale and funeral march, close the work.

Mickiewicz's *Konrad Wallenrod* was beloved of the Poles, who read it as something of a nationalistic proclamation or credo. Unsurprisingly, for the Russians Mickiewicz was a threat, a mole, a "monster of thanklessness" according to one surviving police report: emblematic of the Poles who worked in Russia but subverted it from within. The author of that report on *Konrad* was Senator Nikolay Nikolayevich Novosiltsev (who had been the interrogator of the Philomats), a long-standing and suspicious adversary of Mickiewicz; despite his strong feelings on the threat Mickiewicz posed, however, internal rivalries between Novosiltsev and other Russian officials

---

30. Karol Berger, "Chopin's Ballade Op. 23 and the Revolution of the Intellectuals," in *Chopin Studies 2*, ed. John Rink and Jim Samson (Cambridge: Cambridge University Press, 1994), 73.

Ex. 3.9. Chopin, Ballade no. 1, op. 23, mm. 243–248.

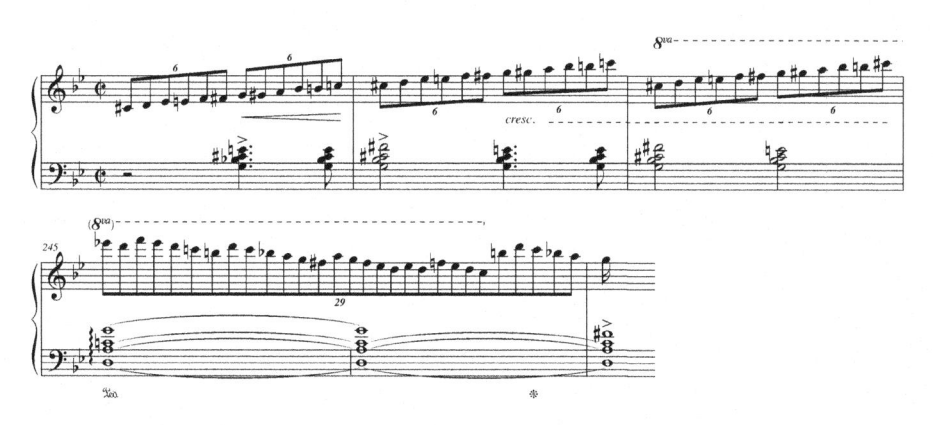

led to the suppression of the report and a lack of punishment for Mickiewicz.[31] The poet was also under the protection of Prince Dimitri Vladimirovich Golitsyn (1771–1844), the military governor-general of Moscow, which of course did not hurt either. That this poem was so influential, that it was a source of such concern within Russia, and that is was of such signal importance to the Polish people testifies to its centrality in the Polish nationalist narrative, and its eminent suitability as a subject for a musical work by a Polish composer—say, Chopin.

The idea that Chopin's First Ballade may have been a reflection of or meditation upon *Konrad Wallenrod* is thus both plausible and attractive. Not only would the poem have made an apt basis for a contemporary nationalistic work, but both the musical styles and unfolding form fit not Mickiewicz's actual poem but—more realistically—a concise "treatment" of its story very neatly, and they fit no other preexistent musical form at all. Plausible or not, however, the absence of external documentation before the year 1900 connecting the poem and Chopin's op. 23 means that absent new information, no actual "solution" is possible; there is no record of Chopin's ever asserting or implying that the poem inspired his work. That in and of itself also means nothing, though, because this was not the sort of information he liked to offer anyway. There is a famous anecdote about Chopin's intending to call the G Minor Nocturne, op. 15 no. 3, "After a Performance of *Hamlet*" but then deciding to "let them guess for themselves."[32] Like many other

---

31. Konstanty Zantuan, "Mickiewicz in Russia," *Russian Review* 23/3 (July 1964), 242.

32. Several sources reference this anecdote, which is discussed in Eigeldinger, *Chopin: Pianist and Teacher*, 79, 153.

composers, Chopin didn't advertise underlying stories or impressions, whether they were present or not.

We can go no further than this with Chopin's intention or inspiration; the extramusical sources cannot support further speculation. The main question raised in this chapter instead has to be how the musical narrative itself might have been heard, particularly among the Polish community. The side-by-side comparison of this ballade with the most powerful episodes of the story, unconsciously supported by Johanna Kinkel, demonstrates how this tale might have been "told"—made comprehensible—by style and musical materials, with the key episodes being connected by near-cinematic fades rather than the cruder cadences and pauses characteristic of the earlier, amateur-level descriptive piano works. A composer could thus recount a story made up of significant episodes, lingering at some points and skipping over others, with seamless and almost unnoticed transitions.

We cannot go too far with this hearing, however. Thousands of performances of this work have proven—as does Kinkel's own account—that the piece clearly communicates to listeners with no a priori knowledge of Mickiewicz's poem or any other story. This is not to say that the story doesn't matter; it just underscores the truism that music communicates on a multiplicity of levels, and differently to different people, something it is admittedly easy to forget when advocating for a particular interpretation or point of view. But truisms aside, familiarity with musical language is centrally important, because seeking to understand stylistic gestures as a composer's contemporaries did tells us far more about musical works and how they communicated than do the bland assertions of artistic timelessness and universality that often mask ignorance of historical style. In his time, Chopin was seen as a unique individual, widely understood to be not just a pianist but a Polish pianist, in the same way that Mickiewicz was a kind of exiled Polish bard (though, of course, he was really of Lithuanian descent). Chopin's brand of musical nationalism was, however, not universally agreed upon even by contemporaries. Without some knowledge of the relevant styles we leave ourselves quite ill-equipped make sound judgments, to distinguish among kinds of nationalism, personal motivations, and the complex kinds of stories that needed to be told.

Of course, the historical record is fragmentary. The correspondence, diary entries, and above all conversations of the time which could have testified to many, many things that "everyone knew" or that "were completely obvious" about the work have simply vanished, and in our very different age these ideas elude reconstruction. We can only go so far, in sum, but we must not fear to go that far.

What the First Ballade demonstrates above all is that narrative structure, dramatic trajectory, and the indication of specific subject matter through the use of musical topics and styles are far more likely strategies for a work titled "Ballade" than a received musical form with another generic title, however reconfigured. It is this idea that opens the door to the hermeneutic approach I want to bring to Chopin's Second Ballade, op. 38, a work for whose "meaning" there was better contemporary external acknowledgment. By the time the First Ballade was published in 1836, there was a general understanding that Chopin's music had political significance and extramusical content, content beyond the mere use of mazurka and polonaise, and the calls for him to compose an opera on a Polish subject were growing ever more shrill. It never happened, but that he was repeatedly called upon to do so by fellow Poles illustrates the dramatic, narrative context in which his music was heard—and heard particularly strongly, it is fair to say, in a piece titled "Ballade."

4

OP. 38 AND THE GENRE ISSUE

A Formal Overview of Chopin's Second Ballade

The bulk of the analysis of Chopin's Second Ballade, op. 38, will be found in chapter 6, which will address the work's musical topics and referents and the way Chopin uses them. Because the subject of this chapter is form and genre, however, a brief overview of the piece is necessary to enable us to compare it to possible formal models and antecedents. It is structured very differently from the First Ballade, so it seems that with the use of the title "Ballade" Chopin was not positing a specific form so much as a process, and probably an aesthetic or dramatic stance also.

The work divides itself into five sections. The first of these is the self-contained siciliano section discussed in chapter 1 (the opening of which was given in ex. 1.2), which works like a character piece, beginning and ending in F major. This is followed in m. 47—after a pause, but no actual modulation—by the tempestuous second section, beginning in A minor, the first eight measures of which are repeated sequencelike in G minor immediately afterward (see ex. 4.1). A modulatory section using the siciliano rhythm follows, starting in D minor in m. 63 and ending on the dominant of A-flat minor in m. 71, a harmony that is sustained over a pedal for nearly ten measures. The expected resolution is avoided, and a quick modulation results in the return of the F major siciliano in m. 83. This second section, beginning in A minor and ending on the dominant of A-flat minor (until the final harmonic sleight of hand that brings it back to F major), cannot be considered to be "in" any single key in the same way that the first section had a single tonic of F major. We first hear the stormy music in A minor, but it soon moves elsewhere, and the ten

Ex. 4.1. Chopin, Ballade no. 2, op. 38, mm. 47–58.

measures that oscillate between an E-flat dominant seventh harmony and A-flat minor cannot realistically be called a necessary part of the journey from D minor to F major.

The return to the opening material and tonic key signals the beginning of the middle section. The siciliano theme is not heard in its entirety, but rather in two relatively lengthy snippets, one five and a half and the other seven measures long, separated by a fermata. A deceptive cadence on the downbeat of m. 96 prepares the way for a new theme (see ex. 4.2), which is combined with the siciliano for the balance of this harmonically and dramatically unstable central section. Beginning with the appearance of the third theme, the remainder of the section is constructed in roughly identical halves: the first proceeds through flat-side sonorities (D-flat major, G-flat major, and B-flat major), eventually pausing placidly in E major; the second proceeds through more uninflected keys (C major, F

Ex. 4.2. Chopin, Ballade no. 2, op. 38, mm. 98–102.

major, and G minor). The close of the middle section touches briefly on the dominant of D minor, as elision to what follows.

This following section, the fourth, begins with the stormy B material over a second-inversion D minor harmony, with the sequential repetition returning to A minor. This key was the first heard after the F major siciliano, and it is where the section (and the piece itself) will now stay; with only a slight stretch, this fourth section can be viewed as the first since the opening siciliano that remains in a single key (the D minor harmony with which it begins can be interpreted as the subdominant over an A minor tonic pedal, even though D minor was the harmony that was prepared). Following some fragmentary statements of the siciliano over an E pedal, a descending scale in unison trills signals the closing section, which begins in m. 169. This section is entirely in A minor and consists of almost thirty bars of agitato virtuosity that halts on a fermata; finally, with a defeated wisp of the opening siciliano theme in A minor, the piece comes to a bleak close.

In structural terms, Chopin's Second Ballade resembles neither the First nor anything else that had to that point appeared on the pianistic scene. The opening section is not introductory; it is detachable and independently viable (as we saw in chapter 1), which is extraordinary. In contrast, the entire remainder of the piece—more than three-quarters of it—is *not* independently viable; without the opening siciliano section it makes no sense at all, despite the convenience of beginning and ending in the same key. The harmonic oddity of op. 38 is much more complex than a mere two-key anomaly; all the harmonic instabilities seem, inexplicably, to be part of the journey from the sudden A minor of m. 47 to the A minor of the close (i.e., no distance at all). For the actual key change of mm.

46–47, F major to A minor, however, Chopin gives us not a conventional modulation, but instead a rather clever (if brusque) triple-common-tone device: the smorzando repeated quarter-note A pitches of m. 46 become the tonic of the new harmony; the fifth of the old tonic (C) becomes the third of the new; and F, the old tonic, becomes the defining dissonance, the half-step upper appoggiatura to the fifth of the new key, and the most important pitch in the measure—indeed, the entire passage—after the A. Obviously, conventional harmonic plans and explanations will be of little use here.

Beyond the extraordinary harmonic strategies, the Second Ballade has a prevailing discontinuity resulting from neither the short, often stock gestures of the programmatic piano pieces nor the thematic fragments used in sonata-form development. Instead, there is a sense of interruption, sudden and not wholly welcome surprises such as the violent B material, and passages that are for some reason prevented from playing out coherently, such as the return of the siciliano—not exactly fragmentary but still discontinuous—in mm. 83–96. We hear it again at the high-and-dry close of the entire piece (see ex. 4.3), but although it is all too tempting to call this A minor fragment (one and a half bars of unison vamp to prepare a scant two bars of actual theme) a "return," it is really as deemphasized as possible, a background reminiscence. This fragment, which follows not a dominant chord but rather a pregnant French-sixth chord in m. 197, is really an interruption of a coherent harmonic progression, an expansion of the V_5^6/V–vii_7°/V–i_4^6–V_7–i heard just before in mm. 191–193, a closing cadence that would make more structural sense without the fermata and

Ex. 4.3. Chopin, Ballade no. 2, op. 38, mm. 195–end.

broken reminiscence of the first theme. Despite a wide variety of such formal oddities, though, the entire piece is so compelling that it represents a ringing challenge to virtually all academic conventions of form and genre.

The Second Ballade and the Sonata Problem

Chopin's First Ballade was the first solo instrumental work to bear that title. From that point forward the generic associations of ballades were growing one piece at a time, and there was certainly no consensus about what these new pieces actually were. Until James Parakilas's pioneering study of 1992, in fact, surprisingly little had been done with respect to the ballade genre.[1] Consider the following oddity from the first two editions of the *Harvard Dictionary of Music*, edited by Willi Apel, in the article "Ballade": "Chopin and Brahms used the term for piano pieces written in the ternary ABA form frequently found in the nineteenth-century character piece. Here the highly dramatic character of A and the lyrical characters of B would seem to portray heroic deeds and knightly love, thus justifying the title *Ballade*."[2] From a source that aspired to authority, the description of Chopin's ballades as ABA character pieces is astounding—in fact, too far off for more than a perplexed mention.[3] Charles Rosen was more direct: "When 'ternary' is applied to one of Chopin's Ballades..., it is actively misleading. Our technical vocabulary is ludicrous when it comes to dealing with Chopin's inventions."[4] A more common view of the ballades, beginning with Hugo Leichtentritt's Chopin analyses of the early 1920s, has taken sonata form as a structural referent.[5] This model has the advantage of familiar concepts and terminology that can be brought to the analytical discussion: first and second subjects, first and second key areas, initial statements and returns, and so on. It also offers a context for the real-time unfolding of the work: the sonata process, the ways in which the thematic and harmonic dialectics are worked out, and how materials are "developed." Jim Samson's statement on this subject has spoken for many: "We need to recognize [sonata form] as the essential

---

1. Parakilas, *Ballads without Words*.
2. Willi Apel, ed., *Harvard Dictionary of Music*, 2nd ed., revised and enlarged (Cambridge, MA: Harvard University Press, 1972), 71.
3. Heroic deeds and knightly love are less far off, in certain cases (particularly in view of the discussion of *Konrad Wallenrod* in the previous chapter), but the definition hopelessly confuses literary content and musical form.
4. Charles Rosen, *The Romantic Generation* (Cambridge, MA: Harvard University Press, 1995), 284.
5. Parakilas, *Ballads without Words*, 84–86.

reference point for all four ballades—the 'ideal type' or archetype against which unique statements have been counterpointed."[6]

David Witten has offered an example of a sonata-based approach to op. 38, in which he begins with the sonata archetype and then proceeds to the unique elements in the work:

> Does this Ballade bear any resemblance at all to sonata form? In conventional sonata movements, the initial theme establishes a tonal center, against which the second theme introduces a state of tension by arriving in a contrasting key area. In the Second Ballade, these contrasting themes are present, but their functions are reversed. A minor, the key of the second theme, turns out to be the true tonic of the piece, the key to which the first theme must be reconciled. The recapitulation, then, does serve the conventional function of resolving the tension created in the exposition, with the important difference that the tonality of the first theme is subordinate to that of the second theme.[7]

The rather obvious fly in the ointment is that if one were to link Chopin's ballades in any way with sonata form, then Chopin's *own* sonata movements would have to be the primary points of reference, not "conventional sonata movements" or textbook models or any other such abstract template the composer may or may not have known. As Anatole Leikin has pointed out, Chopin's mature sonata movements (the first movements of the Second and Third Piano Sonatas, opp. 35 and 58, and the Sonata for Piano and Cello, op. 65) are large-scale binary forms in which recapitulation occurs when the tonic key, which was irrefutably established with the first theme, returns with the *second* theme.[8] The opening themes return, if at all, as fragmentary reminiscences. In other words, if op. 38 bore any relation to a Chopinesque sonatalike form, the F major music would not be given a treatment so complete that the entire section amounts to an independent character piece, which in this case it clearly does, and the A minor music would have to return at some late point in F major, after which the piece would close. A transitional passage would lead from F major to the second thematic material and key area, and other, more important structural points in the piece would be articulated more clearly than the end of this first section.

---

6. Samson, *Chopin: The Four Ballades*, 45.
7. Witten, "Coda," 150.
8. Anatole Leikin, "The Sonatas," in *The Cambridge Companion to Chopin*, ed. Jim Samson (London: Cambridge University Press, 1992), 170.

There are other problems inherent in viewing op. 38 as even a distant relative of sonata-allegro form. One is that if the function of the first and second themes is reversed, as Witten suggests, then the A minor music would have to do a better job of establishing the tonic than its opening six noncadential measures, after which the key disappears for the rest of the section. Another is that the F major music behaves like a first theme, returning in its own key of F major, in mm. 83–96. This return is interrupted and truncated, true, but it is not strictly speaking fragmentary either. Although not a full recapitulation, it is thirteen bars in length, it finishes with a cadence (minus the actual tonic chord) in F major, where it began, and it sets up the affect of the entire middle section (where it is heard in fragmentary form). As its role plays out, it becomes clear that this first theme has no musical function that can be persuasively argued within the framework of sonata form.

Finally, there is the third theme, a little pastoral figure first introduced in mm. 98–102 (see ex. 4.2), which has essentially been ignored in the literature, perhaps because it is usually assumed to be derived from the siciliano. Although the first and third themes share a tempo and overall mood, they share little actual musical content; nowhere does the new theme have the siciliano's characteristic dotted eighth–sixteenth–eighth rhythm, and it moves entirely by stepwise motion, while the siciliano melody has many leaps. Moreover, the new theme's most salient element, the repeating pitch, is absent from the first theme unless one counts part of the opening vamp. The general mood of the themes is similar, but Chopin clearly treats them as discrete entities.

This new idea appears in the central section of the work, which would correspond to the development in a sonata form, and it controls the entire section: it is heard about twenty-eight times and appears in a variety of keys, lastly—it is worth stressing—in F major. Not only does the theme never appear in A minor at all, which would argue for an F major tonic for the work as a whole, but it appears in neither the opening nor closing sections. By the mid-1830s new themes could certainly appear in sonata developments (the first movements of Mozart's Piano Concerto in A Major, K. 488, and Beethoven's Third Symphony are famous cases), but if they had any structural importance they would return in the recapitulation too, whether they first appeared in the exposition or development. Here we have an entire central section in a one-movement work which is based on a theme that appears in neither opening nor closing sections.

Still another problem is the mirrorlike structure of this central section. It does not seem progressive, moving either swiftly or deliberately to the point of furthest harmonic remove and then back to the tonic, because such "progress" as exists is stopped dead by the siciliano fragment, which swamps the C theme. It modulates, ultimately to F major (so far so good), but makes a sudden turn to D minor in mm. 139–140 for the return of the storm music, only afterward settling in A minor. The harmonic business of a sonata development may be summarized as "there and back again"— the trip from the tonic to the second key area and back to tonic—but the agenda behind this central section is clearly quite different. Taken together, all these extraordinary formal strategies prove that a process other than the familiar and too easily cited sonata-allegro form is at work.

If one insists upon finding points of similarity between the ballades and sonata form (or simply has no other available options to hand), a quick overview of the ballades will of course reveal contrasting themes and keys in the opening sections of all four, but such similarities are only superficial. For the most part, sonata form has always been more concerned with formal process and rhetorical strategy than with topical or affective content (or even number of themes, as eighteenth-century monothematic movements and later nineteenth-century "theme groups" demonstrate), and as a process it is not well suited to a narrative genre with its roots in poetry, programmatic music, and opera (more on that third generic antecedent shortly). Rhetorically logical presentation and yarn spinning are, after all, very different things. The assumption that two contrasting themes must imply a sonata model thus betrays a certain habit, even a want of analytical imagination. So many things in op. 38 openly negate any kind of sonata-allegro form that attempts to view it that way seem almost eccentric.

Speaking of the ballades more generally, Gerald Abraham's general description of ballade form acknowledges the too-problematic relationship between the two genres. For him, Chopin's ballades represented "a new and entirely individual form, a form that politely touches its hat to the superficial features of the classical 'first movement' but quietly ignores most of its underlying principles."[9] This idea bears some consideration (though one might even dispute the idea of "politely touching its hat"). One familiar principle negated is that in none of the four ballades does the contrasting material appear in the expected second key area. Another is that, in the first two ballades at least, not only is there much new material in the central sections, but it is musically framed to highlight its significance to the whole rather than being given subordinate status. This material—the stormy passagework in the First, mm. 126–166 (framed by statements of the second theme) and the aforementioned third theme in the Second (framed by storm music, the true second theme)—is neither transitional nor truly developmental, and thus does not have the

9. Abraham, *Chopin's Musical Style*, 54–55.

rhetorical function necessary of a sonata form's development section. Finally, the emotional climaxes of the First, Second, and Fourth Ballades have nothing to do, in terms of theme or motive, with any of the previous material. The persistence of the use of the word "coda"—a term of structural deemphasis rather than climax or culmination[10]—to designate these sections only demonstrates how the sonata terminology has shaped the reception of these pieces. Parakilas's "reckoning" is structurally, dramatically, and narratologically far more appropriate,[11] because the closing sections are as unavoidable as fate itself, crucial to the unfolding dramas of each of these works, yet in the First and Second Ballades they recapitulate no thematic material previously heard. The krakowiak topic of the First is entirely new, while in the Second the topic is still the storm, although it is new material; these sections are thus neither recapitulatory nor structurally nonessential, as a true "coda" is. Ultimately, the sonata model does not clarify anything about these works beyond the analysts' force of habit.

Ballade as Genre

"Ballade" is a generic title, and as such has certain implications in accordance with Jeffrey Kallberg's "generic contract,"[12] which is the idea that giving a piece a generic title such as sonata, nocturne, waltz, or even ballade would intentionally indicate to the listener something of what to expect in terms of tone, form, and approach. The gray area with ballade, of course, is what these implied expectations might have been, because the ballad was a genre of poetry and vocal music, but at the time that the future op. 38 was taking shape Chopin would have known precisely one other instrumental ballade—his own op. 23 in G minor. Beside that single example, Parakilas identifies a couple of other roughly contemporaneous proto-ballades, including Clara Wieck's ballade from her *Soirées musicales*, op. 6, no. 2. The piece, which recalls Chopin's nocturnes with its stable accompaniment and Italianate, operatic melody, is full of languishing sighs, vocalistic emphases, and *fioriture*, and was published the year Chopin first heard her play it in Leipzig (on the same September 1836 visit as when he saw Schumann and played him the

---

10. See chapter 3, n. 14.
11. Parakilas, *Ballads without Words*, 74–76.
12. Jeffrey Kallberg, "The Rhetoric of Genre: Chopin's Nocturne in G Minor," *Nineteenth-Century Music* 11/3 (Spring 1988), 243.

alternate version of op. 38). At the time, Chopin praised her latest work—though whether he had heard and knew this piece is not known.[13]

A kind of response to Wieck's piece or to the ballade idea itself—to judge from the title—might have been Robert Schumann's "Balladenmäßig" (roughly translatable as "Balladelike") from the op. 6 *Davidsbündlertänze*, written about September 1837; neither vocal nor narrative, it is a short, galloping character piece, 3/4 versus 6/8 time throughout, that seems to hint at the kind of heroic action that might appear in a poetic ballad (though it doesn't do much else).[14] From these three piano pieces alone it cannot really be said that a generic pattern was developing, though a certain thread does connect them.

What those pieces and vocal settings have in common is that they all can be seen to have something to do with storytelling. Whether it is the sentimental evocation of a storyteller at work, an excerpt from a tale, or the whole of the tale itself—the grim consequences of a flouted taboo, a grandly heroic and mythic epic, a ghost story or demonic tale—what is common to all is the implied subjective view of the story. Chopin's narrator-framed op. 23 epic, Clara Wieck's singer baring her soul (an arialike reaction to the part of the love story where her lover wrongs her?), and Schumann's wisp of days-of-yore heroism are all part of a larger family, even sharing a kind of proto-generic contract, though the protocols were as yet uncodified. Compare this emerging ballade form with what might be called an "invisible" form such as a minuet and trio (ABA, because that was convention's dictate) or the more complex sonata-allegro (where the contrast, ordering, and presentation of musical ideas is prescribed from the outset to work in certain ways).

Parakilas identifies three distinct strains of the nineteenth-century piano ballade: the narrative ballade, the lyrical ballade (a kind of character piece, with a subcategory of salon ballad, not technically challenging and with perhaps a hint of archaic, plain-style sincerity), and the folksong ballade, all of which evolved in the 1840s and 1850s.[15] Chopin's op. 23 is the *Fons et origo* of the narrative approach, while both Wieck's and Schumann's pieces fit neatly into the second category—"one episode in a ballade," as Parakilas puts it,[16] with the single episode symbolizing the whole in a kind of synecdoche. Although by the 1830s the entire idea of governing protocols in musical genres was giving way to the individual utterance of compositional genius, at least to some extent, it is also

---

13. A perceptive treatment of the piece appears in Parakilas, *Ballads without Words*, 130–33.
14. Ibid., 133–35.
15. Ibid., chapters 4–6.
16. Ibid., 133.

possible to see the genres themselves as gaining a flexibility that would still allow for a kind of contract without the restrictive formal template. The nascent ballade is a good example of this evolution.

This variety of ballade subtypes, incidentally, enables us to understand how a small part of op. 38, the opening forty-six measures, could still be considered a ballade or even a work (instead of a fragment) when Chopin chose to perform it without the rest. The different ballade subgenres, as explained by Parakilas, made such a thing unproblematic. Parakilas has described the salon ballade: "The attraction of the title [i.e. ballade] evidently lay in its suggestion of cultivated simplicity. The themes of these ballades have the melodic simplicity of contemporary sentimental or operatic ballades, not that of folk ballads. The salon ballade may in fact have developed partly out of the tradition of published piano arrangements of the musical numbers from operas."[17] Salon ballades were also "sentimental rather than dramatic, shorter and easier to perform and simpler in form" than a narrative ballade would have been.[18] The accompaniments of salon ballades tended to be plain, which meant that "in a salon ballade everything depends on the attractive melody," and that "the whole repertory is characterized by simplicity of form: themes in salon ballades are not worked over, developed, transposed, or transformed."[19]

This description fits the opening paragraph of op. 38 perfectly (and we remember that it was published separately in 1876 as "Baladine"). It is simple and technically accessible to amateurs, and it is nostalgic and ingenuous but not really folk*like* so much as like an operatic idealization of the Folk themselves. ("What can be finer than the simple strains of the opening section!" effused Niecks. "They sound as if they had been drawn from the people's storehouse of song."[20]) Op. 38, in both versions, thus functions as a true ballade in several ways that do not completely overlap: content, affect, and simplicity in the short version, and contents, affects, narrative structure, and tragic outcome in the published version. To see it in these different lights requires a kind of generic contract that reaches beyond formal road map, which is a good thing, because it frees analysis from such binarisms as "work" (or not), "complete" (or not), and especially the "correct version," like the *Fassung letzter Hand* or any other

---

17. Parakilas, *Ballads without Words*, 135.
18. Parakilas, preface to *The Nineteenth-Century Piano Ballade: An Anthology* (Madison, WI: A-R Editions, 1990), ix. In this passage Parakilas is specifically comparing salon ballades to Ignaz Moscheles's op. 100, but he had just described that piece as "evidently engaged in a project much like Chopin's: to convey in wordless music a balladlike 'story,' somber in tone and rich in dramatic contrasts."
19. Parakilas, *Ballads without Words*, 135–36.
20. Niecks, *Chopin as a Man and Musician*, 2:269.

such idea that would create a hierarchy among versions of a work that may not be relevant to the work's own life or musical culture.

The ballade as an instrumental genre in the 1830s was thus, because it was only emerging, somewhat in flux; as there were different associations with ballad poetry, only some of which had to do with structure and process, so there was a variety of possibilities for what an instrumental work called "ballade" might be like. In some ways, as Fink pointed out in his 1837 review of op. 23 in the *Allgemeine musikalische Zeitung*, the case is not so different from other generic titles, such as Mendelssohn's *Songs without Words* (first published under that title in 1835, though he had been composing them since the late 1820s) or Jan Václav Tomásek's *Eclogues* or *Dithyrambs*: specifically vocal or poetic designations given to music with no words. In cases like this, some kind of generic contract must be implied—why use the generic designation otherwise?—though it must be something very different from that implied by a more familiar, specifically musical form such as fugue or sonata. With ballades, the ideas of the past, a recounted story, and an attractive, unspoiled simplicity are central, as are the narrative tone and posture.

The Operatic Ballade to 1831

One further piece of the generic puzzle warrants examination, though. Since his youth in Warsaw, Chopin had been devoted to the opera, and the influences of this genre show up in his music in a variety of ways.[21] A number of his letters chronicle the different operas he attended, and he effuses about the relative merits of such singers as Giuditta Pasta, Laure Cinti-Damoreau, Maria Malibran, and Henriette Sontag.[22] Of course, many of the operas he saw are rarely or never performed today, including works by Auber, François-Adrien Boïeldieu, Louis Hérold, Étienne Méhul, Giacomo Meyerbeer, and others (although he attended performances of Mozart and Rossini also). Chopin's correspondence suggests that he was drawn more to the operatic medium and theatrical dramas than he was to the Viennese instrumental repertoire that has dominated music history as it is conventionally taught, and against which his music tends to be measured. His affinity for vocal music should of course not be

---

21. In addition to the various discussions in Chopin's correspondence, a good overview of his operatic interest is to be found in Eigeldinger, *Chopin: Pianist and Teacher*, 110–11 n. 75. For his use of operatic principles and his relationship to piano-vocal scores, see Kasunic, "Chopin and the Singing Voice."

22. See, for example, Hedley, *Selected Correspondence*, 44–52, 58–61, and 97–104.

oversimplified, nor should his commitment to instrumental music (piano music especially) be minimized or dismissed, but it is unquestionable that certain operatic formulas and strategies for musical storytelling are as relevant as anything in the instrumental literature to understanding the thick musical context relevant to his ballades.

The operatic ballade is an important generic antecedent. Among the operas Chopin mentions in correspondence or is known to have attended, several have numbers that either are titled "Ballade" or are given other designations (e.g., "couplets") yet possess a ballade's dramatic function and structure.[23] This function is a narrative one, and such a piece is constructed in such a way as to enable a character to tell a story of events that took place long before the opera begins, perhaps a tale of prophetic or fateful import, that will color and inform the rest of the plot. The structure is antiphonal: the stanzas of the narrator's story alternate with a reaction either from the listeners or of the singer himself or herself, so it is really a boiled-down, theatrical summary of a poetic ballad: a tale of moment and a sympathetic or shocked audience reaction from the listeners onstage, or, alternatively, an earnest, moralizing refrain from the singer, repeated just enough times for the real audience to learn the story and internalize the dramatic effect of the stanzaic structure. The additional dramatic function was essentially that of a cinematic flashback: providing crucial backstory in a short amount of time.

Operatic forerunners of the ballade had existed since the eighteenth century. A famous example of the narrative posture with a story of long ago is the romance from act 3 of Mozart's *Entführung aus dem Serail*, "Im Mohrenland gefangen war" (Once upon a time in Arabia), a sort of three-stanza mirror-commentary on the plot, functioning somewhat as do the bardic lays in canto 4 of *Konrad Wallenrod*. Jean-Jacques Rousseau, in his *Dictionnaire de musique* of 1768, described romances as having a "simple and touching style" and a "slightly antique character,"[24] and Mozart's "Im Mohrenland" certainly has both, its stylized archaism reflected in its siciliano rhythm, shifting tonic, and subdominant modulation via the subtonic triad. Because the opera is a Singspiel, the narrative-within-narrative of the romance works as a charming device but not a threatening one. The audience understands the gestures, both the archaic

---

23. Here I am indebted to the work of David Kasunic, in particular his 2003 article "Chopin's Operas," in *Chopin and His Work in the Context of Culture*, ed. Irena Poniatowska (Kraków: Musica Iagellonica, 2003), 387–402, and his 2004 dissertation, "Chopin and the Singing Voice."

24. Jean-Jacques Rousseau, *Dictionnaire de musique* [1768] (Hildesheim: G. Olms, 1969), s.v. "Romance," 420. The source piece for the simple and pseudo-medieval romance was "Un fièvre brûlante," from Grétry's *Richard Coeur-de-Lion* of 1784.

ones and those elements that resonate with the plot currently under way, but there is no hint of approaching doom.

A growing taste for gothic morbidity, though, soon had an effect on the operatic repertoire (one obvious example being Weber's 1821 opera *Der Freischütz*). What the romance—now indistinguishable from a ballade—could become in this German context is illustrated by Emmy's romance from Heinrich Märschner's opera *Der Vampyr* (1828), which warns of a vampire and the way his melancholy glance proves to be a young girl's undoing. After a short introductory recitative (which, incidentally, prefigures Chopin's G Minor Nocturne, op. 37 no. 1), the spooky tale is sung—prepared, accompanied, and closed with prominent tremolo effects. This is more like the later ballade structure in that the chorus answers her with a warning after every stanza: God should be with her, she should not end up a vampire like him, and so on. The end is a foregone conclusion, and the listeners' fruitless entreaties against the inevitable are central to the dramatic function and effect.[25]

Over time, the straightforward stanzaic narrative of the operatic ballade evolved and became more sophisticated, and we will see that the developing genre had a substantial influence on the musical content, formal structure, and even rhetoric of Chopin's Second Ballade. In order to trace this development, David Kasunic has identified four ballades from contemporary French operas known to Chopin, pointing out the ways in which their compositional strategies and character deepened and grew in subtlety.[26] The first of these is Jenny's "Ballad of the White Lady" from Boïeldieu's *opéra-comique La dame blanche* of 1825, which is about a benevolent ghost who watches over young girls who put their trust in faithless men. The opening of the first stanza is given in example 4.4, and a certain lightness and good humor soon become evident; following the mock horror of the opening strain (B-flat minor, upward leaps of a minor sixth, etc.), Jenny breaks into a French Revolutionary march in the parallel major mode to trumpet the merits of the White Lady, and it is that triumphant and jolly strain that the chorus will happily echo after each stanza. Not only does the contrast between major and minor modes signal the affective change in the narrative, but there are dramatic framing sections for the ballad proper—shushing to open and thanks to finish—and the introduction consists of harp arpeggios that, in the absence of an actual bard, at least hint at a bardic topic. All the dramatic elements of the ballade are in place, though here it is all in the service of what is ultimately a fairly cheerful story, unlike

---

25. A good treatment of operatic romances and ballades, including the reproduction of the piano-vocal score of Emmy's romance, is to be found in Carolyn Abbate, *Unsung Voices* (Princeton, NJ: Princeton University Press, 1991), 69–85.
26. See Kasunic, "Chopin's Operas."

Ex. 4.4. François-Adrien Boïeldieu, *La dame blanche*, act 1, "Ballad of the White Lady," mm. 10–29.

Märschner's aforementioned *Vampyr* or the Hérold and Meyerbeer examples to be discussed shortly.

Zerline's ballade-romance (designated "couplets") "Voyez sur cette roche" from Daniel Auber's *Fra Diavolo* of 1830 maintains the major-minor contrast, with the tremolo-laden G minor introductory passage setting up and punctuating a more tuneful G major ballad about the bandit Fra Diavolo. There is no listeners' response composed into this number, but operagoers were especially aware of the "audience," the theatrical function of the listeners who react to the narrative, because Fra Diavolo himself is among them, in disguise as the "Marquis of San Marco"; he even sings the third verse. Although it too is in a lighter vein, this number maintains several of the narrative conventions that have evolved: major-minor contrast, a kind of audience response to the tale (ironic, here, in that it's from the villain), and the kind of dramatic foreshadowing that gives such pieces their dramatic place.

The "Ballad of Alice Manfredi," from Ferdinand Hérold's opera *Zampa* of 1831, is sung early in the first act by Camilla, the opera's ingénue. This ballad is about a perfidious count who seduces and then abandons a sixteen-year-old girl named Alice Manfredi, fleeing Italy and taking to the sea as a pirate. Alice is afterward befriended by a businessman from Sicily named Lugano, and when she subsequently dies, brokenhearted, he has a statue erected in her honor, which is revered in that country in the same way that the statue of a saint might be. The climax of the opera has the statue interfering with a marriage ceremony between the pirate and Camilla, who is Lugano's daughter, and—in a clear echo of the Commendatore and Don Giovanni at the end of Mozart's opera—bearing the guilty pirate away.

Hérold's opera is not a comedy, so the ballade takes itself a bit more seriously. Like Auber's ballade-romance, it does not incorporate any ensemble response, but the singer punctuates her story after each verse with a musettelike refrain beseeching "Saint Alice" to "save us from a similar fate," so the familiar antiphonal structure remains.[27] Moreover, although the first two of three couplets are identical, consisting of a sweetly idealized, French pseudo–folk song in major mode with short, repeated phrases and an affective inflection to the parallel minor, the third is different. Here the text is about Alice's death and the locals' belief that when the wind blows at night her statue murmurs the name of the guilty lover, and as if in response the harmony changes, becoming more chromatic and colored by inflections by the minor mode, and tremolos appear in the accompaniment (see exx. 4.5a and 4.5b). Though the stanzaic structure is maintained, then, the third stanza itself changes to reflect the mood of the story and the ballade's prophetic function in the opera, the integrity of traditional, repetitious ballad structure here giving way to dramatic exigency.

---

27. This short refrain seems directly reminiscent of J. S. Bach's musette for the Gavotte of the English Suite in G Minor, and thus communicates Alice's youthful innocence and unsophistication.

Ex. 4.5a. Louis Hérold, *Zampa*, act 1, Camilla's ballade, first couplet.

A quantum leap beyond the foregoing numbers is the first-act ballade from Giacomo Meyerbeer's *Robert le diable*, which also premiered in 1831, a few months after *Zampa*. Because this ballade is more involved musically—a culmination of the genre, at least until Senta's ballad in Wagner's *Fliegender Holländer*—it will merit a more detailed treatment.

Ex. 4.5b. Hérold, *Zampa*, act 1, Camilla's ballade, third couplet.

Ex. 4.6. Giacomo Meyerbeer, *Robert le diable*, act 1, Raimbaut's ballade, mm. 1–20.

[Musical score: Allegretto molto moderato, with vocal line marked RAIMBAULT beginning at m. 12, text: "Ja-dis ré-gnait en Nor-man-di-e un prin-ce no-ble et va-leur-eux; sa fil-le, Ber-the la jo-li-e, dé-dai-gnait tous les a-mour-eux;"]

After seeing the opera, Chopin considered the hugely successful *Robert le diable* to be "a masterpiece of the modern school" and "a sensation,"[28] so it is fair to assume that this ballade, the first solo in the work, would certainly have caught his attention.

Robert le diable opens, after a short instrumental introduction, with Robert, the duke of Normandy, his mysterious friend Bertram, and Robert's knights all involved in a celebration. The knights sing a lusty paean to wine (the performance indication is "allegro bachique"), and some entertainers from Normandy ("joyeux pèlerins," joyful pilgrims) arrive, including Raimbaut, who would like to sing a song for the duke. Not counting the scene-setting drunken chorus, Raimbaut's ballade, "Jadis

---

28. See Hedley, *Selected Correspondence*, 100, 103.

régnait en Normandie," is the first discernible plot development, and provides the premise for the entire opera.

Raimbaut's ballade begins as a sweet, siciliano-inflected C major pastorale, and in the first stanza we learn that long ago a brave and noble prince ruled Normandy, and that his beautiful daughter Berthe disdained all suitors until a warrior, an unknown prince, presented himself at her father's court and she fell in love with him (ex. 4.6). Here the character of the music changes, and Raimbaut (now in C minor) tells the knights, with a mysterious air, that it was a fateful error: this warrior was a demon. The knightly chorus echoes these words in disbelief (ex. 4.7).

Back in C major—but a C major now colored by a troubled sixteenth-note accompaniment and chromatic alterations in the melody—the second stanza explains that this warrior is really a servant of Satan, and that, owing to the naïveté of both Berthe and her father, she and the demon

Ex. 4.7. Meyerbeer, *Robert le diable*, act 1, Raimbaut's ballade, mm. 32–42.

Ex. 4.8. Meyerbeer, *Robert le diable,* act 1, Raimbaut's ballade, second stanza, mm. 51–60.

lover were wed in church (ex. 4.8). Another C minor passage of commentary ("Funeste erreur!") and knightly reactions follow. The music returns to C major for the third and final stanza, which is now accompanied by roiling tremolos, and Raimbaut only partially sings the melody, sometimes singing nervous fragments around the orchestra's rendering of it (ex. 4.9). This union resulted in a son named Robert, ill-starred and dangerous, kidnapper of women and the cause of much suffering in families. The C minor section that follows is a warning to the "young shepherds" that, it is presumed, usually hear such a ballade: flee! The number ends when Robert explodes wrathfully, telling the pilgrim that *he* is Robert and that the penalty for the insult will be death by hanging. The rest of the opera will follow the evil machinations of Bertram, Robert's dark companion (who turns out to be his demonic father), and Robert's eventual redemption through the efforts of his foster sister Alice. This ballade is thus different in that although its story does overshadow

Ex. 4.9. Meyerbeer, *Robert le diable,* act 1, Raimbaut's ballade, third stanza, mm. 91–98.

and define the opera's plot, its dire message turns out not to be binding; its prophetic warning is taken, and tragic consequences are avoided.

To set the tone for his opera, Meyerbeer thus composed a ballade that drew upon the dramatic and musical devices of the earlier ballades, incorporating them in a more developed and substantial way. On the most obvious level, he used a two-key structure (really a two-mode structure in both cases, with parallel minor and major modes on the same tone), as did Boïeldieu in *La dame blanche,* to reflect both the change in mood of the ballade's story and to set the story itself apart from the reactions of the listeners. Beginning in minor and ending in major, as Boïeldieu does in Jenny's ballade, is not particularly surprising; that had been done in instrumental music for centuries already. However, reversing the modes, as Meyerbeer does in Raimbaut's ballade, thus enabling the minor-mode forebodings of the interpolated commentary and response sections to completely swamp the idealized once-upon-a-time of the beginning, is less common but dramatically more effective. Knowing op. 38, we may surmise that this particular lesson was not lost on Chopin.

The matter of periodic response to the story being recounted is also of interest. In Jenny's ballade, the chorus of listeners merely echoes Jenny's earnest warning about the White Lady's watching out for feminine virtue. In the ballade of Alice Manfredi, Hérold has no listener response but, rather, recurrent moralizing commentary from the narrator herself: "Saint Alice, protect us; we will pray for you." Meyerbeer combines both approaches in his minor-mode responses to the major-mode tale of Raimbaut's ballade: first the singer moralizes ("Fateful error! Fatal delusion!" and, after the third verse, "Flee, shepherds!"), and only afterward is he joined by the knights, who echo his reactions. This is a more nuanced approach to the narrator-listener relationship, because it shows the listeners not only to be caught up in the story, but also to be internalizing the lessons the narrator desires them to draw from it.

A third and crucially important development in Raimbaut's ballade was seen in more tentative form in Hérold's Alice Manfredi ballade. What had been a noticeable musical change toward the end now becomes, with Meyerbeer, a process that extends throughout the piece, as if, in Kasunic's words, "the ballade's strophic music seems to begin to *hear* its words."[29] The orchestral accompaniment and the melody itself begin to reflect listeners' reactions (listeners onstage and in the audience alike), so the drama of the story becomes more vivid, the reactions more guided and controlled. The original C major innocence with which Raimbaut's ballade begins never returns unspoiled, because by the second stanza the music is already registering the demonic threat. This is still another lesson that Chopin clearly took to heart: beyond merely recounting a story, Meyerbeer's piece offers musical strategies for imparting longer range dramatic significance. It is, in other words, an apt musical evocation of the oral-poetic process, and as such makes plain its significance for the nascent instrumental ballade. As Kasunic described it, "Compositionally, the Meyerbeerian ballade presented Chopin with a large-scale form in which two principal melodies, of contrasting modes and characters, alternated and evolved across a dramatic trajectory charted and defined by these melodies."[30] (Compare Charles Rosen's comment on the tonal

---

29. Kasunic, "Chopin's Operas," 394.
30. Kasunic, "Playing Opera at the Piano: Chopin and the Piano-Vocal Score," paper given at the Seventieth Annual Meeting of the American Musicological Society, Seattle, WA, 11–14 November 2004.

process in op. 38: "The opening of the Second Ballade is a model of how to allow one tonality to grow out of another without the formal modulation and opposition of a sonata exposition.")[31] Of the contrasting materials used, Kasunic observes that "Meyerbeer's innovation is to treat these affectively different musics as an opposition to be reconciled."[32] Another Meyerbeerian stroke was to use reminiscences of the ballade later in the opera, so that its dramatic foreshadowing could be deployed in the music, a strategy that—as will be seen—likewise did not go unnoticed by Chopin.

This model was fresh and contemporary with the first two Chopin ballades, relevant to the Second especially, and is manifestly distant from preexistent instrumental forms such as the sonata. It is not that the ballades were the only operatic material relevant to Chopin (or, indeed, used by him); rather, they provided a kind of basic approach that he, unencumbered by actual texts, singers' preferences, or the formulaic expectations of opera audiences, could fashion into musical narratives far subtler and more effective than either actual operatic ballades or vague sonata derivatives.

The conventions of the operatic ballade suggest very strongly that Chopin's use of the term "ballade" as a genre designation was anything but capricious, and that the sonata process was in no way a point of departure or reference for his ballades. In op. 38, we will see that a tale is told clearly enough that certain contemporaries understood it more or less literally, which must mean that the musical content was sufficiently familiar and the narrative strategies sufficiently coherent for that to happen. The necessary background is to be found in the contemporary musical and cultural realms, which will illuminate what the musical language and narrative strategy are seeking to express—what the story actually is.

One key to this puzzle is provided by the informal designation of Raimbaut's ballade as the Pilgrim's Ballade. This nickname is based on the reference to Raimbaut as a "joyeux pèlerin"; the piece is called this in a review of newly published music that appeared in the January 1833 issue of the *Harmonicon*.[33] The Pilgrim's Ballade, the summa of operatic ballades at least up to Chopin's early years in Paris, cast a long shadow,[34]

---

31. Charles Rosen, *The Romantic Generation* (Cambridge, MA: Harvard University Press, 1995), 332.

32. Kasunic, "Chopin and the Singing Voice," 232.

33. *Harmonicon* 2/1 (January 1833), 13–14. The short notice is a review of five different arrangements of music from Meyerbeer's *Robert le diable*, one of which was "The Pilgrim's Ballad, 'Jadis regnait in Normandie,' from the same [i.e. *Robert*], arranged with Variations, by Charles Czerny. (Chappell.)"

34. A measure of just how long a shadow was cast by Meyerbeer's ballade is seen in the ballade from Daniel Auber's comic opera *Le cheval de bronze* (1835). This rather ludicrous early essay in *chinoiserie* (which involves trips to Venus on a flying horse made of bronze) has

one that reached beyond the world of opera. Despite the tendency among more recent commentators to distance Chopin from Meyerbeer and downplay his early appreciative reactions to *Robert le diable*, it will become clear just how much influence on the Second Ballade, op. 38, this one operatic number had.

---

a three-stanza ballade, of somewhat less dramatic moment than the other ballades discussed in this chapter, that prominently includes the word "pèlerin" in two of its three verses.

5

THE POLISH PILGRIMS AND THE OPERATIC IMPERATIVE

A Pilgrims' Ballade; a Polish Ballade

It ought to be becoming clear, now, that not one but two formal models made significant contributions Chopin's new genre of the piano ballade. One is that of programmatic piano pieces, in which a succession of musical excerpts in familiar styles can narrate a story for the informed listener (though scores for such pieces tended to have the episodes explicitly subtitled). Our understanding of this approach can be sharpened past its initial accessibility (or obviousness) by the philosophy of a Kurpiński, as discussed in chapter 2, which explains and endorses the principle of reminiscence. In reminiscence, not only familiar styles, but also quotations or near-quotations of familiar pieces are understood to call up a variety of associations in the minds of listeners, thus deepening the emotional content of the musical narrative. The other formal plan is that of the operatic ballade, where a different strategy was evolving for evoking both the tale itself and listeners' responses to it, with the deepening seriousness of the story being reflected in the gradual transformation of the musical material. It will become clear that both approaches inform Chopin's Second Ballade, op. 38, and its musical content and structural eccentricities.

As we begin to ask what story Chopin needed to tell, some guidance is fortunately provided by two pieces of contemporary documentation. The first of these is a letter from Heinrich Albert Probst, the Parisian agent for Breitkopf und Härtel to his employers. The Breitkopf und Härtel firm was Chopin's primary German publisher, so Probst was hardly a random contact, and he was in the process of negotiating for certain of Chopin's works (and he thought Chopin's asking prices were too high). Among these works was a ballade, called the "Seconde Ballade" in the letter of

2 May 1839 and "a Pilgrims' Ballade" in the letter of 10 May.[1] A note on translation is necessary here: Probst's letter mixes languages, referring to the piece as "eine Ballade des Pèlerins." As it happens, both French and German words for *ballad* are feminine and end in *e*: *Ballade*. If we take the first three words as German, allowing for the natural capitalization of German nouns (applied also to the French one at the end; the German word for pilgrim is *Pilger*), and consider the German writer to have given the French *pèlerin* a German genitive *-s*, the phrase means "a pilgrim's ballad," and that is how it is usually translated in the literature. If, instead, we take the three words after the German article as French, capitalized both as a German author might naturally do or as the actual title of a piece would require, we have "a ballad of the pilgrims" or "pilgrims' ballad," which seems better for a couple of reasons. The phrase is still an obvious play on the ballade of Raimbaut the Pilgrim from Meyerbeer's *Robert le diable* (which had already gained the nickname "Pilgrim's Ballade"[2] and with which, we will see in chapter 6, Chopin's op. 38 has several points of correspondence), yet the plural possessive does not require an ending from one language grafted onto the noun of another, and—particularly given the cultural context—makes more sense. The First Ballade had been in print for three years already, and the "pilgrims' ballade" reference seems to be a nickname, now applied to the future op. 38, of the kind found elsewhere with Chopin's music. (Jeffrey Kallberg, for example, has discussed another such, the so-called Polish People's Prayer.)[3]

A very different kind of testimony had been provided some months earlier in a newspaper tribute, published in *Le revue et gazette musicale de Paris* on 9 September 1838. Written by Félicien Mallefille, who at the time was George Sand's lover but was apparently in the process of being supplanted by Chopin, the piece consists of a letter of appreciation ("To Mr. F. Chopin, About His Polish Ballade") and a brief dramatic scene involving a group of Polish exiles.[4] (The entire text is given, in the original French and my English translation, in the appendix.)

---

1. The correspondence between Probst and his publisher is quoted in Wilhelm Hitzig, "'Pariser Briefe': Ein Beitrag zur Arbeit des deutschen Musikverlags aus den Jahren 1833–40," in *De Bär: Jahrbuch von Breitkopf & Härtel, 1929–30* (Leipzig, 1930), 65. Jeffrey Kallberg discusses it in his dissertation, "The Chopin Sources: Variants and Versions in Later Manuscripts" (Ph.D. diss., University of Chicago, 1982), 93–100.

2. See chapter 4, note 33.

3. Kallberg, "Chopin's March, Chopin's Death," *Nineteenth-Century Music* 25/1 (Spring 2001), 23.

4. "A M. F. Chopin, sur sa Ballade polonaise," *Revue et gazette musicale de Paris* 5/36 (1838), 362–64.

Mallefille begins by saying that recently Chopin had favored a group of intimates, "sympathetic and congenial souls," with "this Polish Ballade we love so much." This implies both that Mallefille was not hearing the ballade for the first time and that the nickname "Polish Ballade" was something Chopin and others would understand. Among the listeners, Mallefille identifies two besides himself. First was the Skeptic, "who had always retained so lively a passion in love and art," and who after the performance was "looking vaguely in front of him, head on his shoulder and mouth parted slightly in a sad smile; I imagined that he had to be dreaming of murmuring brooks, and of gloomy farewells exchanged on somber forest paths." The other was "the old Believer, to whose evangelical word we listen with such respectful admiration"; this man "had his hands joined, his eyes closed, his face furrowed with wrinkles, seemingly interrogating Dante, his ancestor, on the secrets of the heavens and the destinies of the world." It is generally accepted that the Skeptic ("so lively a passion in love and art") was the painter Eugène Delacroix, who was friends with Chopin and Sand at this time, and the Believer ("seemingly interrogating Dante, his ancestor") was the poet Adam Mickiewicz himself. As for Mallefille himself, he tells us, "Hidden on the darkest side of the room, I wept to follow the thought of the desolate images that you put before me. Upon returning to my room, I tried to render, in my own way, the following lines. Read them with indulgence, and if I have somehow misinterpreted your Ballade, recognize this offering as a proof of my affection for you and my sympathy for your heroic fatherland."

The playlet, titled "The Exiles.—A Path," runs as follows. Following an introductory statement by the Choir ("Farewell, Poland!"), a bitter Young Man of defeatist temperament is confronted in turn by an Old Man, a Child (the Old Man's orphaned grandson), and a Priest, all of whom nurture hope for the future, whether it offers vengeance or redemption. The Young Man—angry, despairing, and suicidal—is unpersuaded and lets the group depart without him. It is not until he converses with an amoral and opportunistic Passer-by, who feels no loyalty to his own parents, his native land, or anything else, that the Young Man perceives the error of his ways and turns to follow his brethren, calling "Poland, Holy Poland... to you, forever!" Mallefille's scene seems clearly to be set *after* the ballade's story has taken place ("I wept to follow the thought of the desolate images you put before me"), among the wandering Polish exiles and a sophisticated and urbane—perhaps French—non-Pole. French liberal and intellectual circles were in sympathy with the Polish people, and so this document, in addition to providing a fascinating account of how the Second Ballade was heard and understood by one proximate and well-informed listener (three years before its publication), captures a certain amount of the contemporary French cultural zeitgeist as well. Poland had been in travail, and although the French government had remained on the sidelines, there was a good deal of support in the literary and artistic communities.

The Great Migration and Polish Culture in Exile

By the 1830s Poland had been in a steadily worsening crisis for decades. Politically and administratively, the Polish-Lithuanian Commonwealth had in the previous century been growing increasingly dysfunctional, which made it vulnerable to its opportunistic neighbors Prussia, Russia, and Austria. The Baltic Lithuanians and Slavic Poles had been more or less peaceably united since the late fourteenth century, but in the course of the Polish partitions (1772, 1793, and 1795), when Poland was dismembered into subject political entities, Lithuania fell to the Russians. This history is probably a good part of the explanation for Mickiewicz's sympathy for and identification with the Poles, especially following the disastrous events of 1831.

After the partitions, a series of political maneuvers continued to weaken Poland as a sovereign state, and by 1830 it was at the point of powerlessness. In 1815 the Congress of Vienna had formalized the tripartite partition of Poland into the Grand Duchy of Posen (Poznań), which was under the ultimate control of the Prussians; the Free State of Kraków; and the so-called Congress Kingdom of Poland (based upon but smaller than the former Grand Duchy of Warsaw), which was united with the Russian empire. Polish nationalists reserved their greatest hopes for this last, which had the most trappings of independence (a parliament called the Sejm, official use of the Polish language, a separate administration, and its own army). The rule of Tsar Alexander I, however, became ever more absolute, and in 1819 censorship was introduced into the Congress Kingdom. From 1820 to 1825 the tsar did not convene the Sejm a single time, and secret revolutionary societies began to be formed (and in turn persecuted). In Russia, tensions were raised by the Decembrist Revolt of 26 December 1825, an attempted military action against the new Tsar Nicholas I when, following the death of Alexander, his brother Constantine (1779–1831, later Grand Duke and commander-in-chief of the Polish Army) removed himself from the line of accession. This revolt took place without Polish involvement, but previous connections between Polish and Russian revolutionaries were subsequently discovered, and the Poles came under greater suspicion and scrutiny.

At the same time, throughout the 1820s, Polish literary Romanticism flourished through the pens of Mickiewicz, Julius Słowacki, and others, and nationalist consciousness continued to grow among students, workers, and soldiers, especially those in the Cadet School in Warsaw. The breadth of Mickiewicz's work suggests that Polish nationalistic tastes encompassed epic, dramatic, and lyric tones, and that both the heroic tale and the idyll spoke to the national yearning and nostalgia. At the same time, the Poles continued to chafe with growing bitterness under the increasingly strict, Russian-controlled government and disintegrating economic conditions, so the urge to be free of the Russian yoke was building simultaneously with the flowering of national consciousness in Polish poetry and music.

Throughout 1829 pressure for Poland to wrest itself from Russian domination was at a peak, in part because two seemingly successful revolutions elsewhere in Europe offered the possibility of a free Polish future. In Paris the July Revolution was the response of the populace to the increasingly autocratic behavior of the Bourbon King Charles X, who had suspended freedom of the press, dissolved the elected Chamber of Deputies, and announced that he would thereafter rule by ordinance. The three-day revolution installed Louis-Philippe, the so-called citizen king, an Orléans cousin who also had a claim to the throne. All of this was watched with great interest by the French-speaking Catholic Walloons in Belgium, who felt unrepresented and helpless against the decrees of the Dutch Calvinist king and Dutch ruling party. On 25 August 1830 it was an operatic performance in Brussels that sparked the revolution: following the duet "Amour sacré de la patrie" from Daniel Auber's *Muette de Portici*, the inflamed audience hit the streets and took over government buildings, and eventually Belgium successfully seceded from the Netherlands.[5] (There will be more on Auber's *Muette* further on.) To the Poles, of course, these revolutions were very hopeful developments, and particularly the operatic angle of the second would have struck the national imagination.

The first salvo in the attempted Polish revolution was the incompetently executed armed uprising of 29 November 1830, which had little immediate political impact; there were too many tactical lapses, including too small and insignificant an opening signal fire, an absence of leadership among the revolutionary groups, and a failed student attack on the Belvedere palace, where the Grand Duke Constantine was hidden away by his servants for protection. On 30 November the Administrative

---

5. Rey Longyear, "La Muette de Portici," *Music Review* 19 (1958), 45; and Anthony Arblaster, *Viva la Libertà! Politics in Opera* (London: Verso, 1992), 49.

Council (which acted on behalf of the tsar) condemned the events of the previous night and, in an effort to restore social and political order, announced that such Polish stalwarts as Prince Adam Czartoryski (1770–1861), Prince Michał Radziwiłł (1778–1850), and Julian Ursyn Niemcewicz (1757–1841) would be joining the council.

By early December negotiations with the tsar were being opened up, and it seemed as if concessions might be won from the Russians and political damage kept to a minimum. Prominent Poles sought a peaceful solution to the hostilities, if for no other reason than that a military confrontation with a power the size of Russia would certainly end badly. In reality, though, when he first became aware of the violence in Warsaw the tsar had ordered the preparation of a military response, so the confrontation and crushing of Poland had been a foregone conclusion from the start. He dispatched a large military force, which crossed the border in February 1831 and engaged the Polish forces in several costly battles. After initial defeats, though, a Polish victory came in late March over the Russian 6th Corps. Although the Polish government saw reason to hope, their military failed to capitalize on this success.

A seven-month period of inconclusive political, diplomatic, and military maneuvering followed, during which time it became clear that hoped-for support from England and France, which were more or less sympathetic but not eager to antagonize Russia, would not materialize. Finally, in September 1831, Russia's final, overpowering attack on Warsaw finished off any remaining hope for Polish independence, and the Polish forces surrendered. Poland thus became even more of a shadow country, with great national sentiment but no autonomy; the years following saw the tightening of the Russian control on Polish political and cultural life, at least cultural life at home.

The direct result of this upheaval was the so-called Great Migration (sometimes called the Great Emigration). Following the violence, many Poles, including students, military cadets, and members of noble families, fled their homeland, fearing Russian reprisal for their involvement in the various revolutionary events. These exiles were called the Polish Pilgrims, and their tribunes were poets such as Mickiewicz and Słowacki, who continued to give voice to the ferment of frustrated national feeling. Many of the Polish expatriates settled in Paris, becoming known as "northern Frenchmen,"[6] and began to separate into two main parties. These were the right-wing Hotel Lambert faction, headed by Prince Adam Czartoryski, and the left-wing Democratic Society, headed by the

---

6. Niecks, *Chopin as a Man and Musician*, 2:289 n. 21. In a letter of 6 August 1848, Chopin refers to his fellow Pole Antoni Kontski as a northern Frenchman.

historian Joachim Lelewel; issues about which they disagreed included the abolition of serfdom and whether the newly freed peasants would support Polish efforts against Russia.[7] Still, disagreements aside, the reality of the migration was an exodus of the Polish educated and literary elite, who came to maintain a kind of Polish culture-in-exile that was followed with interest by the literate Polish community at home. In time, a distinct cultural outlook and psychology began to emerge.[8]

As it evolved and flowered in Paris, this outlook, Polish cultural Romanticism, had a variety of components. One, of course, was a mixture of anger, resentment, and desire for revenge, which could be seen in the hallowing of such texts as Mickiewicz's earlier *Konrad Wallenrod*. Another was grief and nostalgia for vanquished, betrayed Poland and a sense of permanent separation from the idyllic land of childhood. Mallefille's published reaction to Chopin's Second Ballade reflects an awareness of this perspective (though he was of course French); an almost painfully idealized image of pre-Russified Poland, Arcadian in its innocence, seems to boil out of the Young Man's anguished description of people in the years before the Cossacks: "They had houses where they were able to rest in peace, trees which would cover them with their cool shadows, and their harvests were the reward of the sweat of their brow.... They had parents who came to rejoice with them on feast days, friends who consoled them in days of sadness, children who smiled at them every day."

Mallefille, writing in 1838, was drawing on what by this point were established Polish literary traditions. Mickiewicz's 1834 epic poem *Pan Tadeusz*, to choose one vast example, reflects this rose-colored hindsight throughout. The first four lines of this work are a bittersweet salute to the poet's homeland; as in *Konrad Wallenrod*, he speaks of Lithuania, or more properly the old Polish-Lithuanian Kingdom, but knowing readers read "Polonia!" for "Litwo!":

> Oh Lithuania, my country, thou
> art like good health; I never knew till now
> How precious, till I lost thee. Now I see
> Thy beauty whole, because I yearn for thee.[9]

---

7. Dorota Zakrzewska, "Alienation and Powerlessness: Adam Mickiewicz's Ballady and Chopin's Ballades," *Polish Music Journal* 2/1–2 (Summer–Winter 1999), subsection "The Ideology of the Great Emigration." http://www.usc.edu/dept/polish_music/PMJ/archives.html.

8. Further discussion of the cultural preoccupations of the émigré community can be found in Berger, "Chopin's Ballade Op. 23," 72–83, and particularly in Zakrzewska: "Alienation and Powerlessness." A superb treatment that emphasizes the mythic and mystical aspects is Goldberg, "'Remembering That Tale of Grief.'"

9. "Litwo! Ojczyzno moja! ty jesteś jak zdrowie; / Ile cię trzeba cenić, ten tylko się dowie, / Kto cię stracił. Dziś piękność twą w całej ozdobie / Widzę i opisuję, bo tęsknię po

Remembering a mortally threatening childhood illness and a pilgrimage made in gratitude for his recovery, he continues:

> Those little wooded hills, those fields beside
> The azure Niemen, spreading green and wide
> The vari-painted cornfields like a quilt,
> The silver of the rye, the wheatfields' gilt;
> Where amber trefoil, buckwheat white as snow,
> And clover with her maiden blushes grow,
> And all is girdled with a grassy band
> Of green, whereon the silent pear trees stand.[10]

An entire epic later, in lines 93–105 of the twelfth and closing book of the work, we find a similar image. All disagreements have been solved, a number of the single characters properly paired off, and all conflict swept away before the food, drink, and music of the marriage celebration. Mickiewicz closes as he began, with a pastoral idyll:

> By now the sun was sinking in the west;
> 'twas warm and still, the circle of the sky
> Was rosy to the westward, blue on high,
> And strewn with little clouds—these were a sign,
> Being bright and fleecy, that it would be fine,
> Like flocks of sheep asleep upon the grass,
> Or groups of teal. Across the west a mass,
> Transparent purple, edged with pearl and gold,
> Hung like a curtain draped with ample fold;
> Still with the western light it glowed and burned,
> Till slowly yellowing to gray it turned:
> The sun had drawn the cloud around his bed,
> And with one last warm sigh laid down his head.[11]

---

tobie." Adam Mickiewicz, *Pan Tadeusz*, book 1, lines 1–4; translation in Mickiewicz, *Pan Tadeusz*, trans. Kenneth Mackenzie (New York: Hippocrene Books, 1986), 2–3.

10. "Tymczasem przenoś moję duszę utęsknioną / Do tych pagórków leśnych, do tych łąk zielonych, / Szeroko nad błękitnym Niemnem rozciągnionych; / Do tych pól malowanych zbożem rozmaitem, / Wyzłacanych pszenicą, posrebrzanych żytem; / Gdzie bursztynowy świerzop, gryka jak śnieg biała, / Gdzie panieńskim rumieńcem dzięcielina pała, / A wszystko przepasane, jakby wstęgą, miedzą / Zieloną, na niej z rzadka ciche grusze siedzą." Mickiewicz, *Pan Tadeusz*, book 1, lines 14–22, trans. Mackenzie, 2–3.

11. "Słońce już gasło, wieczór był ciepły i cichy; / Okrąg niebios gdzieniegdzie chmurkami zasłany, / U góry błękitnawy, na zachód różany; / Chmurki wróżą pogodę, lekkie i świecące, / Tam jako trzody owiec na murawie śpiące, / Ówdzie nieco drobniejsze, jak stada cyranek. / Na zachód obłok na kształt rąbkowych firanek, / Przejrzysty, sfałdowany, po wierzchu perłowy, / Po brzegach pozłacany, w głębi purpurowy, / Jeszcze blaskiem zachodu tlił się i rozżarzał, / Aż powoli pożółkniał, zbladnął i poszarzał; / Słońce

Even if the clouds instead symbolize the coming catastrophe, as has been suggested,[12] Mickiewicz still draws the curtain in an atmosphere of warm nostalgia. The mood changes somewhat in the epilogue, a section the poet had intended to follow immediately upon the epic proper but did not finish in time for publication. (It did not see print until after Mickiewicz's death, in 1860.) In function and effect, it seems rather beautifully analogous to Robert Schumann's *Scenes from Childhood* (1838), where a series of idealized childhood memories in the form of discrete character pieces closes with "The Poet Speaks," a gentle farewell from composer directly to listener that is ostensibly not "about" anything else. Here, after the entirety of *Pan Tadeusz* had unfolded, the narrator was to step out of storytelling mode and mix his nostalgia with a full measure of a Pilgrim's grief and bitterness (and, incidentally, making clear what the first word of his poem, "Litwo!," really meant):

> Alas for us who fled in times of pest
> And, timid souls, took refuge in the west![13]
>
> ...
>
> O Mother Poland, thou that in this hour
> Art laid within the grave—What man hath power
> To speak of thee today?[14]
>
> ...
>
> For us unbidden guests in every clime
> From the beginning to the end of time
> There is but one place in this planet whole
> Where happiness may be for every Pole—
> The land of childhood!
> That shall aye endure
> As holy as a first love and as pure.[15]
>
> ...

---

spuściło głowę, obłok zasunęło / I raz ciepłym powiewem westchnąwszy—usnęło." Mickiewicz, *Pan Tadeusz*, book 12, lines 851–63; trans. Mackenzie, 572–73.

12. Mickiewicz, *Pan Tadeusz*, trans. Leonard Kress (Perrysburg, OH: Harrowgate, 2006; http://www.harrowgatepress.com/pan.pdf, 276 n. 113.

13. "Biada nam zbiegi, żeśmy w czas morowy / Lękliwe nieśli za granicę głowy!" Mickiewicz, *Pan Tadeusz*, epilogue, lines 5–6; trans. Mackenzie, 578–79.

14. "O Matko Polsko! Ty tak świeżo w grobie / Złożona—nie ma sił mówić o tobie!" Mickiewicz, *Pan Tadeusz*, epilogue, lines 40–41; trans. Mackenzie, 580–81.

15. "Dziś dla nas, w świecie nieproszonych gości, / W całej przeszłości i w całej przyszłości / Jedna już tylko jest kraina taka, / W której jest trochę szczęścia dla Polaka, / Kraj lat dziecinnych! On zawsze zostanie / Święty i czysty, jak pierwsze kochanie." Mickiewicz, *Pan Tadeusz*, epilogue, lines 64–69; trans. Mackenzie, 582–83.

That happy country, happy, poor and small!
The world is God's but that was ours—ours all,
And all belonged to us that lay around.
How we remember everything we found,
The linden with her crown magnificent,
That to the village children shadow lent,
And every little rivulet and stone.
How every little corner of the place was known,
And far as the next house was all our own![16]

So the Polish consciousness was fundamentally diasporic. Poles endlessly mourned their lost homeland, the memory of which was borne by the Pilgrims much as the Jews carried the Law with them in exile. This is the link to the third part of the Pilgrim mindset: after wounded rage and profound nostalgia, there was a conscious affiliation with the ancient Hebrews, banished from the promised land and forever singing the Lord's song in faraway places.[17] Jews formed a sizable minority of the Polish populace, and many aspects of the Jewish worldview were well-known to educated Poles. More to the point, Mickiewicz's wife, Céline, daughter of the pianist Maria Szymanowska, was from a Frankist family (the Frankists being a Jewish splinter sect that followed the eighteenth-century messianist Jacob Frank), and Mickiewicz's mother may well have been also, so the Romantic attraction to cultural Judaica found in Mickiewicz's writings (and political actions in later life) may have had some ancestral and filial basis.[18] One of the most famous examples of this affinity is found in the twelfth book of *Pan Tadeusz*, where the Jewish tavernkeeper and dulcimer virtuoso (this would be a hammer dulcimer, related to the Hungarian cimbalom) Jankiel performs a Polish patriotic fantasy that, the poet tells us, astounds the audience and moves the performer himself to tears: "He sobbed, the honest Jew; he loved our country like a patriot true."[19] Another artifact of Polish Hebraism is the vision, from Mickiewicz's *Dziady* ("Forefathers' Eve"), of the messiah who will save Poland:

---

16. "Ten kraj szczęśliwy, ubogi i ciasny! / Jak świat jest boży, tak on był nasz własny! / Jakże tam wszystko do nas należało, / Jak pomnim wszystko, co nas otaczało: / Od lipy, która koroną wspaniałą / Całej wsi dzieciom użyczała cienia / Aż do każdego strumienia, kamienia, / Jak każdy kątek ziemi był znajomy / Aż po granicę, po sąsiadów domy." Mickiewicz, *Pan Tadeusz*, epilogue, lines 79–87; trans. Mackenzie, 582–83.

17. Andrej Walicki, *Philosophy and Romantic Nationalism* (Oxford: Clarendon Press, 1982), 265–67; Ilya Prizel, *National Identity and Foreign Policy: Nationalism and Leadership in Poland, Russia, and Ukraine* (Cambridge: Cambridge University Press, 1998), 45; and Goldberg, "'Remembering That Tale of Grief,'" 58–59.

18. Walicki, *Philosophy and Romantic Nationalism*, 267.

19. "Mówiąk, ciągle szlochał, Żyd poczciwy Ojczyznę jako Polak kochał!" Mickiewicz, *Pan Tadeusz*, book 12, lines 755–56; trans. Mackenzie, 568–69.

> Born of a foreign mother, in his veins
> The blood of ancient warriors—and his name
> Shall be forty and four.[20]

The number "forty and four" has inspired a good deal of debate. The operative concept here is *Gematria*, the numeric values associated with the letters of the Hebrew alphabet, and the Jewish tradition of symbolism and exegesis that results from the study and manipulation of the numbers. In this case there is no agreed-upon answer; "Adam" (*aleph-dalet-mem*) = 45, so the theory that Mickiewicz was writing about himself requires the first aleph to be somehow excluded from the reckoning. Another theory is based on the initials of "Dovid Melech" (King David), which adds up to 44, and his *grand* mother was Ruth the Moabite. In later years, Mickiewicz told his son—I have to imagine there was some disingenuousness here, after the way this Hebraic messianism turned out—that the matter was a mystery to him.[21] (My own suspicion is that it has something to do with the word "blood" in the previous line, because *dam*—blood in Hebrew—is spelled *dalet-mem*, 44.) This Hebrew esoterica is important because of its resonance in émigré culture; it was subsequently appropriated by Andrzej Towiański (1799–1878), a Lithuanian mystic who arrived in Paris in December 1840 and, preaching a Polish messianism, for a while enjoyed a substantial Polish following.[22] The circle of those around Towiański began to take on cultlike characteristics, though, and at his declaration that the Polish battle had been won on the spiritual plane, Mickiewicz and others broke with him. Chopin's comments about the situation, in a letter of 23 March 1845 to the poet Stefan Witwicki, must rank among the great understatements of the epoch: "In short, there is discord—they will surely come to a bad end, and it won't be long either. Apart from that everything is as usual."[23]

The year 1845 was, of course, well after the composition of the Second Ballade, op. 38. What is clear in virtually all aspects of the expatriate community during these two decades is psychological desperation: the disagreements, the clutching at mystical, messianic straws, and above all the preoccupation with their own plight and their yearning for deliverance. This anguish is captured in Mickiewicz's earlier quasi-biblical poetry, written to inspire and comfort the exiles: *The Books of the*

---

20. Quoted in Walicki, *Philosophy and Romantic Nationalism*, 247.

21. A detailed analysis of possible Kabbalistic subtexts in *Forefathers' Eve*, part III, including some attention to the importance of blood, is given in Stuart Goldberg, "Konrad and Jacob: A Hypothetical Kabbalistic Subtext in Adam Mickiewicz's *Forefathers' Eve*, Part III," *Slavic and East European Journal* 45/4 (Winter 2001), 695–715, especially 708.

22. Walicki, *Philosophy and Romantic Nationalism*, 253–57.

23. Hedley, *Selected Correspondence*, 246.

Polish Nation and the Books of the Polish Pilgrims, published in 1832. The following excerpt from *The Books of the Polish Pilgrims* illustrates Mickiewicz's concern for Polish unity and the biblical magnitude the community accorded its own suffering. It also demonstrates that Félicien Mallefille's playlet "The Exiles" was an artistic response to Mickiewicz's concerns about the Polish diaspora in general, and dissension among the Pilgrims in particular, not just to Chopin's performance of his ballade.

> Ye are on your pilgrimage in a strange land, as was God's people in the wilderness.
>
> Guard yourselves on the pilgrimage against murmuring and complaining and doubting. These are sins.
>
> Ye know that when God's people were returning to the land of their fathers, to the Holy Land, at that time they journeyed in the desert, and many of God's people repined and said: "Let us return to Egypt; there we shall be in the land of bondage, but yet we shall have abundance of meat and onions."
>
> And Holy Scripture declareth that God, being offended, prolonged the pilgrimage of the nation until all those who had repined had died in the wilderness; for none of them was to see the Holy Land.
>
> Ye know that there were others among God's people who did not have faith in their prophets, and who said: "But how shall we conquer the land of our fathers, when we have against us mighty kings and men like men of a giant race?"
>
> And Holy Scripture declareth that God, being offended by this unbelief, again prolonged the pilgrimage of the nation, until all those who had doubted perished in the wilderness; for none of them was to see the Holy Land.
>
> And not only those who murmured and doubted aloud, but even those who in their hearts murmured and doubted, died also; for God readeth in hearts as in an open book, although to others that book is closed.
>
> For which reason, guard yourselves from the sin of murmuring and doubting, that ye may not prolong the days of your pilgrimage.[24]

The tragic images multiplied: Poland as the Hebrew nation in the wilderness, as the Suffering Servant, later as Jesus on the cross (the "Christ of the Nations"), and as the broken victim being consoled by Mary Misericordia.

---

24. Adam Mickiewicz, *The Books of the Polish Pilgrims*, trans. Dorothy Prall Radin, in *Poems by Adam Mickiewicz*, ed. George Rapall Noyes (New York: Polish Institute of Arts and Sciences in America, 1944), 403–4.

The Parisian Polish community grieved and fumed and fought with each other; though the Poles had sympathetic artistic fellow-travelers like Mallefille, they got no political or government support against the tsar. Inspired by their artists but otherwise powerless and adrift, the Poles desperately sought a mechanism for their own deliverance.

Personal Anguish and Literary Apotheosis

For a time, some of those most prominent Poles thought that the linchpin of this mechanism might be a new arrival, a young Warsaw pianist of refined mien who came to Paris in late 1831. Fryderyk Chopin had left Poland to pursue his musical career weeks before the insurrection, so like Mickiewicz he was not, properly speaking, a refugee in the same way the exiled Pilgrims were, but at the piano he could sing the grieving nostalgia and patriotic fury of wounded Polonia with unprecedented power. He was invited to the homes of prominent Poles, as he was to the homes of influential non-Poles such as the Baron de Rothschild. Chopin's unique compositions, and especially his way of playing them, made him a valued guest, someone other influential people would go out of their way to hear, so this made him a desirable draw for a soirée.

His precise place in the Polish community, though, is hard to gauge and easy to oversimplify. Jolanta Pekacz has persuasively argued that while Chopin maintained ties to the Polish community, the nobility never really considered him an equal.[25] Not by nature a revolutionary (nor even particularly political), he was more comfortable with the conservative Czartoryski wing, where the Polish aristocracy tended to feel more at home, and where he didn't have to feign sympathy for radical solutions and could indulge his taste for elegance and occupy himself with matters of art. (On their side, though they liked to have him nearby, he was always still just a musician to them, i.e., not of the same caste.) He shared the community's affection for its poet laureates; his teacher Elsner felt music to be essentially impossible without poetry and vice versa, and given Elsner's sympathies for the poetry and nationalistic fervor of the emergent Polish Romantic poets it seems likely that Chopin felt similarly, if in a more general way.[26] It was the work of these poets that he set in his own art songs, and he maintained connections with three of them (Stefan

---

25. Jolanta Pekacz, "Deconstructing a 'National Composer': Chopin and Polish Exiles in Paris, 1831-49," *Nineteenth-Century Music* 24/2 (Fall 2000), 161-72.
26. See Anne Swartz, "Elsner, Chopin, and Musical Narrative as Symbols of Nation," *Polish Review* 39/4 (1994), 445-56.

Witwicki, Bohdan Zaleski, and even to a lesser extent Mickiewicz) who were members of the Polish literary circle there. He also taught the Polish Princess Marceline (Radziwiłł) Czartoryska, a gifted pianist.

Chopin also, however, taught countesses from other countries, including Russia. Pekacz points out that in Chopin's whole life he dedicated fewer than a dozen pieces to Poles,[27] which is surprising only if one imagines him to be something other than a professional musician and pedagogue. He truly missed Poland (especially his family) and maintained Polish connections, but he did acclimate himself to the thriving pianistic world in Paris, associating with other musicians and partaking of musical life. For however much he missed Poland, he required more than Poland—or, in fact, Poles—to be happy, else he would not have left in the first place.

One searches long and hard in the Chopin biographical materials and secondary literature for any indication that he participated actively in the political arguments or the intellectual debates of the time. As Schumann pointed out, he was not even comfortable discussing his own music. This is not to suggest that he was an artistic primitive or that his was an exclusively intuitive mind; he did apparently have fruitful artistic discussions with Eugène Delacroix, and he attended Mickiewicz's literature lectures with George Sand. It is, rather, to say that he is most likely to have empathized with the emotional intensity of the emigré community, and to have shared the concern and feelings of helplessness, while being far less interested in the Polish nationalists' logistical disagreements and (even further afield) the eccentric pseudo-Hebraism and Kabbalistic dreams of Mickiewicz. Chopin and Mickiewicz were very different personalities, and it is no surprise that they never really became close; Mickiewicz dreamed on an epic scale and sought to bear the Polish standard before the world's peoples; Chopin worried about people he loved but mostly wanted to play, teach, and write for the piano.

Nonetheless, his own personal feelings of helplessness and concern for Poland should not be downplayed. His rage was genuine, and he was tormented by his inability to contribute to the Polish cause. "Oh God... Thou art and avengest Thyself not!" Chopin wrote after hearing about the fall of Warsaw to Russian troops.[28] "Thou hast still not enough of the Russian crimes; or, or Thou art Thyself a Russian!" And later, "Why could I not slay even a single Russian?"[29]

These remarks are from a lengthy series of entries that are full of impotent rage and morbid fantasy. Particularly striking is the way Chopin

---

27. Pekacz, "Deconstructing a 'National Composer,'" 168.
28. Warsaw fell on 8 September 1831.
29. Quoted in Hedley, *Selected Correspondence*, 90.

exhibits a distinctly operatic psyche: the political crisis is experienced as a tragic personal story, in which the political events intervene—a formula typical in Chopin's beloved French grand opera of the 1820s and '30s. Upon hearing news of the original uprising, for example, he wrote the following theatrical passages. The first is about his family: "Perhaps I have no mother; perhaps some Russian has killed her, murdered—My sisters, raving, resist—father in despair, nothing he can do—and I sit here, useless! And I here with empty hands!"[30] Another is about his adolescent sweetheart, Konstancia Gladkowska:

> What is happening to her? where is she?—poor girl—perhaps in the hands of Moscow. A Russian is seizing her, strangling her, murdering, killing! Oh, my darling! here I am—alone: come to me and I will wipe away your tears. I will heal your wounds by recalling the past, those days when Russia meant nothing—those days when only a few Russians strove to win your favor; but you scorned them because you had me, me—not that Grabowski!"[31]

Józef Grabowski was, in fact, a Warsaw merchant and the man Konstancia eventually married,[32] so the Russians cannot be held responsible for his place in Konstancia's life. Chopin, never of robust health, certainly did not have a warrior's constitution, and there is no suggestion that any of his Polish friends, old or new, thought he should carry a gun for Mother Poland. So his outraged Polish soul would always be in somewhat uneasy balance with the life he would come to enjoy as a top-tier Parisian artist: invitations to the best houses and salons, being petted and praised for his playing and compositions, teaching an exclusive circle of talented and privileged pupils, and attending the opera as much as he could. Predictably, he soon became a favorite with the Polish exiles in Paris, including (for a time) Mickiewicz himself, in whose company nationalistic ardor could naturally be given musical voice.

Chopin sought to further himself as a musician, but Poland-in-exile wanted a *wieszcz* (pronounced, in one quick syllable, "v'YESH-tch"), one whose art would enlighten and inspire the wounded Poles like a revelation. The clearest image of a *wieszcz*, in the Polish consciousness, was Jankiel, the Jewish dulcimer virtuoso of *Pan Tadeusz*. Halina Goldberg's study "'Remembering That Tale of Grief': The Prophetic Voice in Chopin's Music" is especially useful here because it provides a vivid picture of what the exile community imagined they wanted from a Chopin, whether

---

30. E. L. Voynich, ed., *Chopin's Letters* [1931] (New York: Vienna House, 1971), 149.
31. Hedley, *Selected Correspondence*, 90–91.
32. Huneker, *Chopin: The Man and His Music*, 16.

or not they themselves could articulate it this clearly: understandable, inspiring national music that could produce a powerful audience reaction. (Perhaps that would mean, for example, a reaction like that of the Walloons in Brussels.)

A *wieszcz* such as Jankiel guided the people "to other spiritual or temporal realms," to "revelation."[33] Jankiel himself is Mickiewicz's alter ego, and lies within the tradition of virtuoso musicians described in virtuoso literary passages, where an author—who is perhaps not a musician—rhapsodizes about the transcendent power of a master musician. Goldberg notes that Jankiel's musical performance, in the section Mickiewicz calls the "Concert of Concerts," is not all original: it is an improvisation made up of familiar Polish songs joined with dramatic gestures. What Mickiewicz describes is, in fact, not far from a Polish version of Steibelt's *Journée d'Ulm*, discussed in chapter 2, where a specific story is told through the use of familiar melodies, realized and elaborated in particularly expressive ways. Jankiel's Concert of Concerts is thus worth a closer look: it is essentially a primer in the art of a *wieszcz*, both the actual music making and the audience reaction. Mickiewicz paints a very clear picture of just how his version of a *wieszcz* was able to galvanize a crowd.

We enter the scene at a wedding celebration, where the Jewish virtuoso has just been induced to play for the crowd only because the bride Zosia, who had always been dear to him, asked him to. He allows a couple of pupils (who seem to have miraculously appeared) to prepare and tune the instrument, and after seating himself, he starts by playing

> a triumphal strain... but this was but a trial
> He suddenly stopped and raised the sticks awhile.

Then:

> He played again: the hammers on the strings
> Trembled as lightly as mosquito's wings
> And made a humming sound that was so soft
> 'twas hardly heard.

Another pause, until:

> A sudden crash bursts forth from many strings
> As when a band of janissaries rings

---

33. Goldberg, "'Remembering That Tale of Grief,'" 55.

> With cymbals, bells and drums. And now resounds
> *The Polonaise of May the Third.*[34]

This famous polonaise was not just any familiar patriotic song. The date of 3 May 1791 was the day the Glorious Constitution was ratified, and Mickiewicz tells us that all the old men present remembered that day, when people shouted "Long live the King, long live the Sejm!" and "Long live the Nation!" for sheer joy. This poetic gloss is crucially important: the poet not only describes the musical performance, he explains how the familiar song was heard and what it meant to the listeners. The story, sadly, was far from over:

> The music ever louder grew and faster,
> Then suddenly a false chord—from the master!
> Like hissing snakes or shattering glass, that chilled
> Their hearts and with a dire foreboding filled.
> Dismayed and wondering the audience heard:
> Was the instrument ill-tuned? or had he erred?
> He had not erred! He struck repeatedly
> That treacherous string and broke the melody,
> And ever louder smote that sullen wire,
> That dared against the melody conspire,
> Until the Warden, hiding face in hand,
> Cried out, "I know that sound, I understand;
> It's *Targowica*!" Suddenly, as he speaks, the string
>   with evil-omened hissing breaks;
> At once the hammers to the treble race,
> Confused the rhythm, hurry to the bass.

The Confederacy of Targowica of 27 April 1792, signed in St. Petersburg by a group of Polish-Lithuanian nobles who had opposed the 3 May Constitution because of the limitations it placed on the nobility (and supported by Empress Catherine II of Russia), was regarded by many as the ultimate betrayal of the Polish nation. In an ensuing battle, the Confederacy's forces defeated those of the Polish-Lithuanian Commonwealth as it then stood, which led ultimately to the Second Partition (1793) and then the final dismemberment of Poland in 1795. The Confederates, for the most part, had hoped for a return to the noble privileges

---

34. "The Polonaise recalls the history of Poland since the proclamation of the glorious Constitution of the Third of May, 1791: the treacherous Confederacy of Targowicz which called in the Russians to overthrow the Constitution, and the massacre at Praga, a suburb of Warsaw; the final partition of Poland in 1795, the great emigration, and the formation of the Polish Legions in the service of Napoleon by Dąbrowski." Mackenzie, translator's note, in Mickiewicz, *Pan Tadeusz*, 564.

they had enjoyed before the constitution and had not looked to become a dependent vassal state at all. Noteworthy in Mickiewicz's passage is that it is not a famous piece that evokes the treachery and tragedy of the event, but rather a sound effect, "a false chord... like hissing snakes or shattering glass." Again, this recalls the programmatic piano solos discussed in chapter 2: real-world events expressed onomatopoetically by notes. Though the audience is mystified, the Warden understands the significance of this gesture, and (again) an explanation is given to the audience as to how it should be interpreted. The musical depiction continues:

> And ever louder grew the music's roar,
> And you could hear the tramp of marching, war,
> Attack, a storm, the boom of guns, the moans
> Of children, and a weeping mother's groans.
> So splendidly the master's art resembled
> The horror of a storm, the women trembled,
> Remembering with tears that tale of grief,
> *The Massacre of Praga*; with relief
> They heard the master's final thunder hushed,
> As if the voices of the strings were crushed.

Clearly, Jankiel's improvisation is now in the world of depictive music. The 1794 massacre of Praga, a Warsaw suburb, was the final event in the Kosciuszko uprising, which followed the Second Partition; the Russian forces slaughtered thousands of Polish civilians (hence the mention of mothers' groans and children's moans). It is significant that not once but twice (lines 3 and 6) the horror of battle is described generally as "storm" (*szturm*). Certainly, this is a typical way to describe military action (cf. "storm troopers," etc.). Storm itself, though, had a well-understood group of musical gestures associated with it already, as one hears in, for example, Beethoven's Sixth Symphony and operatic storm scenes such as that of Rossini's *Barbiere di Siviglia*. Chopin was well versed in this tradition; the middle section of his Nocturne in F Major, op. 15 no. 1, is very clearly a storm scene (with pastoral bliss on either side), and the nickname of his Etude in A Minor, op. 25 no. 11 ("Winter Wind"), demonstrates the familiar associations with this kind of writing. I cannot say if the "Massacre at Praga" ("Rzeź Pragi") was a familiar song or piece of the time; Mickiewicz presents it as if it might be, but it would certainly fall within poetic license if it were a product of his own imagination, or just a musical depiction of the onslaught. For our purposes, what matters is that the audience in Mickiewicz's concert-within-a-poem recognized this music and what it was about—and reacted accordingly. It also seems fair to mention that the different elements Mickiewicz lists (marching, guns, moans, etc.) were all standard features of contemporary programmatic piano works.

> Then the mood changes again:
> They've scarce recovered from their marveling,
> The music changes and a murmuring
> Begins: at first a few thin strings complain
> Like flies that struggle in the web in vain,
> But more and more come up and forming line,
> The scattered notes in troops of chords combine;
> And now with measured pace they march along
> To make the mournful tune of that old song:
> *The wandering soldier through the forest goes,*
> *And often faints with hunger and with woes,*
> *At last he falls beside his charger brave,*
> *That with his hoof-beat digs his master's grave.*
> A poor old song, to Polish troops so dear!
> The soldiers recognized it, crowding near
> Around the master; listening, they recall
> That dreadful hour when o'er their country's fall
> They sang this song, and went to distant climes;
> And to their minds came memories of those times,
> Of wandering through frosts and burning sands
> And seas, when oft in camps in foreign lands
> This Polish song had cheered and comforted.
> Such were their thoughts, and each man bowed his head.

"The Wandering Soldier" was a real song (or cluster of variant folk songs) dating back to the seventeenth century. Again, Mickiewicz does not just mention the song that Jankiel chooses; he explains who recognized it (the old soldiers), what it meant to them originally—comfort in time of woe, both before leaving Poland as Polish Pilgrims and when suffering privation far from home—and the reverence it now inspires. Leaving his audience in warm and somewhat maudlin reverie, however, would not have been sufficient for Jankiel, and so the mood changes one final time:

> But soon they lifted up their heads again,
> The master raised the pitch and changed the strain.
> He, looking down once more, the strings surveyed,
> And, joining hands, with both the hammers played:
> Each blow was struck so deftly and so hard,
> That all the strings like brazen trumpets blared,
> And from the trumpets to the heavens sped
> that march of triumph: *Poland is not dead!*
> *Dąbrowski, march to Poland!* With one accord,
> They clapped their hands, and "March, Dąbrowski!" roared.[35]

---

35. The entire Concert of Concerts episode appears in Mickiewicz, *Pan Tadeusz*, trans. Mackenzie, 562–68.

Dąbrowski's mazurka, also known as "The Marching Song of the Polish Legions," is the most famous patriotic song of all—the national anthem, in fact—with its line of "Poland is not [yet] dead!" There is even an incomplete arrangement of the song in Chopin's hand (as was mentioned in chapter 2). This song closes the Concert of Concerts episode, and General Dąbrowski, who is present, kindly allows Jankiel to kiss his hand.

Of course, this segment of *Pan Tadeusz* is well-known among Poles, and it is central, as Goldberg has shown, to the concept of the *wieszcz* and to what the Pilgrim community hoped for from a national musician. Perhaps the expectation was not that far off, as far as Chopin was concerned; we recall again Bohdan Zaleski's 1844 description of just such a Chopinesque improvisation: "finally, in my honor, [he played] an improvisation in which he evoked all the sweet and sorrowful voices of the past. He sang the tears of the *dumkas* and finished with the national anthem, 'Poland is not [yet] dead' [*Jeszcze Polska nie zginęła*], in a whole gamut of different forms and voices, from that of the warrior to those of children and angels. I could have written a whole book about this improvisation."[36]

It is completely plausible that the musician who, eight years before, had told Schumann he had been inspired by "some poems of Mickiewicz" might end an improvisation the way Mickiewicz's own Jankiel did in *Pan Tadeusz*. The method, moreover, is clear; Józef Elsner, Chopin's composition teacher, had recalled the way the youthful Chopin had transformed a chorus of devils into a choir of angels. Of course, "warriors," "angels," "moans," and so on are all topics that can be found in contemporary amateur and pedagogical music. The improvisation for Zaleski, in other words, was probably something like a typical programmatic piano piece of the time—with the not inconsiderable difference, because it was by Chopin, of being incomparably better in every way: gestural vocabulary, melodic content, transitions and continuity, harmonic resources, and overall sophistication. Chopin's musical saga would have been, of course, by a virtuoso artist, not a composer of bland, predictable musical product for those of modest gifts and discernment. Its approach, though, would have been familiar to any listener.[37]

Incidentally, it is no great stretch to imagine that Mickiewicz's effusive musical fantasy in *Pan Tadeusz* was based on something he had heard

---

36. Bohdan Zaleski, from a diary entry of 2 February 1844, quoted in Eigeldinger, *Chopin: Pianist and Teacher*, 283–84.

37. Indeed, the succession of patriotic tunes might have been a favorite and significantly Polish way of affirming national identity. One case where it happened—seemingly spontaneously—in real life is reported by Halina Goldberg, who quotes a review of an opera performance from the 1827–28 season in Warsaw. Here, the orchestra for Elsner's *Leszek the White, or the Witch of the Bald Mountain*, with the composer himself on the podium, responded to audience shouts for "Polish music!" with a krakowiak, then a mazur, then Kościuszko's polonaise, and finally the national anthem, Dąbrowski's mazurka. "Legs moved as in dance,

Chopin do. Both men had been resident in Paris and socializing in related Polish circles when the Concert of Concerts passage was written, and we know both that Chopin was a master improviser and that at least on occasion his improvisations worked very much the way Mickiewicz describes. I am inclined to agree with Bożena Shallcross and Halina Goldberg that Mickiewicz fashioned Jankiel, consciously or unconsciously, as his alter ego, a Romantic master of improvisation who inspires listeners to enlightenment,[38] but it is likewise my strong suspicion that the strictly musical part of his description of Jankiel's performance owes a great deal to Chopin.

The close correspondence between Jankiel's improvisation and extant musical forms enables us to reconceive the former in light of the latter. Chopin himself had already produced his op. 13, the *Grand Fantasy on Polish Airs*; such pieces had both patriotic and entertainment value. Let us pause just a moment to imagine Jankiel's piece as a work something like Schubert's *"Wanderer" Fantasy*, in the four sections Mickiewicz describes, perhaps labeled *Trionfo—Scherzo diabolico—Lamento—Trionfo*, played attaca. Or perhaps it would seem more natural to see it as a programmatic work (dulcimer standing in for olden-days piano, much as Liszt would conceive the relationship between piano and Hungarian cimbalom) with sections such as "Rejoicing: The Constitution Guarantees a Free Poland.—Betrayal by the Confederacy.—Treachery of the Russian Forces.—Massacre at Praga (groans of the mothers and moans of the children)—Lament of the Dispersed Soldiers.—Anthem of Hope: *Poland Is Not Dead*." And for a title, Jankiel's piece might have borne the name *The Destruction of Poland: Triumph to Treachery and Grief to Hope Reborn*, for it narrates the crucial episodes in the history of Poland, from 1791 through post-1795, for the approving listeners.

Of course, Chopin did not give his pieces such titles. Briefly daydreaming about them does point up, though, the close correspondence between Jankiel's improvisation, the entire genre of programmatic piano pieces, and Chopin's improvisation for Bohdan Zaleski (which finished with variations on the same song). This idea of a virtuoso version of an amateur programmatic piano piece—a boundlessly poetic and inspiring nationalistic fantasy intended to stir the hearts of listeners, a veritable apotheosis of a middlebrow genre—is one we must keep near to hand.

---

spurs rang, hearts were filled with emotion, and eyes glistened with tears. The exalted moment affected everyone. Only after the love offering to the homeland was completed could the overture of the opera be performed." Goldberg, *Music in Chopin's Warsaw*, 235–37.

38. Bożena Shallcross, "'Wondrous Fire': Adam Mickiewicz's *Pan Tadeusz* and the Romantic Improvisation," *East European Politics and Societies* 9/3 (Fall 1995), 532.

Sapienti Pauca

Among the Polish exiles in Paris, it was the Great Polish Opera that was wanted, not a piano fantasy, since opera was the primary narrative musical form. Stories of grand and historic sweep could be told onstage in powerful, moving, and above all entertaining ways, with attractive music and astounding theatrical effects ensuring that the historical spectacle—and, more important, a specific interpretation of it—would attract a great number of people. That a popular opera could carry a significant political punch was proven, as we have seen, by Auber's *Muette de Portici* (1828), a tragic love story set against the 1647 Neapolitan insurrection against Spain. It was an opera Chopin saw several times.

This highly influential work opens with the wedding of Alfonso, the son of the Spanish viceroy in Naples, and the Spanish princess Elvira. Alfonso, it is soon discovered, has seduced and then abandoned the mute girl Fenella. Fenella's tragic helplessness (she can communicate only by gestures) and her relation to the newly wedded couple (Alfonso's guilt, Elvira's initial protection of the poor girl and subsequent discovery of what her new consort has done) form one major plot strain of the opera. It is intertwined with the story of Fenella's brother, Masaniello, a fisherman who incites his fellows to rebel against Spanish tyranny. (The apparently lovely but provocational second-act barcarolle where he does this, with its innocent "Amis, la matinée est belle" opening and "Pêcheur, parle bas!" refrain, might even be heard as a distant, contributory model for the opening of Chopin's op. 38.) The Neapolitans take up the cause and are victorious as a result of terrible violence in the marketplace. Masaniello, who sought liberty only, is filled with revulsion; Fenella, who still has feelings for Alfonso, seeks to protect her former seducer regardless, and Masaniello honors her wishes. So the tragedy inexorably proceeds; Masaniello, poisoned by his onetime friend and coconspirator Pietro, dies saving Elvira, and Fenella, when she receives this news, plunges from a terrace into (where else?) the erupting Mount Vesuvius. Curtain, obviously.

The many indications of the opera's cultural impact include arrangements of its attractive Italianate melodies, books about the Neapolitan uprising that suddenly appeared and catered to the operagoers,[39] and the fact that this blend of the personal and the political proved to be definitive for the Grand Opera genre. Rossini's 1829 opera *Guillaume Tell* (another opera Chopin knew well) sets a love story against the fourteenth-century

---

39. Jane Fulcher, *The Nation's Image: French Grand Opera as Politics and Politicized Art* (Cambridge: Cambridge University Press, 1987), 27–28; Fulcher cites "M. C. F.***," *Masaniello: Histoire du soulèvement de Naples en 1647*.

Swiss struggle for freedom against the Habsburgs, and was widely understood as being in support of contemporary Greek and Italian liberation movements.[40] A few years later, Fromental Halévy's 1835 opera *La Juive* set a tale of frustrated love and tormented filial loyalty against the Spanish Inquisition, Meyerbeer's 1836 *Les Huguenots* did the same with the sixteenth-century French religious wars, and so on. It is the way of successful formulas that they inspire an endless series of imitations.

It cannot have been missed by Polish observers that, as mentioned earlier, the successful Belgian Revolution was quite literally incited by a performance of Auber's *Muette*. As for French sympathies, though, the Poles had a certain advantage. Despite the timing—the Belgian Revolution took place only months before the November Insurrection in Warsaw—it seems that the situation of the Walloons was not as captivating for the French as was that of the Poles. Casimir Périer, Louis-Philippe's minister of interior, said as much in a letter to François Guizot, who would soon assume the same office: "[The Polish cause] is more popular than the Belgian one. Why? Because it is more dramatic. France is at the moment in a sentimental, rather than rational mood."[41] Nonetheless, *La muette de Portici* proved to be so popular, influential, and threatening to the French government that the Poles must have come to feel that any political success would be possible with a sufficiently inspiring national opera to stir up popular feeling about it. Even the future King Louis-Philippe, present at the premiere, said, "Nous dansons sur un volcan" (We're dancing on a volcano), while in 1829 Émile Véron, who would later become the director of the Paris Opéra, said "*La muette de Portici* a tout bouleversé" (*La muette de Portici* has turned everything upside-down).[42]

Our twenty-first-century distance from the repertoire and musical idioms of French grand opera tends to limit our understanding of how culturally definitive it was in its time. Chopin, now living in Paris but drawn to opera since childhood, was not simply a consumer of the genre; he was profoundly involved in it. Since his youth in Warsaw, he had improvised fantasies on opera themes, and he was now publishing works based on them such as the *Grand duo concertant* (composed with his friend August Franchomme) for piano and cello on themes from Meyerbeer's *Robert le diable* and the op. 12 *Variations brillantes* on "Je vends des Scapulaires"—a song currently enjoying mega-popularity—from *Ludovic*, an opera by Hérold and Halévy. Both works were published in 1833, and they are only the most obvious; there is also the

40. Arblaster, *Viva la Libertà!*, 66.
41. Quoted in Pekacz, "Deconstructing a 'National Composer,'" 164.
42. Quoted in Fulcher, *The Nation's Image*, 46, 11. The first chapter of Fulcher's book is entirely devoted to *La muette* and its cultural resonance in Paris.

earlier B-flat Minor Polonaise (1826; middle section based on a theme from Rossini's opera *La gazza ladra*), and his Etude in G-sharp Minor, op. 25 no. 7, which bears close resemblances to "Tenere figli," a melody from his friend Vincenzo Bellini's opera *Norma*.

Equally important, for our purposes, is the way Chopin was able to internalize this operatic repertoire. We tend to assume, without much reflection, that because Chopin attended certain operas, often more than once, he would set the tunes by ear. However, opera's influence on the greater musical culture was effected not primarily through performances, but rather through home entertainment: piano-vocal scores of popular operas, and also rondos and variation sets on opera themes arranged for piano and other instruments in the popular and consumer realms. David Kasunic has called attention to certain illustrative examples, of which two are particularly suggestive. One of these is the theme from Chopin's *Ludovic* variations. Any variation set by Chopin would be notable for the variations themselves, not the theme per se, and Kasunic demonstrates that Chopin's scoring of the theme is lifted almost exactly from L.-V.-E. Rifaut's piano-vocal score. Similarly, Chopin's *Grand Duo Concertant*, on themes from Meyerbeer's *Robert le diable*, is noticeably derivative of the piano parts in Johann Pixis's operatic piano-vocal score in several different places where the themes are stated, and in this case there was a personal connection: Chopin tells his friend Tytus Woyciechowski, in a letter of 12 December 1831, that Pixis was responsible for talking him up to the publisher and getting him the contract.[43]

Perhaps even more important than these specific cases, for the people around Chopin, were the clear operatic influences in Chopin's nocturnes, which are in large part (excepting perhaps the anomalous op. 15 no. 3 in G Minor) idealized, pianistically reimagined arias and duets, lush melodies adorned with shimmering *fioriture* of the sort that real-life bel canto singers could only dream of. Likewise, as was noted by Sikorski, Chopin's music is shot throughout with the almost indefinable Polish *melos* that, in its grander form, is easy to imagine in an operatic context; several themes from the ballades readily spring to mind, as does the description of a friend, the Warsaw physician Ferdynand Dworzaczek:

> One day Chopin was improvising. I was lying on the sofa; I was in ecstasy, listening to him and daydreaming. All of a sudden his music rang out with a song which went to the heart of my soul...a well-known song...a song from the homeland...beloved...from the family home...from childhood years...My heart throbbed with

---

43. Kasunic, "Chopin and the Singing Voice," 204–20.

yearning, tears sprang to my eyes—I leapt up: "Fryderyczku!" I cried, "I know that song from the cradle...my mother used to sing it...I have it in my soul, and you just played it!" He looked round with a strange expression. His eyes shone; his fingers were moving delicately over the keys. "You never heard this tune before!' he declared. "But I have it here, here, in my soul!" I cried, pressing my hand to my breast. "Oh!"—he rose and embraced me—"you have just made me indescribably happy; there are not words for it! You never knew this song...only its spirit: the spirit of the Polish melody! And I am so happy to have been able to grasp and reveal it!"[44]

Even allowing for the somewhat overheated literary style, it is obvious why, in the eyes of many, Chopin was uniquely positioned to compose the Great Polish Opera. The Poles cherished their sense of chosenness and exulted in their national musical style, and many at least conceived their national tragedy as something that should speak to a universal sensibility—that the word should go forth and be spread amongst the nations. Chopin's melodic gifts were obvious, his playing evocative of an almost mystically powerful nationalism, and his involvement with operatic music (including the publishing side) obvious to anyone who knew his works and knew him. That this grand task was expected of him by his compatriots was no secret, and the case was put to him with increasing urgency.

One of the first to pointedly request an opera from Chopin was his friend from Warsaw, the poet Stefan Witwicki, several of whose poems Chopin had set to music (these songs eventually ended up among those of op. 74). In a letter of 6 July 1831, Witwicki thanked Chopin for his songs and then forcefully drew his attention to the possibility of opera. Chopin was not even in Paris yet—the letter was sent to Vienna—and the final Polish defeat had not yet taken place. Witwicki was ill and, like Chopin, unable to fight, a matter about which he complains in the letter, but the main point of the letter becomes clear after two sentences of gratitude for the songs:

> You must really become the creator of Polish opera: I am profoundly convinced that you could do it, and that as a Polish national composer you will open up an unbelievably rich field for your talent, in which you will achieve extraordinary fame. Would that you might keep before your eyes this one thing: national feeling, national feeling and again national feeling—an almost meaningless

---

44. Quoted in Eigeldinger, *Chopin: Pianist and Teacher*, 284. Dworzaczek moved to Paris from Germany in 1835.

expression for ordinary writers, but not for a talent such as yours. There is a native melody as there is a native climate. Hills, forests, rivers and meadows have their native, inward voice, but not everyone's spirit can perceive it. I am convinced that Slavonic opera, called into life by a true talent, by a composer who feels and thinks, will one day shine over the world of music like a new sun, will reach higher than all others, will be as singable as Italian opera, while richer in feeling and incomparably more profound. Whenever I think of this, dear Mr. Fryderyk, I rejoice in the sweet hope that *you* will be the first to draw on the vast treasures of Slavonic folk-song: if you failed to follow this path you would be willfully renouncing the most splendid laurels. Leave imitation to others, let mediocrity occupy itself with *that*. You must be original, national. At first you may not be generally understood, but perseverance and self-development in your chosen field will assure your fame and posterity. Whoever wishes to rise to great heights in any art, and to become a real master, must set himself a great goal. Forgive me for writing this: believe me, these counsels and wishes of mine spring from my sincere friendship and the esteem in which I hold your gifts. Should you go to Italy you would do well to spend some time in Dalmatia and Illyria to get to know the folk-song which is so closely related to our own—go also to Moravia and Bohemia. Seek out the folk-song of the Slavonic nations as a mineralogist hunts for stones and minerals on mountains and plains. You might even think it worth while to write down some of these songs: it would be an extremely useful collection for you yourself and would justify the time spent on it. Once more, please forgive my unasked-for scribblings; I will say no more about it.[45]

Witwicki's view, which seems a century early for its romanticized narrative of a composer's development and almost Bartókian in its emphasis on folk-song collection, is noteworthy for antedating the angst associated with the Polish Pilgrims; the defeat had not yet made exiles of them, and Chopin had not even written his obsessed, semi-hallucinatory "Stuttgart Diary" fragment yet. It is also a bit odd, or undiplomatic, for Witwicki to have called upon Chopin to be the "creator" of Polish national opera when Chopin's beloved German-born teacher Józef Elsner had done a good deal in that area already. A Viennese classicist by training, Elsner had years before composed several operas on national themes (involving historical kings and so on) in which he had sought to

---

45. Hedley, *Selected Correspondence*, 85–86.

integrate Polish elements. Nonetheless, Witwicki's call for a Polish opera with Chopin's name at the head was joined by another persistent voice, and this one not that of a native-born Pole: Elsner himself. In a letter of 27 November 1831, he hinted that Chopin should move toward opera composition. Divining the reference to what was probably a longer history of discussion on this topic between the two, Chopin answered him courteously but directly on 14 December:

> In 1830, although I realized how much I had still to learn and how far I was from being able to follow successfully any of the examples which you offered me (if I had wished to allow myself to be tempted by them), nevertheless I dared to think to myself: "I *will* approach his achievement, in however small a measure, and if I cannot produce an opera like his *Lokietek* [actually *Król Łokietek czyli Wiśliczanki*, Elsner's 1818 opera about Władysław III Łokietek— "the elbow-high"—the fourteenth-century king who unified Poland], perhaps some *Laskonogi* ["Spindle shanks," the nickname of Władysław I, an earlier Polish monarch] will come from my brain. But today, seeing all my hopes in that direction dashed, I am forced to think of making my way in the world as a pianist, postponing only to a later period the loftier artistic aims which you rightly put before me in your letter. To be a *great composer* requires enormous experience which, as you yourself taught me, can be acquired by hearing not only other men's works but one's own.[46]

It is not clear what hopes in this direction he had, or how they were dashed; this may have been diplomacy, a courtly variant of "I am indisposed" or the Bartlebian "I would prefer not to." Chopin goes on to talk of other composers who either sit idly with unproduced operas or who had years of thankless labor before one of their dramatic works saw production. He then alludes to Ferdinand Ries and Louis Spohr, who gained reputations as performers (piano and violin, respectively) before composing operas. He postpones to the vague future any work in this area and gently closes the subject: "I am sure you will not refuse me your blessing when you know on what basis and with what enterprise I shall proceed."

Not for Elsner, though, the Witwickian "I shall say no more." On 13 December 1832 he protests that he is writing only because a friend of Chopin's asked him to, then gets straight to the point:

---

46. Ibid., 102–3; bracketed insertions are my own.

However, I cannot forbear mentioning that my work on *The Meter and Rhythm of the Polish Language* in three volumes (containing my dissertation on Melody, which you already partly know) is now finished. However, it cannot be published just yet, since the question of *Nationalism* obviously occupies the most important place in it, apart from the discussion of the present trend of music.

Nationalism, although it may be dressed up in the most moderate and restrained language, is like a beautiful woman whose very attractions may prevent her from being exhibited in the marketplace, even when heavily veiled.

My third volume deals with the close connection between poetry and music, and to convince you—*Sapienti pauca* [a hint for a wise man]—of how far the development of my thoughts on this topic might be of use, not only to Polish opera-composers but also to those who write German, French, and Italian operas, allow me to quote one short passage from the preface:

"Having carefully considered all this, one must recognize that opera as a stage-spectacle is still far from having reached the peak of its true possibilities, especially from the aesthetic standpoint, wherein it still has to be brought to perfection. To this perfection it must be brought by the combined efforts of the poets and composers of all civilized nations."

What a pity that I cannot debate all this with you and your colleagues—people like Mickiewicz! Well, there you are—I said I must not and could not write, and I have gone and filled the greater part of my paper![47]

Elsner still doesn't manage to stop, quite; he offers the "chorus of devils into angelic chorus" remark quoted earlier, and he even more pointedly mentions Mickiewicz again ("I had only to mention the poet's name, Mickiewicz, and at once Hell with its horrors and Heaven with its hopes arise before my eyes and would make me forget that I am on earth"). This letter is not his final salvo, either; he mentions in a letter of 14 September 1834 that "I would like to live to see an opera of your composition, which would not only increase your fame but benefit the art of music in general, especially if the subject of such an opera were drawn from Polish national history."[48] One suspects that Elsner fantasized about a Mickiewicz-Chopin collaboration, and that he probably wasn't alone in doing so.

47. Hedley, *Selected Correspondence*, 113–14.
48. Ibid., 124.

Nor were those desiring an opera coming only from a Polish perspective; Chopin's biographer Niecks tells the story of the M. le Comte de Perthuis, a close associate of Louis-Philippe, who one day asked Chopin, "Chopin, how is it that you, who have such admirable ideas, do not compose an opera?" (Chopin, avec vos idées admirables, pourquoi ne nous faites-vous pas un opéra?) "Ah, Count, let me compose nothing but music for the pianoforte; I am not learned enough to compose operas!" (Ah, Monsieur le Comte, laissez-moi ne faire que de la musique de piano; pour faire des opéras je ne suis pas assez savant.)[49] Chopin is sticking, here, to the line he offered Elsner: I don't yet know enough. Obviously, this humility is just for public consumption. It is clear that he knew early on that opera composition and production were not for him: the attendant harsh realities of dealing with singers, impresarios, schedules, governmental censors, a fickle public, and investors would require a robust physical stamina, which Chopin had never in his entire life possessed, and a willingness to be dependent on economically interested others in a way he would have found insupportable.

By far the most authoritative voice calling for an opera by Chopin was that of the poetic *wieszcz* himself, Adam Mickiewicz. For all the assumptions of a meeting of minds between the two artists—we just saw one such assumption in the mind of Elsner—Mickiewicz and Chopin, despite obvious admiration of each other's art, never really understood each other at all or connected on a personal level. The sole surviving letter between them is a curt note dated around 1842 from Mickiewicz to Chopin, who was apparently trying to obtain a passport for himself or someone else: "If you must have some certificate in order to get the passport, you could work it out to get a Russian or a German passport from Gutt [Gutmann, a longtime German student of Chopin?]. Whatever you do, be sure not to lose it. I'm here if you need me.—A. Mickiewicz."[50] We must be cautious about reading in too much, here; Mickiewicz could have been terribly busy at that moment, or just disinclined to think about a petty administrative matter, or not wanting to be noticed in any way by any other nations. Still, the tone from one of Poland's greatest artists to another, then or at any other time, seems uncomfortably brittle.

Two anecdotes speak further to this non-meeting of minds. Niecks cites an anecdote told by the Polish painter Teofil Kwiatkowski, who "calling one day on Chopin found him and Mickiewicz in the midst of a very excited discussion. The poet urged the composer to undertake a great work, and not to fritter away his power on trifles; the composer, on the other hand, maintained that he was not in possession of the qualities

---

49. Niecks, *Chopin as a Man and Musician*, 1:277.
50. Quoted in Terry Nathan Martin, "Frederic Chopin and Romantic Nationalism: An Examination of His Correspondence" (Ph.D. diss., Washington University, 1990), 132 n. 22.

requisite for what he was advised to undertake."[51] An even more unpleasant conversation between the two was recounted in a letter from Antoine Dessus, a friend of Mickiewicz's secretary, Armand Levy, to the poet's son Władysław.

> Upon coming to visit your father, I found Chopin in the living room. Your father introduced me to him, and Chopin bowed to me with a barely-discernible bow. His mannerism and politeness were those of a well-studied, upper-class sort. On the request of your mother he sat at the piano and played with great feeling. When he finished, your father ran his hand through his hair, gave a deep sigh, and started to reprimand Chopin with such ferocity that I did not know what to do. "How come, instead of developing in yourself the gift of touching souls, you prance around the Faubourg St. Germain! You could stir crowds, but instead you only exert yourself to tickle the nerves of aristocrats!" The more he yelled, the more Chopin cowered, never uttering a word. Finally, Mickiewicz fell silent, and Chopin started to play folk songs. Your father's brow lightened, and when Chopin stood up, they talked as if nothing had ever happened.[52]

This flare-up happened in 1848, which is well over fifteen years after Witwicki and Elsner were urging Chopin to bend his efforts to opera. Of course, context is important here; the anti-aristocratic tone of the description and image of Chopin as a talented musician but cowering snob might well have been tailored to the sympathies of Dessus's reader. For all Mickiewicz's appreciation of Chopin's art (the Believer in Mallefille's scene being transported out of himself, the admiration that underlay his demands for an opera, etc.), he felt quite differently about Chopin the man, referring to him as George Sand's "evil genius, her moral vampire...who torments her and may well end up by killing her" and observing, "Chopin talks with spirit and gives the ariel view of the universe. Liszt is the eloquent *tribune* to the world of men, a little vulgar and showy certainly, but I like the tribune best."[53] Put beside Chopin's

---

51. Niecks, *Chopin as a Man and Musician*, 1:277.

52. Trans. Felicia Wertz from *Zywot Adama Mickiewicza*, 255; quoted in Martin, "Frederic Chopin and Romantic Nationalism," 49 and 133 n. 1. The version in George R. Marek and Maria Gordon-Smith, *Chopin* (New York: Harper and Row, 1978), 83–84, reads somewhat differently.

53. Both quoted in Martin, "Frederic Chopin and Romantic Nationalism," 50–51. On 133 n. 4 Martin quotes an 1832 usage from the Oxford English Dictionary stating that the word "ariel" refers to an Arabian antelope "known for its light, elegant, and graceful form."

standoffish remark (quoted above) about Mickiewicz's break with Towiański and his obvious reticence to get involved with the more ideological elements in the Polish community, and it becomes clear that any real connection between the two would have been, unfortunately, unsustainable. Chopin was a musician interested in his career, with no interest in "stirring crowds" and disinclined to civil disobedience (Nicholas Chopin would write his son from Warsaw, darkly warning him not to get involved with "rascals"). Mickiewicz's poetic output stopped after 1834. He became increasingly involved in political activism and messianic dreams and died in 1855 (probably of cholera) while trying to set up a Polish-Jewish regiment to fight against Russia in the Crimean War. In some ways, Chopin's feelings about Mickiewicz the man may be summed up by the question he rhetorically asked his friend Julian Fontana in a letter of 12 September 1841: "Have they all gone mad?"[54]

It is clear that no number of words to the wise directed to Chopin by his Polish and French friends inclined to the artistic beau geste would have had any effect. Although he obviously was deeply involved in opera and its world, he knew himself better than to take on the responsibility of writing one. Chopin's Polish compatriots did not understand that his nationalism was of a different sort, and he was neither really *of* the aristocratic world nor completely comfortable outside it. They also didn't really understand his music; the close correspondence between Jankiel's improvisation and Chopin's own, as described by Zaleski (and chapter 6 will put the Second Ballade, op. 38, in a similar light) shows him to be rendering, in tones, almost exactly what might have been expected of a *wieszcz*: nationalistic fervor, tugging heartstrings, a saga by the Bard of the Great Migration. And although Mickiewicz clearly responded strongly to his playing—again, remembering Mallefille's description of the Old Believer sitting deep in thought after hearing op. 38, and Dessus's description of his being mollified by Chopin's playing of national tunes (which might well have been another Jankiel-like improvisation)—the poet wanted Chopin to do something he either was not capable of doing or was constitutionally indisposed to do, and blamed the composer for failing him. He wanted to reinvent Chopin, it seems, as a Jankiel, a musical Mickiewicz, a heroic spirit creating both works and also improvisations that would stir the world, or "the crowds," to active self-liberation. It is hard to avoid the sense that there was a frustrated self-identification here, given Mickiewicz's earlier history as an excellent poetic improviser—this especially during his time in Russia—and his personal lack of musical gifts (one Russian listener wryly commented,

---

54. Hedley, *Selected Correspondence*, 205.

"He improvised in song and had, alas, the voice of a chicken").[55] Perhaps, too, his marriage to the daughter of a famous Polish pianist had something to do with his desire for a musical voice (it was an unhappy enough marriage otherwise); Dessus had mentioned that it was at her request that Chopin had played the piano for Mickiewicz in the first place.

On Chopin's side, there was probably a good deal about Mickiewicz that he ultimately found unsympathetic. Mickiewicz's messianic enthusiasms, his affiliation with Towiański, and perhaps even his quasi-mystical philo-Semitism would certainly have seemed alien and undesirable. Chopin himself could sound viciously anti-Semitic in correspondence, generally in complaining about publishers' business practices (an area in which he himself was no trusting innocent). To be fair, it is not clear how to square this reflexive, perhaps typically Polish, epithet-based anti-Semitism with Chopin's desire that his friend Charles-Valentin Alkan, a reclusive Jewish superpianist and Chopin's neighbor at the square d'Orléans, be one of those entrusted with his incomplete notes for a piano method, and Antoine Marmontel's recollection that "When Chopin died, many of his dearest pupils chose Alkan to continue the late master's tradition."[56] Alkan was a bona fide Talmudist, devoted to the study of Jewish religious writings, so it is hard to see Chopin's friendship with him and ugly epistolary comments about publishers as part of a coherent view of Judaism or Jews. Then again, one does discern a certain aloof distance or even suppressed contempt in the anecdotes involving Chopin and such Jewish musicians and Moscheles and Meyerbeer. In any case, Chopin evidences no particular inclination to view any race as a chosen people—not the Poles, the Jews, the French (Mickiewicz's three choices), or anyone else.

Chopin's nationalism spoke to a personal sensibility rather than a mystical one. His mazurkas especially came to be heard either as psalms—eternally grieving, as in Liszt's identification of a uniquely Polish melancholy, *żal*, in Chopin's music[57]—or politically incendiary. In the view of his student Wilhelm von Lenz, Chopin "represented Poland, *the land of his dreams*, in the Parisian salons under Louis-Philippe—salons which *his* viewpoint allowed him to use as a political platform. Chopin was the *only political* pianist; he *incarnated* Poland, he *set* Poland *to music!*"[58] And Schumann observed:

---

55. Shallcross, "'Wondrous Fire,'" 527.
56. Eigeldinger, *Chopin: Pianist and Teacher*, 134 n. 129.
57. See Franz Liszt, *Frederic Chopin* [1854], trans. Edward N. Waters (London [New York]: Free Press of Glencoe, Collier-Macmillan, 1963), 79–80.
58. Quoted in Kallberg, "Hearing Poland: Chopin and Nationalism," in *Nineteenth-Century Piano Music*, ed. R. Larry Todd, 2nd ed. (New York: Routledge, 2004), 253.

Fate also distinguished Chopin among all others by endowing him with an intensely original nationality, specifically Polish. And because this nationality now goes forth in black raiments, it attracts us all the more firmly to this thoughtful artist.... If the mighty autocratic monarch of the north knew what a dangerous enemy threatened him in Chopin's works, in the simple tunes of his mazurkas, he would forbid this music. Chopin's works are cannons buried in flowers.[59]

Chopin was also called the "Mickiewicz of pianists" and compared with the Irish poet Thomas Moore in that "through their songs, they keep alive the traditions and the love of the country where they were born, and nurse it with a sweet and noble hope of liberation."[60] It is true to an extent, but also simplistic, as many contemporary and later views of Chopin have been.

The picture that emerges of Chopin in the various milieux of mid-1830s Paris is peculiarly contradictory and unassimilated. He was universally recognized among pianists; his works were commercially successful, he was in demand as a teacher, and he inspired an adulation that sometimes bordered on hysteria. At the same time, he seems to have symbolized frustrated Polish aspirations in the sense that his compatriots were not shy about pinning their own hopes and dreams on him, and indeed holding him responsible for them. They approved of his nationalism but demanded more, far more, than he was able to produce, and he was not really an equal; though in demand as a guest, the only Polish salon he came to frequent, after a while, was the more conservative salon of the Czartoryskis.[61] He was considered by non-Poles to have a nationalistic story to tell, but it was a safely distant and exotic one. Although Mallefille and Probst seemed to have had some sense of a nationalistic inspiration for the Second Ballade, most others, non-Poles and Poles alike, needed mazurka rhythms in order to perceive Polish national content and meantime were preoccupied by demanding an opera. Among the Pilgrims, therefore, Chopin was something of a disappointment in his stubborn refusal to produce a major work that was, after all, more the product of their imagination than of his.

What story would Chopin have wanted to tell, and what would his strategy have been for doing so? By this point, it must seem a bit obvious. The most likely potential story—the one preoccupying the Polish

---

59. Ibid., 249.

60. The first quote is from an 1836 Polish review of some mazurkas by Antoni Woykowski; the second is from the *Revue et gazette musicale de Paris* 10 (1843), 179; both are quoted in Kallberg, "Hearing Poland," 249–50.

61. Pekacz, "Deconstructing a 'National Composer,'" 167–69.

community in Paris—was the martyrdom of Poland and ensuing Great Migration, which, not coincidentally, is the story Mallefille and Probst associated with op. 38. Chopin had already composed one clearly narrative work, the First Ballade, op. 23, and whether or not it bore a direct relationship to Mickiewicz's *Konrad Wallenrod*, it was artistically an unqualified success. Indeed, in 1836 Schumann recorded their agreement that it was their favorite work. Composing a second ballade seems a natural choice, given another story that needed telling.

Chopin was, moreover, ideally prepared for the peculiar requirements of such a work. He was familiar with not one but two other, preexistent narrative forms, each of which contributed to op. 38. The first is the amateur programmatic piano piece (Würfel's patriotic Polish fantasy being probably one of the most familiar to him), with its succession of familiar styles and tunes used to tell a story, often specified through subtitles and almost always involving a military battle and its attendant heroism. The second of these genres was the operatic ballade, where the narrative account and listener reaction—two discrete musical ideas—are presented in alternation with each other and woven into a single-movement musical dialectic. The Second Ballade inherits its succession of familiar material from the programmatic piano pieces, especially those using operatic material to tell a new story such as Steibelt's *Journée d'Ulm*. The alternation of contrasting material is inherited from the operatic ballade, though in the case of the ballade the narrator-listener dialectic is concentrated in the A and C sections, while the B sections have to do with the events of the story itself.

Informing all of this is the aesthetic of his older Polish colleague Kurpiński, who openly advocated reminiscences or actual quotations of familiar musical ideas in order to access listeners' emotional associations with them in new contexts. Again, Steibelt's Ulm piece is an apt illustration, and what we know of Chopin's improvisations suggests, tantalizingly, that they may have been early examples of this approach. For choice of material in a grand musical narrative, a narrative by the operatically inclined composer who was nonetheless not inclined to compose an opera himself, what would have been more likely than idioms—and pieces themselves—from familiar operas, which were familiar to Parisian listeners and which had myriad broader connotations in the contemporary culture? It now remains only to identify the musical material and examine Chopin's narrative and formal strategies. This will be the business of chapter 6.

6

MARTYRDOM AND EXILE

The Narrative of Chopin's F Major Ballade

The identification of familiar styles and specific referents in Chopin's musical material brings us, ironically, full circle to the thinking of the purple-penned Edward Baxter Perry and the subsequent "poetic" tradition. This may make us uncomfortable, but it should not. By now, we have seen that communicating with listeners—governing audience response, even—through use of well-known musical gestures and references to more famous works was not only practiced, it was theorized, so in sifting such "internal evidence" (Perry's phrase) we are moving toward the experience of Chopin's listeners and those of subsequent decades, not engaging in some kind of naive and anachronistic amateur hermeneutics. It is, of course, impossible to recreate authentic nineteenth-century ears (to paraphrase a well-known truism), but a lot can be done with regard to reassembling a typical listener's listening experience and context.

Internal Evidence I—the A Material: Siciliano

Example 6.1 gives the entire opening section of Chopin's Second Ballade. The opening theme, which begins after one and a half measures of unison vamp on the fifth scale degree, is clearly a siciliano; the prevailing rhythm (dotted eighth–sixteenth–eighth in compound duple time) and andantino tempo make that clear. Meredith Little identifies the siciliano as a dance with "simple melodies and clear, direct harmonies"—both clearly in evidence in Chopin's piece—and gives its early associations as "pastoral scenes and melancholy emotions,"[1] all of which may be found in numerous seventeenth- and eighteenth-century examples. Again, we are reminded of Samson's description of op. 38 as a narrative of "innocence under threat," and it suits perfectly: a sweet siciliano, harmonically clear, sincere but with a dash of melancholy (especially the jump to A minor in m. 18). Chopin's opening forty-six-bar paragraph seems an evocation of Eden lost: perfect in memory, but memory made more poignant by sad experience.

Ex. 6.1. Chopin, Ballade no. 2, op. 38, mm. 1–46.

1. Meredith Ellis Little, "Siciliana," in *The New Grove Dictionary of Music and Musicians*, 2nd ed., ed. Stanley Sadie (London: Macmillan, 2001), vol. 23, 350–52.

It is not just a pastoral, slightly melancholy siciliano, however; far more is happening in this section than the introduction of a theme (as would be the case in a sonata: after the theme, one would proceed to the modulation, contrasting material, rhetorical development, and so on). What carries the significance in these first forty-six measures is more than the theme itself: it is the theme, its key, the siciliano rhythm, the siciliano topic (including both the siciliano dance and its pastoral affect), and certain aspects of the accompanying texture. The section is in AABA form, where the theme is stated twice, followed by the brief affective jump to A minor (mm. 18–20) on the way to C major (mm. 20–26), before the return to F and the final statement of the theme, which is given some extension material. The original phrasing, which is given here as it appears in Chopin's surviving autograph, is significant. After the opening vamp, the theme is divided into two phrases: a soloistic melody with the range of an octave (mm. 3–6) alternates with a simpler, more static figure with the melodic range of only a fourth, suggestive of a choral response (mm. 6–10).[2] Not only is the melodic range of the choral response simpler, but it has far less stepwise motion, simply oscillating in bagpipe-like fashion. (Example 6.2 gives a cognate figure, the opening four-measure vamp of Chopin's Mazurka in C Major, op. 24 no. 2.) The opening section of this ballade offers, therefore, not only a siciliano-pastorale topic and harmony-defining theme, but also an implied narrative: the ideal bucolic past is presented in the form of a sung, once-upon-a-time description, with murmured punctuation or assent from the "listeners." The operatic inheritance of this piece thus asserts itself immediately.

Of course, the siciliano topic is only part of the story; the specific reference clarifies much more. The primary referent for Chopin's A material, including the siciliano theme, is Raimbaut's ballade ("Jadis régnait en Normandie") from act 1 of Meyerbeer's *Robert le diable*, which is also

Ex. 6.2. Chopin, Mazurka in C Major, op. 24 no. 2, mm. 1–4.

2. For whatever reason, it was reduced to a big legato slur over the entire section in the French first edition, perhaps because the composer thought the textural contrast would make the point sufficiently to perceptive eyes or, alternatively, because he feared that such an explicit notation might result in pianists' exaggeration of the phrase articulation.

Ex. 6.3. Meyerbeer, *Robert le diable*, act 1, Raimbaut's ballade, opening of vocal line.

a siciliano and was discussed in some length in chapter 4. Example 6.3 gives the opening vocal part of Raimbaut's ballade, already seen in example 4.4.

There are good reasons to rely on the piano-vocal score versions of operatic material rather than the full scores; these were the primary vehicles of dissemination of this repertoire, and the vast, hungry market of musical consumers ensured that these were the versions most heard and studied. Chopin's involvement with the world of musical publishing and amateur pianism was discussed in chapter 5; he based several different works on opera themes, and he took his versions of these themes from the piano-vocal scores, not from the full scores. A comparison of the opening theme of op. 38 and Raimbaut's ballade in its piano-vocal arrangement makes the correspondence between them clear: although Raimbaut is a tenor, he has to be played an octave higher on the piano because of the placement of the accompaniment. Both pieces are sweetly innocent, vocalistic sicilianos, similar in range and texture, and similarly introduced by unison vamp figures. (In the second and third verses of Raimbaut's ballade, Meyerbeer puts the vamp on the fifth scale degree, as did Chopin, but at the beginning it is on the third degree.)

So much for the musical correspondence, which is clear enough, and which furthermore reminds us of Probst's 1839 letter and its implied linkage between Chopin's "Pilgrims' Ballade" and Meyerbeer's "Pilgrim's Ballade," juxtaposing the Polish Pilgrims and the "joyeux pèlerin" Raimbaut, who sang of the sweet days of yore in far-off Normandy and the way everything turned tragic there. From a dramatic perspective, Meyerbeer did two very interesting things with his theme: he varied it with each stanza, making it increasingly darker and more disturbed to reflect the events of the story; and he later brought it back twice as a reminiscence. In the opera's opening act, immediately following the ballade (which Raimbaut is prevented from quite finishing by an enraged shout from Robert), there is a furious exchange between Robert, the hapless pilgrim Raimbaut, and Raimbaut's beloved Alice, who happens to be Robert's foster sister. Alice will plead for mercy following Raimbaut's offense, and Alice and Raimbaut are then joined by a chorus of knights. Following this, as Raimbaut is taken into custody, the melody of the ballade is briefly alluded to under the action, in fragmentary form over a disturbing tremolo in the lower strings (see ex. 6.4), this time in F major (the subdominant of the original), as if to remind us, just at the end, what all the emotional upheaval was really about, and reinforce the significance of this opening episode in the unfolding drama.

Even more suggestive is the later reminiscence in E minor, the mediant of the original C major tonic (cf. Chopin's F major/A minor harmonic dialectic in op. 38). In the conversation between Robert and Alice, following Alice's romance (still in act 1), she suddenly spies Bertram and recognizes him as Satan, owing to his resemblance to an image of the archfiend in a painting, in her hometown, of St. Michael striking down the devil (see ex. 6.5). At the sight of him, she begins to tremble and

Ex. 6.4. Meyerbeer, *Robert le diable*, act 1, first reminiscence of Raimbaut's ballade.

stutter; reminiscences of the ballade theme are stated twice in E minor, once in G major, and once in A minor. It is not coincidental, I think, that the main key relationships extending through the statements of Meyerbeer's ballade (the C tonic of the ballade itself to the initial E minor of the second reminiscence, and the F major of the first reminiscence to the ending A minor of the last statement of the second) follow the tonic-to-mediant

EX. 6.5. Meyerbeer, *Robert le diable*, act 1, second reminiscence of Raimbaut's ballade.

progression of Chopin's op. 38, and neither returns to the tonic. These are not major structural points, of course—Raimbaut's ballade itself is the governing statement of that material—but the lack of return to the tonic later on and the repeated tonic-to-mediant journey could well have stuck in Chopin's subconscious. It might be that Chopin's final reference to his siciliano first theme, at the very end of op. 38, owes something to the Meyerbeerian strategy.

Two other well-known opera pieces inform the way Chopin's opening siciliano would have been heard by contemporaries. Masaniello's famous barcarolle from Auber's *Muette de Portici*, mentioned in chapter 5, is a song of both nationalism and plotted insurrection set to a gentle *al fresco* compound duple meter; sounding sweet and innocent, it presages the violence and upheaval to follow. A slightly later piece that may well have been influenced by this barcarolle is the pastorale-chorus of Swiss peasants and archers from act 1 of Rossini's *Guillaume Tell*, an opera that (like Auber's) was seen and admired by Chopin.[3] The chorus begins as a hymn to rural life. Taking a cue from Auber's barcarolle, which begins, "Friends, it's a beautiful day, let's go down to the shore" (Amis, la matinée est belle / Sur le rivage assemblez vous), Rossini's pastorale begins, "The sky foretells a beautiful day; let us celebrate it with our songs!" (Quel jour serein le ciel présage / célébrons le dans nos concerts). This is, of course, before anything in the plot goes wrong, which it of course will—in fact, in the second section of the same number, William Tell alludes to Austrian despotism by singing darkly, "For us, [there is] no more homeland...Switzerland mourns its liberty" (Pour nous, plus de patrie!...L'Helvétie pleure, pleure sa liberté). So the Auber, Rossini, and Meyerbeer pastorales, three well-known operatic numbers, all premiered within four years of each other (and within a decade of the composition of Chopin's op. 38). And they all begin with bucolic sweetness but quickly take on a more sinister character, and thus establish a general expectation of what will follow such statements of nothing-can-go-wrong trust. Although Raimbaut's ballade is certainly the most immediate model for Chopin, all three numbers form the backdrop to the wider perception of Chopin's siciliano-pastorale as both popular in origin and "national" in association (of the People, if not in musical terms specifically the Poles), and their well known dramatic contexts would certainly have influenced the way Chopin's piece was heard and understood.

---

3. Tad Szulc, *Chopin in Paris: The Life and Times of the Romantic Composer* (New York: Scribner, 1998), 94.

Internal Evidence II—the B Material: Storm

Example 6.6 gives the opening measures of the B section of Chopin's op. 38, a violent A minor passage that hinges on the repeating melodic A pitches that echo into silence at the end of the opening section. Jim Samson has used the phrase "confrontation of styles" to describe what he sees as the dialectic of topics in the work: following the F-major siciliano, a "brutal étude-like figuration" in the new key that he reads as a "'narrative' of innocence under threat."[4] Both "confrontation of styles" and "innocence under threat" are perceptive readings of what Chopin gives us; there is neither transition nor harmonic modulation between the opening siciliano and the A minor explosion following, which, in context, can be heard only as cataclysmic. Samson also (correctly, I think) links this figuration with that of the Étude op. 25 no. 11 ("Winter Wind").[5] What the A minor figurations in op. 38 and op. 25 no. 11 share most noticeably is the tonality, a blistering prestissimo descent, and the descending F–E dyad that initiates both passages.

To call this passage "étude-like" seems to miss the mark somewhat. "Étude-like" too easily becomes "étude," as the topic of the passage was

Ex. 6.6. Chopin, Ballade no. 2, op. 38, mm. 47–52.

---

4. Samson, *Chopin*, 156. Chapter 1, note 30, cites Samson's other use of the same phrase.

5. Samson, *Chopin: The Four Ballades*, 14–15; Samson, "Chopin's Alternatives to Monotonality," 41. Dorota Zakrzewska also calls this topic an étude: Zakrzewska, "Alienation and Powerlessness," 6.

subsequently designated by Dorota Zakrzewska;[6] it is the same pattern as when the supposedly "waltz-like" first theme of the First Ballade later becomes, simply, a "waltz." Perhaps more important, this arpeggio-based figuration, which is made up of a combination of single notes and intervals, has relatives throughout Chopin's works; we already saw one such in the First Ballade (mm. 47–56), and the concertos and other concerted works offer a variety of other examples. Clearly, such writing was a standard part of his post-Classical brilliant style arsenal. In contrast, "étude" for Chopin meant a more specialized (or, for lack or a better word, more difficult) figuration: something involving especially challenging stretches, nimble chromatic work, double-note figures, or idiosyncratic schematic patterns. I believe that the only place this Chopinesque single-note/double-note arpeggio mix appears in Chopin's own études is the diabolically antic middle section of op. 25 no. 5, which scrambles over most of the keyboard. More typical examples of this texture (such as the B section of op. 38) would not, seemingly, qualify as an étude style, at least for Chopin.

Samson's linkage of the B section of op. 38 with the "Winter Wind" étude is nonetheless instructive because the two passages do share a topic, though it is not étude but storm. Storm scenes featuring blistering scales, rapid changes of direction, and other effects were quite familiar by the mid-1830s, and Chopin had already written one such passage in the middle section of his very pastoral Nocturne in F Major, op. 15 no. 1; there the scale-work appears in the left hand. Further, the equation of storm music with military assault was also by now a tradition. For proof of this we need look no further than the dulcimer playing of Mickiewicz's Jankiel in *Pan Tadeusz*, who (as we saw in chapter 5) depicts the massacre of Praga ("the tramp of marching, war, attack, a storm ... ").

Chopin's B section is clearly not a typical storm scene, though is certainly manifests storm writing. The booming left-hand octaves in an eccentric line (two ascending fifths and a minor second) can pass for either thunder or cannons, particularly in the midst of the pandemonium that surrounds it. And this pandemonium is meticulously crafted not only of dissonances, furious speed, and rapid changes of direction, but, more important, of polymeters, which retain the chaotic implications they seemed to have in the First Ballade. Though the time signature continues to be 6/8, in the first two measures of this section (mm. 47–48) the right hand in m. 47 is clearly in 3/4 (three groups of four sixteenths), and the left hand in m. 48 is in 12/16 (four groups of three sixteenths). Played as

---

6. Dorota Zakrzewska: "Alienation and Powerlessness: Adam Mickiewicz's Ballady and Chopin's Ballades," *Polish Music Journal* (Online Publication) 2/1–2 (Summer–Winter 1999): http://www.usc.edu/dept/polish_music/PMJ/archives.html.

written and naturally grouped, as opposed to the far more common regularization of the meter (which results, for example, in a senseless accent on the second right-thumb C in m. 47), it becomes utterly, and appropriately, chaotic. Again, Jankiel comes to mind: "At once the hammers to the treble race, confused the rhythm, hurry to the bass."

The operatic referent here is, again, Rossini's *Guillaume Tell*. This popular, influential, and politically charged 1829 work entwines an ultimately triumphant love story with, as was mentioned in chapter 5, the fourteenth-century liberation of Switzerland from Austria, especially as personified by the cruel governor, Gesler. The second section of the opera's overture consists of storm music, foreshadowing the end of the opera's fourth act, which features a storm, a foundering ship, and a final desperate battle between Swiss patriots and Gesler's forces. Example 6.7 gives the relevant passage; not only does the descending chromatic string writing prefigure Chopin's A minor figuration (especially the opening half step), but also the answering ascending eighth-note figures in the bass find their echo in Chopin's mm. 51–52 and analogous places.

For the reckoning of the ballade, Chopin keeps the general storm topic but uses new content. Example 6.8 gives the opening of this section, which begins at m. 168. Here, too, *Guillaume Tell* has provided some musical material: at the close of the first act, the Swiss patriarch Melcthal is captured by Gesler's soldiers. Melcthal is seized, manhandled, bound, and dragged off while the Swiss patriots watch, desperate but weaponless—a scene oddly similar to Chopin's tormented fantasy, recounted in the Stuttgart diary, of helplessly witnessing the brutal Russian treatment of his family and of Konstancia Gladkowska. The relevant passage from the Rossini piano-vocal score is found in example 6.9; the chromatically descending harmony and bass sequence starting in the thirteenth bar of the excerpt are like raw materials from which Chopin crafted a compositionally far better, and more fearsome, maelstrom.

One of the formal impressions left by op. 38 is that of alternation, as in operatic ballades, though it is more apparent than actual. After the initial, self-contained siciliano-pastorale (the A section), the first storm passage (the B section) subsides into a return of the siciliano (at the beginning of the C section, in m. 83), which—after a couple of incomplete statements—expands into something wholly different, still in 6/8, still featuring occasional wisps of the siciliano but in no way a return. This middle section—about which there will be more to say shortly—stumbles back into the storm music of section B, a bona fide return this time. The return of the B material leads in turn to the reckoning, which consists of the new storm music and the pathetic whisper of the siciliano theme at the end. The two

Ex. 6.7. Gioachino Rossini, *Guillaume Tell*, overture, mm. 92–116.

basic moods make clear why op. 38 is considered to be primarily a struggle between two highly contrasting ideas, even though the first is completely overborne by the second. Of the two basic topics, the storm topic has two different sorts of figuration associated with it. Similarly, there is also another pastoral theme (discussed in chapter 4), though I have never seen it discussed, and it is the primary musical content of the middle section.

Ex. 6.8. Chopin, Ballade no. 2, op. 38, mm. 169–183.

Internal Evidence III—the C Theme

Measures 95–102 are given in example 6.10. The first four measures consist of a deceptive cadence (an F major tonic arrival would have been expected on the downbeat of m. 96) and modulation to D-flat major, the key in which the new theme will begin in the second half of m. 98. The theme is presented in stretto, here and everywhere else, and consists simply of a stepwise descent from the sixth scale degree to the third, with use of ornamental suspension tones (though without ties). This little figure is probably most often considered to be more or less derived from the siciliano theme (in the absence of commentary

Ex. 6.9. Rossini, *Guillaume Tell*, instrumental postscript to the finale of act 1.

about it we are left to guess), but there is surprisingly little in common between them. The A theme has far more leaps than steps, no suspension tones, and indeed few repeated notes of any kind, while the C theme has no siciliano rhythm, is all stepwise motion and suspensions, and makes constant use of repeated notes. When it appears, it recalls the opening repeated-note vamp more than it does the siciliano theme itself.

This central section is highly modulatory, but it seems more unsettled and insecure than "exploratory" or "developmental," possibly because of the almost total lack of root-position triads. In mm. 98–108 the C theme is stated in D-flat major and G-flat major; following a distorted and anguished siciliano passage (mm. 108–115) that ends on the dominant seventh of E major (in third inversion), the mood quiets, the tonality slips to the dominant of C major, and the pattern repeats (canonic statements in C and F major) in this new and much more naive-sounding tonal neighborhood.

This seems a minor point, but in fact it is an important one. In the unequal piano temperaments of Chopin's time, the most innocent- and naive-sounding keys were C major and F major; D-flat and G-flat major

Ex. 6.10. Chopin, Ballade no. 2, op. 38, mm. 95–102.

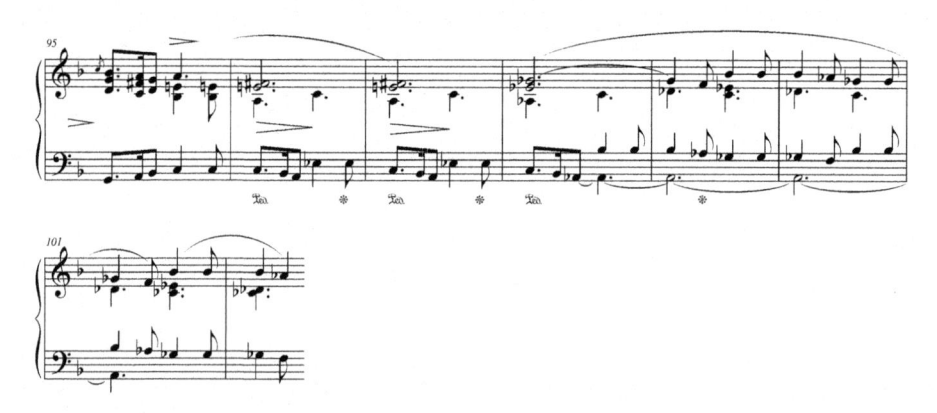

were among the most misty and highly colored.[7] This passage would therefore have registered much more, to the attentive contemporary listener, than just another statement a half step lower; after the tortured siciliano fragment, the naïveté and innocence of the C themelet, stated this time in traditional pastoral keys, would have seemed both more poignant and pathetic, an affect reinforced by the fact that the sequential restatements are likewise a half step lower, never higher. And so it turns out to be: after an even more anguished siciliano statement in mm. 133–140, the storm music proper returns, and it soon becomes apparent that this time there will be no escape from A minor. This ultimately victorious second key was, interestingly, never actually the goal of a modulation; initially it had simply superseded the disappearing echoes of F major, via common tones, and later it appeared after the key that had actually been prepared (D minor), recontextualizing D minor as a subdominant. After a long dominant pedal on E, where the siciliano rhythm is now completely subsumed in a stormy A minor context, the reckoning is reached.

Identifying an operatic referent for the C theme is a bit more difficult than it was for the A and B material. The topical polarity of op. 38 juxtaposes the siciliano-pastorale and storm passages; especially after the troubled returns of the siciliano, the C theme functions a bit like

---

7. Key characteristics and unequal temperaments in the nineteenth century are not an uncontested area, but indications are very strong that the prevailing tonal environment, especially for piano, was something very different from the homogenized equal temperament familiar to us today. Three very helpful sources on this issue are the recent Ross W. Duffin, *How Equal Temperament Ruined Harmony* (New York: W. W. Norton, 2007); Steblin, *A History of Key Characteristics*; and Owen Jorgensen, *Tuning* (East Lansing: Michigan State University Press, 1991). One treatment of unequal temperament in Chopin is Bellman, "Toward a Well-Tempered Chopin," 27–40.

neutral material, pastoral but not as specific as a siciliano, enabling the more recognizable material to communicate its message. A referent for this short theme, while it seems likely that there would be one, may simply be missed because there is no way of knowing every opera or other piece of music that Chopin knew. Possible seeds of musical inspiration seem distant or illusory.

Nonetheless, one excerpt does present itself, shown in example 6.11; it is again from Rossini's *Guillaume Tell*, this time from the act 2 "Oui, vous l'arrachez à mon âme." Here Princess Mathilde (a Habsburg) is singing to her beloved Arnold (a Swiss), "I cannot extinguish my flame; we must both be lost in it" (Je ne puis étouffer ma flamme, dût elle nous perdre, nous perdre tous deux). Arnold will answer, in the same music, with "So her flame answers my flame!" (Oui, sa flamme répond à ma flamme, dût elle nous perdre tous deux). Here is where the love story set against the tale of heroic nationalism comes into relief: the two young people are caught up in historical forces beyond their control, and—realizing that their feelings for each other are requited—they declare themselves in a love-against-the-odds duet. This image is certainly not far from Chopin's rose-colored view of his romantic past as described in the Stuttgart diary, however stale it would have become by the time he was composing op. 38. The scale degrees are slightly different here, beginning 5-4-3-2 as opposed to the 6-5-4-3 of the C theme, but the rhythms and suspensions are rather close, and the little phrase repeats, as does Chopin's. Rossini's tempo is agitato, nothing like that of Chopin's op. 38 middle section, but adapting a similar figure to a slower tempo is well within the possibilities that might occur to a composer ruminating over a vocal score. The applicability of this little figure, via its source aria, to the Polish situation and to Chopin's own experience makes it an apt vehicle for commentary on the unfolding action of the ballade.

It is impossible to know if this particular duet is the one that was "vigorously applauded" when Adolphe Nourrit and Cornélie Falcon sang it, on 5 April 1835, at a benefit concert for Polish refugees at the Théâtre Italien, though it seems likely.[8] The only other possible duet from that opera is not nearly as hopeful and is more given to pure vocal display, which would seemingly make it less appropriate for that kind of event. Chopin was present at this concert and in fact played his E Minor Piano Concerto; although he had known *Guillaume Tell* for years, it is a tantalizing thought that a well-received performance of this one number at a celebration of Polish national aspirations might have stirred his imagination shortly before the Second Ballade would have begun taking shape.

---

8. A review of this concert appeared in the *Revue et gazette musicale de Paris* (12 April 1835), 130–31.

Ex. 6.11. Rossini, *Guillaume Tell*, act 2, "Oui, vous l'arrachez à mon âme," mm. 28–34.

The A material, the B material, and the C theme are the stuff of which Chopin constructed his musical narrative. Beyond the identification of musical content, topical significance, and operatic referents, stylistic analysis of the piece must rest on Chopin's strategies—what he chose to do with that material. With the musical material we have just three ideas, or characters; it is only in the arrangement and treatment of these ideas that Chopin, as *wieszcz*, could present the story that motivated him to compose a second epic ballade.

Chopin's Second Ballade as Narrative of National Martyrdom

To project a coherent ballad narrative, Chopin's ballade has to succeed on two fronts: it must both evoke the telling of a story and recount the events of that story. Relevant to the first of these is Jim Samson's insightful point that despite the huge contrast between the A and B material, Chopin finds different strategic ways to draw connections between themes and sections.[9] Of principal concern, of course, is how: interthematic and intersectional linkages of varying kinds reinforce the narrative process because these

---

9. Samson, *Chopin: The Four Ballades*, 51.

subtle connections between disparate elements subliminally imply a single narrative voice and continuity between them—two requirements of a well-told tale. We already saw how, in the First Ballade, Chopin linked the widely contrasting introduction, first theme, and second theme with the characteristic but well integrated three-note figure consisting of a descending fourth and an ascending minor third. Examples of similarly subtle unifying features found in the Second Ballade are legion. One would be the way Chopin contrives to have the crucially important key of A minor first appear in the opening F major section in mm. 18 ff., as a touch of melancholy foreshadowing. A second would be the way the opening siciliano rhythm itself reappears in the storm music in mm. 63–68. Another would be the E–F dyad, which is prominently placed in both the A and B sections (and the triple common-tone device that connects these sections, discussed in chapter 4). Several more wonderfully resourceful connections are found in the middle section, where the C theme references the opening vamp and affect but not the A theme itself. When the music breaks into anguished siciliano fragments—approaching the storm affect of the B material, but not quite reaching it—it is a figure from the middle of the siciliano melody that is used (that which first appeared in mm. 4–6), not the opening. These and other such moments, which reference disparate parts of the same work, evince a narrative strategy that is subtler and more complex even than that of op. 23.

Chopin's First Ballade, we remember, registered the presence of the bardic narrator only with the improvisatory harplike introduction and the brusque dotted figures and short flourishes that closed the tale. In between these two points, the sense of narrative depended primarily on the artful way the succeeding scenes—the events of the story—proceeded one from another, without narratorial commentary. Even the unifying three-note melodic cell heard at the end of the introduction and in both main themes served to unify the whole more than to specifically recall the introduction. In that sense, op. 23 worked rather like a small play introduced and closed by the narrator; other than those two dramatic intrusions, it proceeded from beginning to end without noticeable narratorial presence.

There is no bardic introduction to the Second Ballade, but the A material evokes both the narrator's role—siciliano melody and bagpipe-like choral response—and his subject: the distant, beloved Poland of childhood memory. Recurrences of this material therefore recall both Poland per se and the narrator's voice in talking about it, which will evolve into a mechanism for narratorial commentary, like a documentary voice-over. The listener is told not only what happened, but also how to feel about it—an approach to narratorial control developed in the operatic ballades, and similar to that of Mickiewicz in the course of Jankiel's Concert of Concerts in *Pan Tadeusz*.

When A minor briefly appears in the opening section, it seems a noteworthy sound event, but we have nothing to relate it to. Its effect is felt later in that its appearance helps set up the new key, stressing the A and C common tones and enabling the sudden shift to the B material in m. 47 to make a kind of intuitive sense. When the opening siciliano rhythm reappears in the second section, the increased tempo transforms it into a diabolical gigue, almost; the listener may sense the connection between the rhythm and the slower section that came before, but it is not sufficient to indicate a return of the voice or stance of the first section. The storm is strong enough to sweep away everything in its path.

In the middle section, however, the excerpts of the A theme at the beginning reestablish the importance of the siciliano rhythm and the presence of the narrator. This rhythm now both introduces the C theme, in mm. 96–98, and then reappears after each pair of canonic statements of it, in mm. 108–115 (see ex. 6.12) and 133–140. As just mentioned, the roiling mood and subtle references to the opening theme represent further connections drawn—B mood beginning to transform A material—and as the themes and moods are made ever more proximate to each other, Chopin uses a strategy similar to that of Meyerbeer in the third verse of Raimbaut's ballade. In that final verse, Meyerbeer has the orchestra carry the actual melody while the Pilgrim finishes his story in hesitant fragments, as if he as the narrator of the tale were slowly being transformed into the listener responding to it, barely managing to proceed to the horrible end. In op. 38, sections of the siciliano theme (signifier of the narrator's evocation of the idealized past) now become portents of impending disaster, as if fragments of Poland herself were responding to and being transformed by the dire circumstances.

Because the C theme shares the pastoral tone of the siciliano material but differs from it in content, there can be a separation between the narrator's voice and the first theme, as there was in Meyerbeer's ballade and the later reminiscences of it, where Alice and Robert converse in recitative over the baleful thematic fragments symbolizing Bertram, Robert's demonic father. The new theme can assume the responsibility of narratorial commentary without speaking only of idealized Poland, and so it now can deepen, so to speak, the story of which the first theme is a part. The narrator can deftly guide the listener through the unsettled and increasingly insecure middle section, which is linked to the main story by the siciliano rhythm in increasingly stormy realization (Poland is remembered sweetly, but then things go from bad to worse) via the glosses of the C theme, which perhaps suggests a hint of the hopefulness of the duet from Rossini's *Guillaume Tell*: Love in Travail, struggling to prevail in the midst of great historical forces. In that latter context, it is hard not to

Ex. 6.12. Chopin, Ballade no. 2, op. 38, mm. 108–115.

remember Mallefille's retrospective image of "gloomy farewells exchanged on somber woodland paths."

When the storm music returns, the C theme is gone forever—hope dashed, seemingly—but the siciliano rhythm returns twice more as a kind of psychological reminiscence. At the end of this fourth section, the siciliano rhythm is stated three times over an E pedal (mm. 157–164) in a sort of expanded i_4^6 passage, which has the ultimate function of establishing, once and for all, that there will be no harmonic escape from the second key: the siciliano rhythm now has a clear role in the A minor cadence that sets up the reckoning—one that cannot be gainsaid. It is present but completely powerless: overborne, its pastoral spirit and characteristic tempo completely gone and controlling absolutely nothing. The siciliano's final, glum appearance, of course, is at the very end: the narrator, singing a bleak A minor farewell to Polonia in the final bars, reminds us that there was no satisfactory ending, and that the tragic story goes on.

Let me now summarize the narrative as concisely as possible. I see, in Chopin's Second Ballade, an explicitly nationalistic tale: the martyrdom of the Poles and their national aspirations told in tones. A variety of factors point to this reading: Chopin's chosen topics, their operatic referents, the extraordinary and unique form of the piece, the Polish cultural zeitgeist in Paris, and the important external clues provided by the tribute of Mallefille and the mention of Probst. The musical gestures and their referents work in concert with each other, in both literal and subtler psychological ways, as the story unfolds:

- First, mm. 1–46 consist of the nostalgic F major siciliano-pastorale, as if sung by a narrator with listeners' soft antiphonal assent. This is Chopin's Poland Before the Fall, in a kind of Edenic state of never-to-be-recaptured beauty and joy. The resemblance to Raimbaut's ballade from Meyerbeer's *Robert le diable* is seen in the introductory unison vamp and melodic and harmonic materials, and that specific reference will be strengthened and made more explicit by later reminiscences throughout the piece. The slightly melancholy, bucolic innocence contributes to the poignant affect: nostalgia for something beautiful but irretrievably lost.
- Second, mm. 47–83 present a sudden, furious storm and battle scene that—with its descending treble gusts answered by ascending eighth-note bursts in the bass—echoes the storm and battle music from Rossini's *Guillaume Tell*, referencing that narrative of struggle for national freedom. It also evokes Jankiel's descriptive playing in Mickiewicz's *Pan Tadeusz*, especially the "storm" of the Russians' 1794 descent upon Praga; the suddenness and fury of the onslaught now call to mind the first Russian response to the Insurrection of November 1830: violent and irresistible.
- Third, we find in mm. 83–140 an unstable middle section, increasingly troubled and inconclusive, beginning with the A theme siciliano but soon dispersing into increasingly wan statements of the C theme. Via the general relationship to the siciliano without the specificity of the rhythm or thematic content, the C theme calls to mind once again the narrator's voice, glossing the ongoing action, perhaps (via the Rossinian operatic referent) sketching a subplot about love in a deepening crisis. The recurrent presence of the siciliano rhythm suggests the unraveling of aspirations and dreams, much like the period between late March and September 1831, when it seemed possible—though the likelihood appeared more and more distant—that the damage with Russia could be minimized. Chopin's subtle vacillation of mood in this section is masterful: the sweet C theme is repeatedly prevented from reaching a proper cadence—now by a quiet wisp of the siciliano, now by an angry and explosive excerpt of it. By the time hopes are finally crushed, the C theme has been stated, hoping against hope, in the too-innocent and harmonically undermined tonic of F major, and neither the theme nor that original tonic key will ever return.
- Fourth, in mm. 141–168 there is a return to the storm music of the second section, the very cataclysm the central section had

been seeking to forestall. The parallels to both the two-stage Russian response to the Insurrection and Mickiewicz's twofold mention of "storm" in Jankiel's performance are striking. This time, the storm does not subside, but instead prepares, via a long harmonic extension, what is clearly to be an A minor apocalypse. In the course of this passage, the thematic fragment with the siciliano rhythm is repeated three times, without resolution, against a dissonant tremolando figure in the right hand (mm. 157–164), almost as if suspended in midair and scourged. The historical parallel with this section, of course, would be the Russians' return, and the musical style and harmonic trajectory tell us that there will be no escape, no return to the beloved Poland of childhood memory.

- Fifth, Chopin presents the ballade's reckoning section in mm. 169–197. In this infinitely improved recasting of the closing music of the first act of *Guillaume Tell*, Chopin seems to evoke the powerlessness of witnessing the horrors befalling friends and loved ones as his nation collapses before the Russian forces, as at the close of Rossini's act 1 and as he had imagined them before, alone and writing in his diary in Stuttgart.
- Sixth and finally, we have the close in mm. 197–204. After a furious diminished-chord sequence, the opening siciliano melody is cast up, exhausted and pathetic, in A minor, the wrong key, the key of the Russians—a key from which, we now realize, there can now be no return. The Polish defeat is complete, and we can almost see Mickiewicz's defeated soldiers from *Pan Tadeusz*, who—following "their country's fall," "went to distant climes ...wandering through frosts and burning sands," as forlorn as the distressed exiles in Mallefille's playlet. The final narratorial word is given when the siciliano feebly interrupts this closing cadence like a sad moral: *and thus, until the Day of Redemption, they will continue to wander.* So the work ends: with the idyllic tones of the opening section transformed and subverted, and a return to the harmonic home base entirely impossible.

A stylistic analysis of the ballade in light of the musical environment in which it was composed and first heard thus suggests a clear program: the Polish version of Eden to the Fall, to the Expulsion, and finally to the Pilgrims bearing the agonizing memory as they wanly sing the Lord's song in a strange land. This reading is completely in keeping with contemporary Polish cultural imagery in Paris and explains the grim ending-without-an-ending that accounts for the two-key structure so puzzling to many: as long as Poland was still in a stranglehold, there was no returning home for the Pilgrims—thus, no return to the tonic. It is also consistent with Mallefille's effusive, Mickiewicz-influenced dramatic scene, evoking the national paroxysm for which the scene serves as moralizing postlude: only after the Pilgrims are exiled and wandering could the scene, with its "desolate images" and morally instructive conversations (which echo Mickiewicz's *Books of the Polish Nation and the Books of the Polish Pilgrims*), take place. As a Frenchman close to George Sand, Mallefille would have been, of course, fully aware of both the plight of Chopin's countrymen and the musical idioms of which he was making use.

Chopin's Second Ballade amounts to a stupendously successful assimilation of preexistent approaches, as pointed out in chapter 4. It combines the formal processes of the programmatic piano piece, with its succession of depictive gestures and direct quotations (or more general reminiscences) of familiar music that could, through association, allow the listener to comprehend a new narrative, and the operatic ballade, with its alternation of material representing the accepted strategy to evoke not only a momentous story but the recounting of it. Significantly, the ballade also deploys and elevates a variety of middlebrow musical gestures and strategies to produce an artwork of the very highest order, an artwork that—not coincidentally, I am convinced—mirrors the spirit and aesthetic of Jankiel's Concert of Concerts from *Pan Tadeusz*. Chopin could have become familiar with Mickiewicz's passage only in the mid-1830s, around the time the ballade was taking shape, and whether he was using Mickiewicz as inspiration, as he told Schumann, or Mickiewicz was idealizing something he had heard Chopin do (or both) is less important than the explicit Polishness of Chopin's approach to recounting this ballade's tale.

Unavoidably, my approach to the analysis of this work will strike some as naive, a return to a long-discredited way of thinking and writing about music. There is probably no way for one to advance a narrative interpretation without opening oneself up to this criticism. Yet potential criticism is no excuse for intellectual reticence. This interpretation is in no way ahistorical: every compositional strategy in op. 38, including the use of topics and styles, the evocation of a bardic, subtly narratorial presence encompassing commentary as well as the recounting of events, and even the use of melodies close enough to well-known music to call forth a variety of associations into the listener's mind are evident in works composed in the years before. It would be less credible to pretend that Chopin was somehow *not* aware of these strategies, or aware of music that told explicit stories, or that he was *not* willing or able to appropriate, improve, and use such devices in much more sophisticated ways in his own music. In overlooking earlier, more literal, middlebrow repertories we retrospectively narrow Chopin's musical world, limiting his options and musical influences because of what amounts to our own aesthetic insecurity. Too often, we earnestly remake Chopin in our own musical image and stress the high seriousness of his Bach and Mozart influences (or, in the case of the ballades, fabricate a respectable sonata model) while refusing to acknowledge and examine the other music that was a major part of his musical environment in Paris, and to a large extent probably in Poland also, because—nearing two centuries later—we are uncomfortable with it. Surely this is the most naive perspective of all.

It is somewhat ironic that the Poles back home did not hear the same nationalistic narrative in the Second Ballade that Mallefille and his fellow listeners did. Even an admirer such as Józef Sikorski, a music critic writing in 1849, sensed a life-or-death struggle but assumed the story was Germanic in origin—a spectacular miss born of the ballade's lack of specifically Polish folkloric musical inflections. He described the work as

> one of those through which Chopin entered into mystery most deeply. What a delectable legend! Not like our national ones, taken through the genius of Mickiewicz from the mouth of the folk, gentle [and] playful; but rather menacing and forcefully urgent, like inescapable fate [Sikorksi uses the Latin word *fatum*]. This [urgency and menace are] characteristic of German ballads, such as those of Bürger, a relic of a harsh feudalism almost unknown here [and] of superstition born of German character. In [the German ballade], you have foreseen but unavoidable necessity, in ours—chance; there grief and horror, here submission and, in it, hope. This is because [in the German ballade, one finds] the sufferance of mystery, [and in ours] openness of fantasy; there poison, tomb, skeletons, and ghosts, here water-nymphs, frolicking, and at the most an impish German who can be easily fooled. To finish: there, helpless anguish; and here, deeply felt faith. The image of our legends resides in many of Chopin's mazurs; his ballades have nothing in common with them and only show the path onto which strays the inward-turned imagination, forced by suffering into this prison.[10]

Even more surprising is that these remarks appeared in the context of a theoretical treatment of Chopin's musical nationalism, in which Sikorski asserted that (in Zofia Chechlińska's paraphrase) "the national character

---

10. Józef Sikorski, "Wspomnienie Chopina" [Recollections of Chopin], *Biblioteka Warszawska* 4 (1849), 544–45. I am grateful to Halina Goldberg for this translation. A good discussion of Sikorski's article is found in Chechlińska, "Chopin's Reception as Reflected in Nineteenth-Century Polish Periodicals," 249–54.

of art does not depend on the use of folk melodies but on capturing the real spirit of national music."[11] Actual folk songs were not necessary, in other words, but a kind of recognizable Polish *melos* was—conveniently enough, the kind found in "Chopin's mazurs" but not, he felt, in the ballades. Even though Sikorski required no specific national dances or melodies, the implication remains that "the real spirit of national music" would have to be recognizable, somehow, to Poles. This is where the paradoxical nature of the Poles' expectations of Chopin are most evident, and he himself probably realized that there was no way to satisfy those who clamored for an opera in their own musical language that would still somehow be effective at spreading the word of their plight to the nations. The musical language of the Second Ballade would obviously have been inappropriate because its gestures are not Polish; its musical materials come instead from the world of opera, especially French opera. Unsurprisingly, the "national" character of this ballade was apparently more comprehensible to Western Europeans, and what might have been Chopin's most concentrated nationalistic statement went largely unremarked in his homeland.

Hard as it is to believe in the face of the ongoing celebration that constitutes Polish Chopin reception today, the Poles were not always so open to all of Chopin's music, and their understanding of it seems to have been rather two-dimensional. Zofia Chechlińska's surveys of the nineteenth-century periodical literature show that before Chopin's death he was by no means the most often performed composer in Warsaw, and indeed interest in his music (before his death and the emergence of the Chopin cult) was surprisingly limited.[12] Performances of his larger works were rare, and although the First Ballade, op. 23 was appreciated, the others did not receive the same approval. Chechlińska concludes—going where angels fear to tread—that "the level of musical culture in nineteenth-century Poland was low, and the circle of musical cognoscenti narrow."[13] Chopin's most obviously nationalistic music was beloved, but his other works, such as, for example, those influenced by salon dance forms, Italian opera vocalism, the sonata genre, or the narrative impulse, did not speak as immediately to the Polish musical public as they

---

11. Chechlińska, "Chopin's Reception as Reflected in Nineteenth-Century Polish Periodicals," 250.

12. Zofia Chechlińska, "Chopin Reception in Nineteenth-Century Poland," in *The Chopin Companion*, ed. Jim Samson (Cambridge: Cambridge University Press, 1992), 206–21; and Chechlińska, "Chopin's Reception as Reflected in Nineteenth-Century Polish Periodicals," 247–58.

13. Chechlińska, "Chopin Reception in Nineteenth-Century Poland," 211, 213, 214, 221.

would later. Because he chose not to limit himself to the familiar musical calling cards of mazurka, polonaise, and krakowiak, a large portion of Chopin's music seems to have been better appreciated outside Poland. Unless we count Mickiewicz's reveries in Mallefille's description of Chopin's performance of this ballade, there is no indication that the Poles ever understood what he was doing with op. 38. They wanted a Polish opera, and nothing less, and whatever else he accomplished, there would always be a lingering disappointment that he had never composed one.

For all its demonstrable connections with opera, programmatic music, and ballad poetry, and aside from the way a Mickiewicz or a Mallefille might have been expected to understand it, Chopin must have known that many listeners would only be able or inclined to understand the Second Ballade on a musical level, without knowing the broader context and referents. Such nonnarrative listening would, of course, become increasingly common as the nineteenth century drew to a close and the twentieth progressed. Arthur Hedley's view of the tradition of assigning a specific Mickiewicz poem was reassuring in its dismissiveness: "The listener who has never heard of Mickiewicz or his poem need not worry. The Ballade exists for the whole world as beautiful and convincing music in its own right."[14] Never mind, the message is, you're free to like Chopin on your own terms, with or without the broader context.

And this is true, to a point; one need not read an entire book of historical research and stylistic analysis about a masterpiece such as op. 38 for it to communicate as a work of art. But for those who reach beyond the most casual level of understanding, especially those performing such music, this comfortable enjoyment does not go far enough. If the pianist understands Chopin's Second Ballade only in the familiar, two-dimensional way (the lovely siciliano and contrasting fast, stormy material, arranged in some order or other), then the interpretation is likely to be aesthetically haphazard. The storm topic becomes étude, as Samson implied and Zakrzewska stated outright, which means—to any pianist—that it is to be played ever faster, more accurately, and effortlessly. Effortless is, undoubtedly, is the precise opposite of what storm should sound like. Similarly, the siciliano—a dance type with rather specific associations—becomes simply pretty, familiar in a general way but devoid of nostalgia or poignancy. There is no confrontation of styles, in other words, but merely a kind of random juxtaposition of contrasting but increasingly distorted ideas, and the work is no longer conceived and heard as a narrative—a "ballade"—but rather just as a series of familiar

---

14. Hedley, *Chopin*, 174–75.

musical gestures and technical challenges. Readings of that kind, although common, devalue their artworks.

However much we cling to the idea of absolute or abstract music, music that does not seek to "express" or "mean" or "signify" anything, it is above all a modern idea. It is true that Chopin was notoriously reluctant to discuss extramusical meaning in his own work, but that cannot be taken to mean that there was none. Both the Henry F. Chorley passage that heads the introduction to this book and Mallefille's little dramatic scene from the *Revue et gazette musicale de Paris* demonstrate that listening for a work's inner narrative was not atypical in the mid-1830s. Mallefille's letter demonstrates that he had every confidence that he and his fellow listeners that evening understood what they were hearing, and that his readers would understand the linkage between Chopin, the work in question, and the composer's "heroic fatherland."

Now that I have put forward what I believe to be the story of Chopin's Second Ballade, op. 38, it seems appropriate to revisit the three vexed questions that arose from Schumann's 1841 review of the piece, with which this study began, and to reflect a bit about what the greater context of the Second Ballade means for our understanding of Chopin in particular and (if it doesn't seem too grandiose) what is usually called "the repertoire" of Western art music more generally.

Versions, Tonic Keys, and Mickiewicz Revisited

The simplest explanation for Schumann's reference to an earlier version of the Second Ballade and the persistent stories of its continued presence is without question that given in chapter 1 (and suggested by Jim Samson in 1992):[15] the composer and certain students after him retained the option of playing the opening forty-six measures as a complete work, an alternative to playing the whole as published. There is no need, given the historical sources, to posit some kind of "extended version" of the opening section (speculation about which seems to have begun only a century or so after the fact); playing the first section as an independent piece is consistent with all comments about early performances, including Schumann's. Because Chopin performed the piece both ways, there is every reason for the shorter version to be considered appropriate for performance, perhaps as part of a group of short pieces. Both versions therefore qualify as works in the meaningful sense, as valid alternative

---

15. Samson, *Chopin: The Four Ballades*, 53.

readings of the same piece (however curious that seems). Each might be considered a different *kind* of work, though the complication here is that both short and long versions, radically different as they are, bore the designation "ballade" in Chopin's lifetime; the long version was of course published that way, and when he played the shortened version in concert in England and Scotland in 1848 the generic title still appeared in the printed programs. That in turn means, as was suggested in chapter 4, that the short and long versions of the Second Ballade point toward what became different ballade traditions, the salon ballade and the narrative ballade, and even if it wasn't until later that these two subcategories came to be defined by the newer members of a growing genre, this work still qualifies as a kind of progenitor of both.

As for tonic key, the case for F major, especially given the fact that the shorter version never leaves this key, seems ironclad. The one oddity that advocates for an F major tonic must explain is the anomalous off-tonic end, and it is quite possible for them to do so: Op. 38 clearly presents a functional F major tonic for five-sixths or so of its length but is unable to effect a final return there, and instead ends—bleakly, as if washed up after a shipwreck—in the mediant. The stylistic analysis and implied program provide the obvious answer: Poland, the main subject of the work—originally characterized by a sweet and nostalgic F major siciliano—now wanders in exile, forever transformed by the A minor horrors visited upon it. It is a tragic narrative, a story incompatible with a happy ending and a return to the tonic. One might as well politely request of Shakespeare that Romeo and Juliet be returned to life.[16]

In contrast, because advocates for an A minor tonic insist that the final harmony heard must necessarily be the tonic key, they must formulate a persuasive view of the piece that explains all harmonic phenomena up to that point in ways consistent with that view. These, however, border on the preposterous. The entire opening section (the whole of the shorter version, remember) is considered to be secondary material, "the submediant of an incomplete progression," and the clear return of the A material in m. 83 is no return at all, but rather something that "merely teases."[17] The entire structure of the work (again, comparisons with Meyerbeer's ballade are helpful) depends on a governing F major tonic: the key in which the work clearly begins, and the key it departs from and

---

16. This would equate attempts to recompose the end of the full version of op. 38 to return to F major with the Victorian rewrites of *Romeo and Juliet* to have a happy ending. A hilarious satire of this practice is David Edgar's award-winning dramatization of Charles Dickens's *The Life and Adventures of Nicholas Nickleby*, which was broadcast on television in the early 1980s.

17. Sheveloff, "A Masterpiece from an Inhibition," 286.

returns to. Though the final return is denied, it is because of the violence of the narrative, not a mistaken conception of the form and tonality; the form is still entirely coherent without that final return. The Second Ballade thus offers an apt warning to analysts who let textbook assumptions about form overrule common sense.

Schumann's third point, that of Mickiewicz's role as inspiration for the first two ballades, also seems to have a relatively simple explanation: Chopin was being completely honest about how "certain poems of Mickiewicz suggested his ballades to him," but he was not making any more specific claims. The greater lesson here is that Mickiewicz's much-disputed inspiration is problematic only if one extrapolates from Schumann's remark that said inspiration must have meant that a single poem provided the story for each ballade—something there is no record of Chopin's ever having said or implied. When we can put aside the idea of this or that specific poem, it becomes easier to appreciate the extent to which Mickiewicz and Chopin were connected by their fellow Poles, in Paris and Warsaw both. The aesthetic of each encompassed both miniatures and works of epic sweep, and the works of both were clearly informed by wounded national feelings and painful levels of nostalgia. A few words Mickiewicz intended for *Pan Tadeusz* bear remembering:

> The land of childhood!
> That shall aye endure
> As holy as a first love and as pure...
> That happy country, happy, poor and small!
> The world is God's but that was ours—ours all,
> And all belonged to us that lay around.

Chopin may well not have known these precise lines, coming as they do from the unpublished epilogue to *Pan Tadeusz*, but they evoke a realm he knew well already: the promised land, the indescribably sweet, unspoiled homeland that time, distance, and events had forever cut off from the living but that would bloom forever in the expatriate consciousness. The same can be said of the poem's introductory paean to *Litwo!*, quoted and discussed in chapter 5: the scene is set, but it will be twenty-six lines before we segue into the world of Mickiewicz's characters, so in a sense the passage is self-standing, separate from the hurly-burly of the epic's narrative, though its relationship to the narrative is clear. Just as Mickiewicz's introduction functions outside the greater continuity of *Pan Tadeusz*, then, so does Chopin's opening section of op. 38 work as an independent entity, an almost impossibly beautiful evocation of a childhood paradise lost. The full version of the Second Ballade can be heard to reflect much of Mickiewicz's anguish about the Polish Pilgrims, of course, but the bittersweet nostalgia of the opening section in no way depends on it. So the imagery and cultural vocabulary of both versions of the piece—and the First Ballade too, for that matter—have much of Mickiewicz in them, exactly as Schumann remembered Chopin said: as inspiration. However persuaded the reader is by the specifics of my narrative readings of the First and Second Ballades, Chopin's suggestion that the two works were inspired by "certain poems of Mickiewicz" is completely plausible, and ought now to be beyond question.

The Forest and the Trees

This study has focused primarily on one work, and it has been my goal to demonstrate that, for all its popularity, one of the primary reasons that a great deal of its relevant musical and cultural context has remained hidden is a widespread, and rather curious, lack of scholarly interest in the musical surface and a reluctance to glean information from the stylistic gestures found there. The topics (the siciliano and the storm in this ballade) are apparent to those familiar with the art-music repertoire, yet only rather recently have people begun to suspect that style per se might be worth analytical attention. Jim Samson's "confrontation of styles" formulation is a good indication of this still-nascent trend: he sees the styles as defining features, not ancillary ones. And one of the main lessons from Sikorski's earnest appreciation of the piece is that without awareness of style, analysis is adrift; for all his love of op. 38 he really had little to say about it because it did not do what he expected a Chopin work to do. Overlooking musical style leads commentators to focus on nonessentials: for Sikorski, it was the rumination on Polish versus German legends, and more recent attention has centered on identifying the specific Mickiewicz poem that supposedly inspired the ballade, or teasing out a relationship to sonata-allegro form. None of these issues is helpful in parsing Chopin's piece, and their persistence in the literature generates much more heat than light.

We see, finally, what results when general questions are asked of "the ballades" as a whole and not of opp. 23, 38, 47, and 52 individually. The idea that each of the works to which Chopin gave this generic title must be like the others in predictable ways is a natural outgrowth of privileging general over specific, of genre over individual pieces—in other words, of comprehending the ballades first and foremost as they relate to each other, not (say) to other music, or the wider culture, or especially in terms of what is extraordinary about each. Certainly, this is a very common approach in musicological writing; books on Haydn's string quartets or Brahms's symphonies fill not only commercial and disciplinary niches, they neatly reflect our intellectual patterns as well: it is natural to mentally organize the repertoire in chunks that may be conceptualized in a consistent way so that the informed person will have some idea what to expect when he or she hears or studies an unfamiliar Haydn quartet or Brahms symphony. The Chopin ballades make even likelier candidates for this kind of overview because they essentially defined the entire instrumental ballade genre, and there are only four of them. Looking at music—Chopin's ballades especially—in terms of generic commonalities, expectations, and even "generic contracts" thus seems a natural, even commonsensical way to proceed.

It is too easy to forget, though, that musical works are composed and performed—in blood and sweat and tears, I cannot forebear to add—one at a time, not as complete genres. Looking at genres or any other grouping of works almost always forces one to scant the unique qualities of each work in order to make generalizations about the family resemblances of the group. Although there can be astounding formal and rhetorical differences between works of the same genre (Haydn's symphonies or Beethoven's piano sonatas, for instance), it is still the general patterns more than the idiosyncratic flashes of genius that lodge most firmly in our consciousness and remain as "knowledge."

The common caution not to miss the forest for the trees—not to miss the big picture by getting bogged down in individual cases or minutiae—can thus be a stumbling block. Privileging form, motivic deployment, and so on in the study of music enables broad patterns to be discerned and generalizations to be made across vast amounts of repertoire—all the symphonies, all the sonatas, all the string quartets—but too often these become the bromides of the music-appreciation classroom and historical survey, the too rarely questioned platitudes of our discipline. When misapplied this way, a generic contract becomes an artificially straitening yet still binding series of assumptions based upon not the whole of a genre, but rather a very limited subsection of it, and often the subsection includes only the best-known and most predictable examples.

When Chopin wrote his Second Ballade, there was virtually no generic history for the piano ballade outside the First. Still, so forceful is the habit of thought—as we saw in chapter 1—that Gerald Abraham was led to posit something like a generic contract for a new piano ballade based on that sole preexistent example, insisting on an original form for the Second Ballade that closely mirrored that of the First: "And it seems to me highly probable that this or something like it *was* the original form of the piece that Schumann heard." Far better would be to take the generic contract this far, at least for the first ten or fifteen years of the genre's existence: because of its title, the piano ballade can be assumed to evoke storytelling in some way. It might depict or suggest a scene with a storyteller in it, it might recount a whole epic, or it might partake of elements of both. Perhaps a familiar story is being told, or, alternatively, one that lives only in the composer's mind. It is the style or styles of the piece that lead us to the story or image: a narrator's harp and vocal declamation, perhaps, or explicit words implied in the melodic rhythm, or the antiphony of narrator and audience reaction, or a series of musical gestures that evoke a particular historical episode. The stylistic analysis of the First Ballade given in chapter 3 points up a variety of narrative devices, most of which are different from those of the Second Ballade. The forms of the two works are very different, as are the key relationships, as are the number and function of themes in each. Yet, both works are clearly narrative, though in different ways, and a thorough examination of each is needed for us to tease out such common threads as are shared between them as well as, and even more important, the unique elements of each.

Put differently: tree by tree, one learns about the forest, and in the case of the ballades we have been deficient in scrutinizing the individual trees. We learn from Chopin's op. 38 that making musical style a central part of any common-practice analysis has the possibility to allow us, via cognate styles and referents, to establish what (generally speaking, of course) a piece is *about*, and from that point we can proceed to examine and evaluate all the organizational and rhetorical means used for communicating those ideas. Content and form were, in the common-practice period, profoundly interconnected, despite our contemporary tendency to analyze only in terms of one or two aspects or according to a given system.[18] The "forest" of any given generic repertoire (sonatas, string quartets, ballades), often appears to be an undifferentiated mass, through force of accrued theoretical habit. Were we instead to take more time examining individual trees, inquiring after the special aspects of each, we might better understand forests as aggregates of unique trees rather than understanding a tree as an otherwise unremarkable part of a forest. With art—if I may (paradoxically) close with a generalization—it is the individual work that provides the life-changing experience, not the entire genre. The patient study of musical works one at a time, the same way they are learned, performed, and heard, offers individual insights that the forest of other works too easily obscures.

---

18. One of the relatively rare attempts (and a highly effective one) to synthesize both in an analytical framework is to be found in the early chapters of John Daverio, *Nineteenth-Century Music and German Romantic Ideology* (New York: Schirmer, 1993).

APPENDIX

"A M. F. Chopin, sur sa Ballade polonaise," by Félicien Mallefille

Revue et gazette musicale de Paris 5/36 (9 Septembre 1838), 362–64.

(Diplomatic Transcription)

A M. F. CHOPIN
SUR SA BALLADE POLONAISE.

Mon cher ami,

Il y a peu de temps, dans une de ces soirées où, entoure de sympathies choisies, vous vous abandonnez sans méfiance à votre inspiration, vous nous avez fait entendre cette ballade polonaise que nous aimons tant. A peine le génie melancolique enfermé dans votre instrument, reconnaissant les mains qui ont seules le pouvoir de le faire parler, eut-il commencé à nous raconter ses douleurs mystérieuses, qui nous tombâmes tous dans une profonde rêverie. Et quand vous eûtes fini, nous restâmes silencieux et pensifs, écoutant encore le chant sublime dont la dernière note s'était depuis longtemps perdue dans l'espace. De quoi songions-nous donc ainsi tous ensemble, et quelles pensées avait eveillées dans nos âmes la la [sic] voix mélodieuse de votre piano? Je ne puis le dire; car, chacun voit dans la musique, comme dans les nuages, des choses différentes. Seulement en voyant notre ami le Sceptique, qui a pourtant conservé une foi si vive dans l'amour et dans l'art, regarder vaguement devant lui, la tête penchée sur l'épaule et la bouche entr'ouverte par un triste sourire, je me suis imaginé qu'il devait rêver de ruisseaux murmurants et de mornes adieux échangés sous les sombres allées des bois; tandis que le vieux Croyant, dont nous écoutons avec une admiration si respectueuse la parole évangelique, avec ses mains jointes, ses yeux fermés, son front chargé de rides, semblait interroger le Dante, son aïeul, sur les secrets du ciel et les destinées du monde. Pour moi, caché dans le coin le plus sombre de la chambre, je pleurais en suivant de la pensée les images désolantes que vous m'aviez fait apparaître. En rentrant chez moi, j'ai essayé de les rendre à ma manière dans les lignes suivantes. Lisez-les avec indulgence, et, quand même j'y aurais mal interprété votre ballade, agréez-en l'offrande comme une preuve de mon affection pour vous et de ma sympathie pour votre héroïque patrie.

Revue et gazette musicale de Paris 5/36 (9 September 1838), 362–64.

To Mr. F. Chopin
about his Polish Ballade.

My dear Friend,

It is not long since, in one of those soirées where you were surrounded by sympathetic and congenial souls, you abandoned yourself without distrust to your inspiration and played for us this Polish Ballade we love so much. Scarcely had the melancholy spirit locked in your instrument, recognizing the hands which alone have the power to make it speak, begun to recount to us its mysterious griefs, when we all fell into a profound reverie. And when you had finished, we remained silent and thoughtful, still hearing the sublime melody whose last note had long since been lost in the ether. Of what were we all dreaming together, and what thoughts had the melodious voice of your piano awakened? I am not able to say; for each saw in the music, as we do in clouds, something different. Seeing our friend the Skeptic, who had always retained so lively a passion in love and art, looking vaguely in front of him, his head on his shoulder and his mouth slightly parted in a sad smile, I imagined that he had to be dreaming of murmuring brooks, and of gloomy farewells exchanged on the somber paths of woods; while the old Believer, to whose evangelical word we listen with such respectful admiration, had his hands joined, his eyes closed, his face furrowed with wrinkles, seemingly interrogating Dante, his ancestor, on the secrets of the heavens and the destinies of the world. As for me, hidden on the darkest side of the room, I wept to follow the thought of the desolate images that you put before me. Upon returning to my room, I tried to render, in my own way, the following lines. Read them with indulgence, and, if I have somehow misinterpreted your Ballade, recognize this offering as a proof of my affection for you and of my sympathy for your heroic fatherland.

[The usual identification of the Skeptic is the artist Eugene Delacroix, a friend of Chopin's and Mickiewicz's, and the Believer is Mickiewicz himself (note the reference to the poet Dante, "his ancestor").]

Les Exiles.—Un Chemin. [P. 363]

Le Chœur: Adieu, Pologne, sainte Pologne, tombe de nos aieux, berceau de nos enfants, adieu!

Un Jeune Homme: Mes frères, à quoi bon porter encore ces épées qui n'ont pas su défendre de l'esclavage notre chère patrie? L'étranger dira en les voyant: Que signifient ces insignes aux flancs des vaincus? Pourquoi ceux-ci viennent-ils mendier chez nous, puisqu'ils ont des armes? Il n'y a que le lâche qui soit pauvre avec une épée.

Un Vieillard: Nous gardons nos armes pour le jour de la résurrection. Je ne le verrai pas, moi, ce jour à jamais béni dans le nombre des jours que tu donneras au monde, ô Seigneur. Mais ma vieille poussière se réjouira au bruit des chants de victoire, et mes os frémiront d'orgueil quand mon petit-fils viendra déposer sur mon tombeau mon sabre réhabilité de sa défaite.

Un Enfant: Grand-père, j'ai entendu mon père dire une fois: "Le sang lave la rouille que font les larmes." Je ferai reluire ton sabre, grand-père.

Le Vieillard: Oui, tu renaîtras, Pologne, sainte Pologne, tombe de nos aïeux....

Le Jeune Homme: *l'interrompant.* Tombe de nos enfants, tombe de notre liberté. Pologne, pauvre Pologne, adieu!

Un Prêtre: Qui est-il celui qui défend l'espérance, quand Dieu veille?

Le Jeune Homme: L'espérance est morte, et Dieu est endormi. Enterrons ici nos armes!

Le Vieillard: Jeunes gens, gardez vos armes à vos côtés, et l'espérance dans vos cœurs. L'avenir est riche; il donne à qui sait attendre.

Le Jeune Homme: L'avenir est comme la fortune, il ne donne qu'à ceux qui ont. Puisque tu ne veux pas que nous enterrions nos armes, servons-nous-en pour mourir.

Le Prêtre: La mort est un crime quand ce n'est pas Dieu qui la donne.

Le Jeune Homme: Dieu ne nous donne plus rien.

Le Vieillard: Pas d'impiété, jeune homme! Tu peux vivre; moi, je vis bien.

Le Jeune Homme: Cela vous est facile: vous avez peu de jours devant vous; moi, j'ai beaucoup d'années. Et tous ceux-ci, pourquoi les faire vivre, quand ils n'ont plus ce qui fait la douceur de la vie? Ils avaient des maisons où ils pouvaient reposer en paix, des arbres qui les couvraient de leurs fraîches ombres, et des moissons, prix de leurs sueurs.... Les Cosaques sont venus. Qu'est-il resté? des cendres. Ils avaient des parents qui venaient se réjouir avec eux aux jours de fête, des amis qui les consolaient aux jours de douleur, des enfants

The Exiles.—A Path.

Choir: Farewell, Poland, holy Poland, tomb of our forefathers, cradle of our children, adieu!

A Young Man: Brothers, to what good are we still carrying these swords, which didn't know how to defend our dear country from slavery? On seeing them, the foreigner will say, "What is the meaning of these badges at the sides of the defeated? Why do they come to beg in our country, since they have arms? It is only the coward who is poor with a sword!"

An Old Man: We keep our arms for the day of resurrection. I will not see it, myself, this day forever consecrated in the number of days you gave the world, O Lord. But my old remains will rejoice in the clamor of victory songs, and my bones will tremble in pride when my grandson here comes to place my sword, vindicated from defeat, on my tomb.

A Child: Grandfather, one time I heard my Father say that blood cleanses the rust made from tears... I will make your sword shine, Grandfather.

The Old Man: Yes, you will be reborn, Poland, holy Poland, tomb of our forefathers...

The Young Man (interrupting): Tomb of our children, tomb of our freedom, Poland, poor Poland, adieu!

A Priest: Who is this who forbids hope, when God keeps vigil?

The Young Man: Hope is dead, and God is asleep! Let us bury our arms here.

The Old Man: Young people, keep your arms at your sides, and hope in your hearts. The future is rich, and gives to those who know how to wait for it.

The Young Man: The future is like Fortune: it only gives to those who already have. Since you don't want us to bury our arms, let us turn them on ourselves so that we may die.

The Priest: Death is a crime when God doesn't grant it.

The Young Man: God gives us nothing anymore.

The Old Man: No impiety, young man. You are able to live; for myself, I live well enough.

The Young Man: That's easy for you; you have but few days left before you. I have many years. And for those here, why live those years when they offer none of life's sweetness? They had houses where they were able to rest in peace, trees which would cover them with their cool shadows, and their harvests were the reward of the sweat of their brow... the Cossacks came. What remained? Ashes. They had parents who came to rejoice with them on feast-days, friends

qui leur souriaient tous les jours... Les Cosaques sont venus. Qu'est-il resté? des cadavres. Pologne, pauvre Pologne, tombeau de nos aïeux, tombe de nos enfants, tombe de notre bonheur et de notre liberté, adieu! Pologne, nous voulons mourir!

Le Vieillard: Suivez-moi, enfants; et séparez-vous de celui qui désespère.

Le Prêtre: Éloignez-vous de l'impie; fidèles, suivez la croix.

Le Chœur: *s'éloignant.* Adieu, Pologne, sainte Pologne, tombe de nos aïeux, berceau de nos enfants, adieu!

Un Passant: Que fais-tu là, jeune homme?

Le Jeune Homme: Je creuse une fosse pour moi et mon sabre.

Le Passant: Que dis-tu? toi si jeune et si fort, mourir! Pourquoi donc?

Le Jeune Homme: J'avais une patrie, je l'ai perdue à jamais; et maintenant je ne veux pas accompagner la troupe de mes frères qui s'en vont à l'exil et à la mendicité.

Le Passant: Tu as raison. Laisse-les aller; chacun pour soi dans ce monde. Mais tu ferais une sottise de te tuer maintenant; quand tu n'auras plus ni jeunesse, ni beauté, ni force, à la bonne heure! suis mes conseils, et tu t'en trouveras bien. Ramasse ton sabre et suis-moi.

Le Jeune Homme: Où veux-tu me mener?

Le Passant: Dans une grande ville où tu pourras t'enrichir promptement, si tu le veux; alors tu te donneras tous les plaisirs de la vie; tu auras une bonne table, de belles femmes, de beaux chevaux, tout enfin; et quand tu en seras las, tu feras comme moi, tu voyageras.

Le Jeune Homme: Quoi! tu as une patrie, et tu la quittes?

Le Passant: Que veux-tu que j'y fasse? crois-tu que je doive rester attaché, comme un chien de garde, au seuil de ma vieille maison?

Le Jeune Homme: Tu as une maison, et tu vas dormir ailleurs que sous le toit paternel!

Le Passant: Mon père et ma mère sont d'honnêtes gens, qui ont eu bien soin de mon enfance; mais maintenant j'en sais trop long pour m'entendre avec les gens du siècle passé, et je m'ennuierais à périr si je restais chez eux.

Le Jeune Homme: Je prie Dieu qu'il ne te maudisse pas! mais je ne suis pas le même chemin que l'homme qui laisse aux étrangers le soin de fermer les yeux de ses vieux parents. Va de ton côté, moi, je vais du mien; tu m'auras été utile sans t'en douter; tu m'as montré qu'il est lâche d'abandonner dans le malheur ceux qui nous aiment. Je ne me reconnais plus le droit de mourir, et je vais rejoindre mes compagnons d'infortune; je combattrai pour les faibles, je travaillerai pour les infirmes, je prierai pour

who consoled them in days of sadness, children who smiled at them every day. The Cossacks came. What remained? Corpses. Poland, poor Poland, tomb of our forefathers, tomb of our children, tomb of happiness and liberty, adieu! Poland, we want to die!

THE OLD MAN: Follow me, children, leave him who despairs!

THE PRIEST: Remove yourselves from this unbeliever; Faithful, follow the cross!

CHORUS: (growing more distant) Adieu Poland, holy Poland, tomb of our forefathers, cradle of our children, adieu!

A PASSER-BY: What are you doing here, young man?

THE YOUNG MAN: I'm digging a grave for myself and my sword.

THE PASSER-BY: What are you saying? You, so young and strong, to die? Why?

THE YOUNG MAN: I had a fatherland, and I lost it forever. And now, I don't want to accompany the troupe of my brothers into exile and begging.

THE PASSER-BY: You are right. Let them go; each for himself in this world. But you were speaking foolishness about killing yourself now; when you no longer have any youth remaining, or beauty, or strength . . . at the proper time! Follow my advice and you'll make out fine! Pick up your sword and follow me.

THE YOUNG MAN: Where do you want to lead me?

THE PASSER-BY: To a great city, where you will soon be able to enrich yourself, if you want; you will have the pleasures of life, you will have a full table, beautiful women, good horses, and finally when you are weary of it, like me, you will travel.

THE YOUNG MAN: What! You have a fatherland, and you leave it?

THE PASSER-BY: What do you want me to do? Do you want me to stay tied up at the side of my old home like a watchdog?

THE YOUNG MAN: You have a house, and you go to sleep elsewhere than under the paternal roof?

THE PASSER-BY: My father and mother are honest people, who took great pains for me in my childhood; but I know too much to agree with these people of the past century, and I'm bored to death if I stay with them.

THE YOUNG MAN: I pray to God that he doesn't really finish you off. I am not of the same stuff as someone who leaves the task of closing the eyes of his aged parents to strangers. You go your way, and I'll go mine; you have doubtless been useful; you have shown me that it is cowardly to abandon those you love in the darkest hour. I no longer recognize the right to die, and I go to join my companions in misfortune: I will fight for the weak, I

les désespérés. Adieu, homme de plaisir! adieu, toi qui ne cherches dans l'univers que toi-même! va loin! Frères! attendez-moi! et répétons en chœur: À toi, Pologne! sainte Pologne! tombe de nos aïeux! berceau de nos enfants, à toi toujours!
—Felicien Mallefille.

will work for the infirm, I will pray for the despairing. Goodbye, Man of Pleasure! Farewell, you who looks in the universe only for yourself! Go far! Brothers! Wait for me and let us repeat together, Poland, Holy Poland, tomb of our forefathers, cradle of our children—to you, forever!
—Felicien Mallefille.

BIBLIOGRAPHY

Abbate, Carolyn. *Unsung Voices*. Princeton, NJ: Princeton University Press, 1991.
Abraham, Gerald. *Chopin's Musical Style* [1939]. London: Oxford University Press, 1968.
Altick, Richard D. *The Scholar Adventurers*. New York: Macmillan, 1950.
Apel, Willi, ed. *Harvard Dictionary of Music*. 2nd ed., revised and enlarged. Cambridge, MA: Harvard University Press, 1972.
Arblaster, Anthony. *Viva la Libertà! Politics in Opera*. London: Verso, 1992.
Asikainen, Matti. "'Mickiewicz of the Piano': The National Style of the *Ballades*." In *Interdisciplinary Studies in Musicology: Report from the First Interdisciplinary Conference, Poznán, November 23–24, 1991*, edited by Maciej Jablonski and Jan Steszewski. Poznán: Ars Nova, 1993.
Atwood, William. *Fryderyk Chopin: Pianist from Warsaw*. New York: Columbia University Press, 1987.
Avins, Styra, ed. *Johannes Brahms: Life and Letters*. Oxford and New York: Oxford University Press, 1997.
Azoury, Pierre H. *Chopin through His Contemporaries: Friends, Lovers, and Rivals*. Westport, CT: Greenwood Press, 1999.
Barbedette, Hippolyte. *Chopin: Essai de critique musicale*. Paris: Leiber, 1861.
———. *F. Chopin: Essai de critique musicale*. Paris: Heugel & Cie, 1869.
Bellman, Jonathan. "Toward a Well-Tempered Chopin." In *Chopin in Performance: History, Theory, Practice*, edited by Artur Szklener. Warsaw: Narodowy Instytut Fryderyka Chopina, 2005.
Bennett, Joseph. "The Great Composers: Chopin." *Musical Times*, 1 January 1882, 12–15; 1 February 1882, 70–74; 1 March 1882, 132–35; 1 April 1882, 191–94; 1 May 1882, 256–59; 1 June 1882, 314–17; and 1 July 1882, 372–75.

Berger, Karol. "Chopin's Ballade Op. 23 and the Revolution of the Intellectuals." In *Chopin Studies 2*, edited by John Rink and Jim Samson. Cambridge: Cambridge University Press, 1994.

———. "The Form of Chopin's Ballade, Op. 23." *Nineteenth-Century Music* 20/1 (Summer 1996), 46–71.

Binental, Léopold. *Chopin*. Paris: Éditions Rieder, 1934.

Bourniquel, Camille. *Chopin*. Translated by Sinclair Road. New York: Grove Press, 1960.

Brown, Maurice J. E., and Eric Sams. "Schubert, Franz: Works." In *The New Grove Dictionary of Music and Musicians*, 2nd ed., edited by Stanley Sadie, vol. 22. London: Macmillan, 2001.

Bullivant, Roger, and James Webster. "Coda." In *The New Grove Dictionary of Music and Musicians*, 2nd ed., edited by Stanley Sadie, vol. 6. London: Macmillan, 2001.

Chechlińska, Zofia. "Chopin Reception in Nineteenth-Century Poland." In *The Cambridge Companion to Chopin*, edited by Jim Samson. Cambridge: Cambridge University Press, 1992.

———. "Chopin's Reception as Reflected in Nineteenth-Century Polish Periodicals: General Remarks." In Goldberg, ed., *The Age of Chopin*.

Chomiński, Józef Michał, and Teresa Dalila Turło. *A Catalogue of the Works of Frederick Chopin*. Krákow: Polskie Wydawnictwo Muzyczne, 1960.

Citron, Marcia. *Gender and the Musical Canon*. Cambridge: Cambridge University Press, 1993.

"Coda." In *The Oxford Dictionary of Music*, edited by Michael Kennedy and Joyce Bourne. Oxford: Oxford University Press, 1994.

Coleman, Arthur Prudden, and Marion Moore Coleman. *Mickiewicz in Music: A Study of the Musical Uses to Which the Poems of Adam Mickiewicz Have Been Put, Together with Twenty-Five of the Many Songs Written to the Poet's Words from 1827–1947*. New York: Klub Polski, 1947.

Cone, Edward. "Ambiguity and Reinterpretation in Chopin." In *Chopin Studies 2*, edited by John Rink and Jim Samson. Cambridge: Cambridge University Press, 1994.

Cortot, Alfred. *Chopin Ballads (Students' Edition)*. Translated by David Posonby. Paris: Editions Salabert, 1931.

Dabrowski, Patrice M. "Russian-Polish Relations Revisted, or the ABC's of 'Treason' under Tsarist Rule." *Kritika: Explorations in Russian and Eurasian History* 4/1 (Winter 2003), 177–99.

Dahlhaus, Carl. *Nineteenth-Century Music* [1980]. Translated by J. Bradford Robinson. Berkeley and Los Angeles: University of California Press, 1989.

Daverio, John. *Nineteenth-Century Music and German Romantic Ideology*. New York: Schirmer, 1993.

———. "Schumann's Ossianic Manner." *Nineteenth-Century Music* 21/3 (Spring 1998), 247–73.

Davies, Norman. *God's Playground: A History of Poland*. 2 vols. New York: Columbia University Press, 1982.

Duffin, Ross W. *How Equal Temperament Ruined Harmony.* New York: W. W. Norton, 2007.
Ehlert, Louis. "Frederic Chopin" [1885]. In *From the Tone World*, translated by Helen Tretbar. Freeport, NY: Books for Libraries Press, 1973.
Eigeldinger, Jean-Jacques. *Chopin: Pianist and Teacher* [1970]. 3rd ed. Edited by Roy Howat. Translated by Naomi Shohet, with Krysia Ososotowicz and Roy Howat. Cambridge: Cambridge University Press, 1986.
———. *Frédéric Chopin.* Paris: Fayard, 2003.
Eigeldinger, Jean-Jacques, and Jean-Michel Nectoux. *Frédéric Chopin: Œuvres pour piano: Facsimile de l'exemplaire de Jane W. Stirling avec annotations et corrections de l'auteur.* Paris: Bibliothèque nationale, 1982.
Fink, Gottfried Wilhelm. "Musikalisches Album." *Allgemeine musikalische Zeitung* (January 1837, no. 2), cols. 25–28.
Fulcher, Jane. *The Nation's Image: French Grand Opera and Politics as Politicized Art.* Cambridge: Cambridge University Press, 1987.
Gaillard, Paul-André. "Jugements portés sur Chopin par Mickiewicz, d'après le Journal de Caroline Olivier." *Schweizerische Musikzeitung/Revue musicale suisse* 103/5 (September–October 1963), 289–92.
Gaines, James R. *Evening in the Palace of Reason: Bach Meets Frederick the Great in the Age of Enlightenment.* New York: HarperCollins, 2005.
Ganche, Edouard. *Chopin: Sa vie et ses œuvres* [1913]. Geneva: Minkoff, 1972.
Gerhard, Anselm. "Ballade und Drama: Frédéric Chopins Ballade opus 38 und die französiche Oper um 1830." *Archiv für Musikwissenschaft* 48/2 (1991), 110–25.
Glickman, Sylvia, and Martha Furman Schleifer, eds. *Women Composers: Music through the Ages.* Vol. 3, *Composers Born 1700–1799: Keyboard Music.* New York: G. K. Hall, 1998.
Goldberg, Halina, ed. *The Age of Chopin: Interdisciplinary Inquiries.* Bloomington: Indiana University Press, 2004.
———. *Music in Chopin's Warsaw.* New York: Oxford University Press, 2008.
———. "'Remembering That Tale of Grief': The Prophetic Voice in Chopin's Music." In Goldberg, ed., *The Age of Chopin.*
Goldberg, Stuart. "Konrad and Jacob: A Hypothetical Kabbalistic Subtext in Adam Mickiewicz's Forefathers' Eve, Part III." *Slavic and East European Journal* 45/4 (Winter 2001), 695–715.
Hadden, J. Cuthbert. *Chopin* [1903]. Revised ed. New York: E. P. Dutton, 1934.
Hallé, Charles. *The Autobiography of Charles Hallé, with Correspondence and Diaries.* Edited by Michael Kennedy. London: Elek, 1972.
Harasowski, Adam. *The Skein of Legends around Chopin.* Glasgow: MacLellan, 1967.
Hedley, Arthur. *Chopin* [1947]. New York: Collier Books, 1962.
———, ed. and trans. *Selected Correspondence of Fryderyk Chopin.* London: Heinemann, 1962.
Hipkins, Edith J., and A. J. Hipkins, *How Chopin Played: From Contemporary Impressions Collected from the Diaries and Note-Books of the Late A. J. Hipkins.* London: J. M. Dent & Sons, 1937.

Hitzig, Wilhelm. "'Pariser Briefe': Ein Beitrag zur Arbeit des deutschen Musikverlags aus den Jahren 1833–40." In *De Bär: Jahrbuch von Breitkopf & Härtel, 1929–30*. Leipzig: Breitkopf & Härtel, 1930.
Hoesick, Ferdynand. *Chopin: Życie i twórczość*. 3 vols. Warsaw: F. Hoesick; Cracow: G. Gebethner & Spółka, 1910–11.
Hudson, Richard. *Stolen Time: The History of Tempo Rubato*. Oxford: Oxford University Press, 1994.
Huneker, James. *Chopin: The Man and His Music* [1900]. With new introduction, footnotes, and index by Herbert Weinstock. New York: Dover, 1966.
———. *Unicorns*. New York: Charles Scribner's Sons, 1917.
Jachimecki, Zdzisław. *Frédéric Chopin et son œuvre*. Paris: Librairie Delagrave, 1930.
———. "Polish Music." *Musical Quarterly* 6 (1920), 553–72.
Jorgensen, Owen. *Tuning*. East Lansing: Michigan State University Press, 1991.
Juszka, Antanas, Oskar Kolberg, and Izydor Kopernicki. *Melodje ludowe litewskie* [Lithuanian Folk Melodies]. Kraków: Wydawnictwo Akademji Umiejętności, 1900.
Kallberg, Jeffrey. *Chopin at the Boundaries: Sex, History, and Musical Genre*. Cambridge, MA: Harvard University Press, 1996.
———. "Chopin's March, Chopin's Death." *Nineteenth-Century Music* 25/1 (Spring 2001), 3–26.
———. "The Chopin Sources: Variants and Versions in Later Manuscripts and Printed Editions." Ph.D. diss., University of Chicago, 1982.
———. "Hearing Poland: Chopin and Nationalism." In *Nineteenth-Century Piano Music*, 2nd ed., edited by R. Larry Todd. New York: Routledge, 2004.
———. "The Rhetoric of Genre: Chopin's Nocturne in G Minor." *Nineteenth-Century Music* 11/3 (Spring 1988), 238–61.
Karasowski, Moritz. *Frederic Chopin: His Life and Letters* [1879]. 3rd ed. Translated by Emily Hill [1938]. Westport, CT: Greenwood Press, 1970.
Kasunic, David. "Chopin and the Singing Voice: From the Romantic to the Real." Ph.D. diss., Princeton University, 2004.
———. "Chopin's Operas." In *Chopin and His Work in the Context of Culture*, edited by Irena Poniatowska. Kraków: Musica Iagellonica, 2003.
———. "Playing Opera at the Piano: Chopin and the Piano-Vocal Score." Paper given at the 70th national meeting of the 2004 American Musicological Society, Seattle, WA, 11–14 November, 2004.
Keefer, Lubov. "The Influence of Adam Mickiewicz on the *Ballades* of Chopin." *American Slavic and East European Review* 5/1–2 (May 1946), 35–80.
Kinkel, Johanna. "Friedrich Chopin als Komponist" [1855]. *Deutsche Revue* 27/1 (1902), 93–106, 209–23, 338–60.
Kleczyński, Jean. *Chopin's Greater Works: How They Should Be Understood*. Translated and with additions by Natalie Janotha. London: William Reeves, 1896.
———. *The Works of Frederic Chopin: Their Proper Interpretation* [1880]. Translated by Alfred Whittingham. 6th ed. London: William Reeves, [1913].

Klein, Michael. "Chopin's Fourth Ballade as Musical Narrative." *Music Theory Spectrum* 26 (2004), 23–56.
Kurpiński, Karol. "O expresji muzycznej i naśladowaniu." *Tygodnik muzyczny I dramatyczny* 6 (16 May 1821), 21–22.
Lednicki, W. "Bits of Table Talk on Pushkin, I: One More Polemic of Pushkin with Mickiewicz." *American Slavic and East European Review* 5/1–2 (May 1946), 93–110.
Leikin, Anatole. "The Sonatas." In *The Cambridge Companion to Chopin*, edited by Jim Samson. London: Cambridge University Press, 1992.
Lewalski, Kenneth F. "Mickiewicz'[s] *Konrad Wallenrod*: An Allegory of the Conflict between Politics and Art." *American Slavic and East European Review* 19/3 (October 1960), 423–41.
Liszt, Franz. *Frederic Chopin* [1854]. Translated by Edward N. Waters. London: Free Press of Glencoe; [New York]: Collier-Macmillan, 1963.
Little, Meredith Ellis. "Siciliana." In *The New Grove Dictionary of Music and Musicians,* 2nd ed., edited by Stanley Sadie, vol. 23. London: Macmillan, 2001.
Locke, Ralph P. "Quantity, Quality, Qualities." *Nineteenth-Century Music Review* 1/1 (2004), 3–41.
Loesser, Arthur. *Men, Women, and Pianos*. New York: Simon and Schuster, 1954.
Longyear, Rey. "La Muette de Portici." *Music Review* 19 (1958), 37–46.
Mallefille, Félicien. "A M. F. Chopin, sur sa Ballade polonaise." *Revue et gazette musicale de Paris* 5/36 (1838), 362–64.
Marek, George R., and Maria Gordon-Smith. *Chopin*. New York: Harper & Row, 1978.
Martin, Terry Nathan. "Frederick Chopin and Romantic Nationalism: An Examination of His Correspondence." Ph. D. diss., Washington University, 1990.
Mickiewicz, Adam. *The Books of the Polish Nations* and *The Books of the Polish Pilgrims*. Translated by Dorothy Prall Radin. In *Poems by Adam Mickiewicz*, edited by George Rapall Noyes. New York: Polish Institute of Arts and Sciences in America, 1944.
———. *Dziady* [Forefathers' Eve], Part 3. In *Polish Romantic Drama: Three Plays in English Translation*, edited by Harold B. Segel. Ithaca, NY: Cornell University Press, 1977.
———. *Konrad Wallenrod* [1828] and *Grazyna* [1823]. Translated by Irene Suboczewski. Lanham, MD: University Press of America, 1989.
———. *Pan Tadeusz* [1834]. Translated by Leonard Kress. Perrysburg, OH: Harrowgate Press, 2006. http://www.harrowgatepress.com/pan.pdf.
———. *Pan Tadeusz* [1834]. Translated by Kenneth R. Mackenzie. New York: Hippocrene Books, 1986.
Milewski, Barbara. "Chopin's Mazurkas and the Myth of the Folk." *Nineteenth-Century Music* 23/2 (Fall 1999), 113–35.
Niecks, Frederick. *Frederick Chopin as a Man and Musician* [1902]. 2 vols. New York: Cooper Square, 1973.
Parakilas, James. *Ballads without Words: Chopin and the Tradition of the Instrumental Ballade*. Portland, OR: Amadeus Press, 1992.

———, ed. *The Nineteenth-Century Piano Ballade: An Anthology.* Madison, WI: A-R Editions, 1990.

Pederson, Sanna. "The Missing History of Absolute Music." Paper given at the Seventy-third Annual Meeting of the American Musicological Society, Québec City, Canada, 1–4 November 2007.

Pekacz, Jolanta T. "Deconstructing a 'National Composer': Chopin and Polish Exiles in Paris, 1831–49." *Nineteenth-Century Music* 24/2 (Fall 2000), 161–72.

———. "Memory, History, and Meaning: Musical Biography and Its Discontents." *Journal of Musicological Research* 23/1 (January–March 2004), 39–80.

Perry, Edward Baxter. *Descriptive Analyses of Piano Works.* Philadelphia: Theodore Presser, 1902.

Prizel, Ilya. *National Identity and Foreign Policy: Nationalism and Leadership in Poland, Russia, and Ukraine.* Cambridge: Cambridge University Press, 1998.

Rawsthorne, Alan. "Ballades, Fantasy, and Scherzos." In *The Chopin Companion: Profiles of the Man and Musician* [1966], edited by Alan Walker. New York: Norton, 1973.

Reddaway, W. L., J. H. Penson, O. Halecki, and R. Dyboski., eds. *The Cambridge History of Poland, 1697–1935.* New York: Octagon Books, 1978.

Richards, Annette. *The Free Fantasy and the Musical Picturesque.* Cambridge: Cambridge University Press, 2001.

Rink, John S. "Chopin's Ballades and the Dialectic: Analysis in Historical Perspective." *Music Analysis* 13/1 (March 1994), 99–115.

Rosen, Charles. *The Romantic Generation.* Cambridge, MA: Harvard University Press, 1995.

Rosenblum, Sandra P. "'Effusions of a Master Mind': The Reception of Chopin's Music in Nineteenth-Century America." *Polish Music Journal* 3/2 (Winter 2000). http://www.usc.edu/dept/polish_music/PMJ/issue/3.2.00/rosenblum.html.

Rousseau, Jean-Jacques. *Dictionnaire de musique* [1768]. Hildesheim: G. Olms, 1969.

Saint-Saëns, Camille. "A Chopin M.S.: The F Major Ballade in the Making." In *Outspoken Essays on Music* [1922], translated by Fred Rothwell. Westport, CT: Greenwood Press [1970].

Samson, Jim. *Chopin.* New York: Schirmer, 1997.

———. "Chopin's Alternatives to Monotonality." In *The Second Practice of Nineteenth-Century Tonality,* edited by William Kinderman and Harald Krebs. Lincoln: University of Nebraska Press, 1996.

———. *Chopin: The Four Ballades.* Cambridge: Cambridge University Press, 1992.

———. *The Music of Chopin.* London and Boston: Routledge & Kegan Paul, 1985.

Schumann, Robert. *Neue Ausgabe sämtlicher Werke.* Series 8, vol. 1, *Robert Schumann: Eine Lebenschronik in Bilden und Dokumenten,* edited by Ernst Burger. Mainz: Schott, 1998.

———. "F. Chopin, Zwei Notturnos, Werk 37.—Ballade, Werk 38.—Walzer für Pianoforte, Werk 42." *Neue Zeitschrift für Musik* 15 (1841), 141–42.

———. *On Music and Musicians*. Edited by Konrad Wolff. Translated by Paul Rosenfeld. [New York]: Pantheon, [1946].

———. *Robert Schumanns Briefe: Neue Folge*. 4 vols. Edited by F. Gustav Jansen. Leipzig: Breitkopf & Härtel, 1904.

Schwab, Arnold T. *James Gibbons Huneker: Critic of the Seven Arts*. Stanford, CA: Stanford University Press, 1963.

Shallcross, Bożena. "'Wondrous Fire': Adam Mickiewicz's *Pan Tadeusz* and the Romantic Improvisation." *East European Politics and Societies* 9/3 (Fall 1995), 523–33.

Sheveloff, Joel. "A Masterpiece from an Inhibition: Quashing the 'Inquisitive Savage.'" In Witten, ed., *Nineteenth-Century Piano Music*.

Sikorski, Józef. "Wspomnienie Chopina" [Recollections of Chopin]. *Biblioteka Warszawska* 4 (1849), 544–45.

Stan, J[ean?]. *Les ballades de Chopin*. Paris: Parisis Editions, [1934].

Steblin, Rita. *A History of Key Characteristics of the Eighteenth and Nineteenth Centuries* [1983]. 2nd ed. Rochester, NY: University of Rochester Press, 2002.

Sudolski, Zbigniew. "La poésie romantique et la musique de Chopin." *Revue de musicologie* 75/2 (1989): 171–84.

Swartz, Anne. "Elsner, Chopin, and the Musical Narrative as Symbols of Nation." *Polish Review* 39/4 (1994), 445–56.

Szulc, Tad. *Chopin in Paris: The Life and Times of the Romantic Composer*. New York: Scribner, 1998.

Temperley, Nicholas. "Coda." *The Oxford Companion to Music*. Edited by Alison Latham. New York: Oxford University Press, 2002.

Tomaszewski, Mieczysław, and Bożena Weber. *Fryderyk Chopin: A Diary in Images*. Translated by Rosemary Hunt. Arkady: Polskie Wydawnictwo Muzyczne, 1990.

Tovey, Donald Francis. *Essays in Musical Analysis*. Vol. 4, *Illustrative Music* [1937]. London: Oxford University Press, 1956.

Voynich, E. L., ed. *Chopin's Letters* [1931]. New York: Vienna House, 1971.

Walicki, Andrzej. "Adam Mickiewicz and the Philosophical Debates of His Time." *Dialogue and Universalism* 11–12 (2005), 15–31.

———. *Philosophy and Romantic Nationalism*. Oxford: Clarendon Press, 1982.

———. *The Slavophile Controversy*. Oxford: Clarendon Press, 1975.

Welsh, David. *Adam Mickiewicz*. New York: Twayne, 1966.

Will, Richard. *The Characteristic Symphony in the Age of Haydn and Beethoven*. Cambridge: Cambridge University Press, 2002.

Witten, David. "The Coda Wagging the Dog: Tails and Wedges in the Chopin Ballades." In *Nineteenth-Century Piano Music: Essays in Performance and Analysis*, edited by David Witten. New York: Garland, 1997.

Zakrzewska, Dorota. "Alienation and Powerlessness: Adam Mickiewicz's *Ballady* and Chopin's Ballades." *Polish Music Journal* (Online Publication) 2/1–2 (Summer–Winter 1999). http://www.usc.edu/dept/polish_music/PMJ/archives.html.

Zantuan, Konstanty. "Mickiewicz in Russia." *Russian Review* 23/3 (July 1964), 238–46.

INDEX

Abraham, Gerald, 11, 15, 30, 31, 32, 55, 93, 174
Alexander, Tsar, 114
Alkan, Charles-Valentin, 142
Allgemeine musikalische Zeitung, 56, 97
Altick, Richard, 13n20
Apel, Willi, 90
archaism, 38, 52, 98
Auber, Daniel, 49, 78, 97, 100–101, 115, 132–33, 151
  Le cheval de bronze, 109–10n34
  Fra Diavolo, 100–101
  La muette de Portici, 49, 78, 115, 132, 133, 151

Bach, Johann Sebastian, 36, 101n27, 167
  Capriccio in B-flat Major, BWV 992 ("On the Departure of His Beloved Brother"), 36
ballad poetry, 50, 51, 52, 53, 56, 97, 169
ballade types
  folk-song, 95
  lyric, 95
  narrative, 95, 96, 171
  operatic, 97, 98, 99, 109, 111, 144, 166
  salon (subtype of lyrical), 95, 96, 171
Barbedette, Hyppolyte, 22
bards, bardic imagery, and bardic topos, 20, 50, 52, 58, 62, 67, 70, 76–79, 98, 99, 141, 161, 166

Beethoven, Ludwig van, 17, 25, 38, 39, 40, 47, 72, 92, 128, 174
  Symphony no. 6 in F Major, op. 68 ("Pastoral"), 38, 39
Bellini, Vincenzo, 78, 79, 134
  L'abbandono, 78, 79
  "Tenere figli" (*Norma*), 134
Bennett, Joseph, 12
Berger, Karol, 82
Berlioz, Hector, 38–40, 44
  Symphonie fantastique, 38
Boïeldieu, Adrien, 97, 99–100, 107
  "Ballad of the White Lady" (*La dame blanche*), 99–100, 107, 108
Bourniquel, Camille, 32
Brahms, Johannes, 15, 16, 53, 90, 174
  Piano Sonata no. 2 in F-sharp Minor, op. 2, 53
Breitkopf und Härtel, 15, 111
Brzowski, Józef, 9, 11, 14
Byrd, William, *The Battell*, 36, 42

Cellier, Laurent, 27, 28, 30–32, 73
Challoner, N[eville] B[utler], *The Battle of Waterloo*, 16
Charles X (Bourbon), 115
Chechlińska, Zofia, 167, 168
Chopin, Fryderyk
  Baladine, 10, 11, 96
  Ballade no. 1 in G Minor, op. 23, 3, 4, 5, 7, 12, 20, 23, 27, 30, 32,

Chopin, Fryderyk (*continued*)
  Ballade no. 1 (*continued*)
    35, 53–66, 72, 73, 77–88, 90, 93–95, 112, 144, 153, 161, 168, 173, 175
    metrical plan, 58
    reckoning, 64, 66
    1st theme, 59–64
    2nd theme, 61–64
  Ballade no. 2 in F Major, op. 38, 3–9, 11–15, 19, 20, 22, 23, 24, 28, 30, 31, 32, 44, 47, 48, 53, 54, 58, 85–91, 99, 109–11, 113, 117, 121, 141, 143–45, 159, 160, 161, 163, 166, 167, 168, 169, 170, 171, 172, 174, 175
    alternate version, 3, 6, 7, 9, 12–14, 18, 33, 95, 170
    reckoning, 165
    1st theme (Siciliano), 86, 88, 92, 145, 151, 152, 161, 162, 164, 165, 171, 173
    2nd theme (Storm), 86, 88, 93, 152, 164, 171, 173
    3rd theme (Pastoral), 77, 87, 92, 93, 157, 158, 159, 160, 161, 162, 163, 164
    tonic key, 14–16, 18, 33, 171
  Ballade no. 3 in A-flat Major, op. 47, 22–24, 27, 28
  Ballade no. 4 in F Minor, op. 52, 24–27, 32
  Etude in A Minor, op. 25 no. 11 ("Winter Wind"), 128
  Etude in G-sharp Minor, op. 25 no. 7, 134
  Funeral March in C Minor, 45
  Grand duo concertant, 133
  Grand Fantasy on Polish Airs, op. 13, 131
  Mazurka in A Minor, op. 7 no. 2, 60n8
  Mazurka in C Major, op. 24 no. 2, 147
  mazurkas, 167, 168
  Nocturne in B Major, op. 32 no. 1, 43
  Nocturne in D-flat Major, op. 27 no. 2, 4
  Nocturne in F Major, op. 15 no. 1, 34, 128
  Nocturne in F-sharp Minor, op. 48 no. 2, 43
  Nocturne in G Minor, op. 15 no. 3, 34, 83, 134
  Nocturne in G Minor, op. 37 no. 1, 34, 99
  Polonaise in B-flat Minor, 134
  Preludes, op. 28, 9
  Variations brillantes, op. 12, 133
  Variations sur "Là ci darem la mano" de "Don Juan" de Mozart, op. 2, 39
Chopin, Nicholas, 141
Chorley, Henry F., vii
Cinti-Damoreau, Laure, 97
Constantine (Pavlovich), Russian Grand Duke, 114, 115
Cortot, Alfred, 27–32, 73
Crutchfield, Will, 78
Custine, Marquis de, 9n9
Czartoryska, Princess Marcelline, 12, 13, 124
Czartoryski, Prince Adam, 65, 116, 123, 143

Dąbrowski's mazurka, 130
Delacroix, Eugène, 113, 124
Dessus, Antoine, 140, 141, 142
D'Indy, Vincent, 25
Dorn, Heinrich, 4
Dussek, Jan Ladislav, 42–45
  The Sufferings of the Queen of France, 42
Dworzaczek, Ferdynand, 134

Eigeldinger, Jean-Jacques, 10
Elsner, Józef, 22, 45, 47–48, 123, 130, 136–40
  Król Łokietek czyli Wiśliczanki, 137
  The Meter and Rhythm of the Polish Language, 138

Fétis, François-Joseph, 39
Filtsch, Karl, 13n20
Fink, Gottfried, 56–59, 97
Fontana, Julian, 141
Frankists, 120

Gaines, James R., 18
generic contract, 94–97, 174
Gladkowska, Konstancia, 125, 154
Gluck, Christoph Willibald, 43

Armide, 43
Goldberg, Halina, 41, 46, 48, 125, 131
Golitsyn, Prince Dimitri Vladimirovich, 83
Grabowski, Józef, 125
Great Migration, 114, 116, 141, 144
Grétry, André-Ernest-Modeste, 28, 43, 44
   La caravane de Caire, 44
Guizot, François, 133
Gutmann, Adolph, 43, 139

Harasowski, Adam, 32
Haydn, Joseph, 44, 173, 174
   Symphony no. 100 in G Major ("Military"), 44
Hedley, Arthur, 12, 13, 31, 169
Heine, Heinrich, 28, 32
Hérold, Louis, 97, 100–102, 108, 133
   "Ballade of Alice Manfredi" (*Zampa*), 101, 108
Hiller, Ferdinand, 78
Hipkins, A[lfred] J[ames], 12
Hummel, Johann Nepomuk, Fantaisie, Op. 18, 16
Huneker, James, 23, 24, 25, 26, 27, 30, 31, 32, 55, 66, 72

Jachimecki, Zdzisław, 28, 30, 31
Jankiel (Jewish cimbalom virtuoso in Mickiewicz's *Pan Tadeusz*), 120, 125, 126–31, 141, 153–54, 161, 164–66
Jansen, F. Gustav, 5
Jews, Jewish topos, and Jewish worldview, 120, 121, 125, 126, 141, 142
July Revolution, 115

Kallberg, Jeffrey, 94, 112
kanklės, 80
Karasowski, Mortiz, 22
Kasunic, David, 99, 108, 134
Keefer, Lubov, 29
Kinkel, Johanna, 74, 75, 78, 80–84
Kleczyński, Jean, 22–24, 31, 32
Kosciuszko uprising, 128
Kotzwara, Franz, 42–45, 49
   The Battle of Prague, 42, 47

krakowiak, 41, 48, 64, 82, 94, 169
Kristeva, Julia, 44
Kuhnau, Johann, 36
Kurpiński, Karol, 48, 49, 111, 144
Kwiatkowski, Teofil, 139

Leichtentritt, Hugo, 33, 90
Leikin, Anatole, 91
Lelewel, Joachim, 117
Lenz, Wilhelm von, 142
Lesueur, Jean-François, 52
   Ossian, ou les bardes, 52
Levy, Armand, 140
Lewalski, Kenneth, 76
Liszt, Franz, 131, 140, 142
Little, Meredith, 145
Locke, Ralph P., 41
Louis-Philippe (Orléans), 115, 133, 139, 142

MacPherson, James, 52
Malibran, Maria, 97
Mallefille, Félicien, 47, 112, 113, 117, 122, 123, 140–44, 163–70
   "The Exiles.—A Path," 113, 122
Märschner, Heinrich, *Der Vampyr*, 99, 100
Mathias, Georges, 24, 33, 57, 72
mazurka, 48, 65, 85, 130, 143, 169
Méhul, Étienne, 97
Mendelssohn, Felix, 8, 37, 52, 74, 97
Mendelssohn Hensel, Fanny, 74
   "How Lovely Are the Messengers" (*St. Paul*), 8
   Song without Words in E Major, op. 30 no. 3, 52
Meyerbeer, Giacomo, 97, 100, 102, 105, 107, 108, 109, 110, 112, 133, 134, 142, 147, 148, 150, 151, 162, 164, 171
   Raimbaut's ballade (*Robert le diable*), 104, 105, 107, 108, 109, 147, 148, 149, 151, 162, 164
   Robert le diable, 102, 104, 105, 110, 112, 133, 134, 147, 148, 164
Mickiewicz, Adam, 3, 5, 19–25, 27–33, 55, 61, 66, 67, 71–84, 113–31, 138–44, 153, 161, 164–73

Mickiewicz, Adam (*continued*)
  "The Ballade of Alpuhara," 27, 70, 71, 73, 77
  Ballady, 20, 21
  The Books of the Polish Nation and the Books of the Polish Pilgrims, 122
  Konrad Wallenrod, 22, 23, 27, 30, 31, 32, 55, 66, 67, 68, 72–83, 98, 117, 144
  Pan Tadeusz, 61, 117, 119, 120, 125, 130, 153, 161, 164, 165, 166, 172
  Świteź ("Le lac de willis"), 22, 24, 27, 28, 30, 31, 32
  Świtezianka ("Undine"), 22, 23, 27, 28, 29–32
  Trzech Budrysów, 27, 30, 32
Mickiewicz, Céline (Szymanowska), 120
Mickiewicz, Władysław, 140
Mikuli, Karol, 24
Milewski, Barbara, 41
Moore, Thomas, 143
Moscheles, Ignaz, 142
Mozart, Wolfgang A., 39, 92, 97, 98, 101, 167
  "Im Mohrenland gefangen war" (*Die Entführung aus dem Serail*), 98

Neue Zeitschrift für Musik, 3
Nicholas, Tsar, 114
Niecks, Frederick, 24, 96, 139
Niemcewicz, Julian Ursyn, 116
Novosiltsev, Nikolay Nikolayevich, 82

Ossian, 52

Parakilas, James, 51, 53, 56, 63, 90, 94, 95, 96
Partitions, Polish, 20, 114, 127
Pasta, Giuditta, 97
Peerson, Martin, 35
Pekacz, Jolanta, 123, 124
Perahia, Murray, 15, 16, 32
Périer, Casimir, 133
Perry, Edward Baxter, 25–27, 33, 60, 73, 76, 77, 145
Perthuis, M. le Comte de, 139
Philomats, 67, 82

Piccinni, Nicolò, 43
  Didon, 43
Pixis, Johann, 134
Polish Pilgrims, 111, 112, 116, 120, 122, 123, 129, 136, 143, 148, 165, 166, 172
polonaise, 48, 65, 85, 127, 169
Probst, Heinrich Albert, 111, 112, 143, 144, 148, 163

Radziwiłł, (Prince) Michał, 116
Ratner, Leonard, 33
Rich, Adrienne, 25
Ries, Ferdinand, 137
Rifaut, L.-V.-E., 134
Rink, John, 33
Rosen, Charles, 90, 108
Rossini, Gioachino, 78, 97, 128, 132, 134, 151, 154, 159, 164, 165
  Il Barbiere di Siviglia, 128
  La gazza ladra, 134
  Guillaume Tell, 78, 132, 151, 154, 159, 162, 164, 165
Rothschild, James Mayer de, 123
Rousseau, Jean-Jacques, 98
Rubinstein, Anton, 25
Rudorff, Ernst, 15

Saint-Saëns, Camille, 9, 14, 16, 18
Samson, Jim, 12, 16, 19, 35, 90, 146, 152, 153, 160, 169, 170, 173
Sand, George (Aurore [Dupin] Dudevant), 112, 124, 140, 166
Schubert, Franz, 17–19, 131
  Ganymed, 17
  Der Liedler, 17
  Schöne Müllerin, 17
  Thränenregen, 17
Schumann, Robert, 3–7, 11, 12, 14, 15, 18–24, 30–33, 39, 40, 58, 59, 75, 94, 95, 119, 124, 130, 142, 144, 166, 170–74
  Kinderszenen, 119
  Kreisleriana, 6
Sejm, 114, 127
Shallcross, Bożena, 131
Sheveloff, Joel, 15
Sikorski, Józef, 22, 48, 49, 134, 167, 173
Słowacki, Julius, 115, 116

Sobański, Gotard, 76
sonata, sonata-allegro form, 25, 36, 40, 46, 53, 54, 58, 63, 64, 89, 90–95, 97, 109, 147, 167, 168, 173, 174, 175
Sontag, Henriette, 97
Spohr, Louis, 137
Stan, J[ean?], 29, 30, 73
Steibelt, Daniel, 43, 44, 45, 46, 49, 126, 144
  La journée d'Ulm, 43, 44, 49, 126, 144
Stirling, Jane Wilhelmina, 10, 14
Szulc, Marceli Antoni, 20, 21
Szymanowska, Maria, 28, 29, 120

Tomásek, Jan Václav, 97
Tomaszewski, Mieczyslaw, 14n21
Tovey, Donald Francis, 12, 38
Towiański, Andrzej, 121, 141, 142

Véron, Émile, 133
Viardot-Garcia, Pauline, 9, 11, 14
Vivaldi, Antonio, 36, 37, 40
Voynich, E[thel] L[illian], 28, 30

Wagner, Richard, Senta's ballad (*Der Fliegender Holländer*), 102
Wallenrodism, 72
Weber, Carl Maria von, 37–39, 40, 44, 99
  Conzertstück, 37, 38
  Der Freischütz, 99
Wieck, Clara, 94, 95
wieszcz (Polish prophet-bard), 125–26, 130, 139, 141, 160
Witten, David, 15–16, 91–92
Witwicki, Stefan, 121, 124, 135–37, 140
Woyciechowski, Tytus, 134
Würfel, Wilhelm (Vaclav), 45–46, 49, 144
  Grande fantaisie lugubre au souvenir des trois héros Prince Joseph Poniatowski, Kościuszko, et Dąbrowski, composé et dediée à la nation polonaise, 45

Zakrzewska, Dorota, 153, 169
Zaleski, Bohdan, 47, 124, 130–31, 141
Żywny, Woyciech, 45